Car-Free®
in Boston

The Guide to Public Transit in
Greater Boston & New England

8th Edition, 1993-94

Editors
Robert M. Davis
Robert Gentile
Anne L. McKinnon

Photography
Kenneth Martin

Cover Design
Joseph Ulatowski

Consultants
Peter Bracciotti • Peter Barros • Michael Eads

Publisher
Association for Public Transportation, Inc.

For additional copies send $5.75 plus $1.25 postage and handling to:
APT, P. O. Box 1029, Boston, MA 02205.
A bulk discount is available for orders of 100 or more copies.
Call (617) 482-0282 for more information.

Note: Every effort has been made to obtain accurate information prior to publication. However, transit services and schedules do change. For this reason, we urge you to confirm schedules with the carrier before making your trip.

Contents

Part III. Places to See and Things to Do
Ideas for an afternoon, a day trip, or a weekend in the Boston area and throughout New England

Part IV. Destination Listings
How to get to hundreds of specific destinations

Part V. Routes and Schedules
A guide to every Boston-area transit route

Introduction

"Relocate to Decatur."
—From a list of suggested
ways to avoid hassles
during the Big Dig.

This eighth edition of *Car-Free in Boston* coincides with the beginning of the Big Dig—the depressing of the Central Artery and the building of another cross-harbor tunnel in Boston. As work on these massive public works projects continues, traffic will be re-routed, causing inevitable delays. Motorists preparing for such inconveniences should consider their car-free options.

Revised and expanded, this edition covers these options. For example, the listing of cities and towns in Chapter 16 now includes the addresses for selected park-and-ride facilities, an important alternative for motorists during the Big Dig. The text of this edition is set in a new typeface and, in the interest of clarity and readability, there have been other design changes.

The Big Dig is only the latest reason for being car-free. There are plenty of others: Boston's crooked, narrow, one-way streets that bedevil motorists; bad drivers and high accident rates; difficult parking; vigorously enforced tow zones; restricted street parking in some areas; high garage fees.

It is expensive to own and operate a car in the Boston area. Hidden auto costs, such as maintenance, depreciation, taxes, and insurance are much greater than transit fees. Even with occasional use of taxis and rental cars, it's cheaper not to own a car. If you do own one, you can save money by taking transit. Many families find that, by using transit, they can get by with one car instead of two.

If you add up the time waiting in traffic, hunting for parking, getting lost, shoveling snow, dealing with repairs and insurance, paying tickets, and retrieving towed cars, you may find transit faster in the long run. And transit riders can use their travel time to read, work, or just relax.

Americans have become increasingly aware of the effects of pollution on the environment. Auto exhaust, the source of more than half the air pollution in America, causes lung disease, acid rain, and global warming (the "greenhouse effect"). By taking transit instead of driving, you prevent pollution at the source.

Because so many Bostonians use public transit, many neighborhoods, parks, buildings, and historic areas—sites that might have been bulldozed or imploded for the sake of parking lots—have been preserved. Our excellent transit system keeps the city's shopping areas thriving and prevents traffic congestion during special events. When the Tall Ships visited Boston for a few days during the summer of 1992, the public transit system carried a record-breaking 4 million passengers.

Boston has a transit system that keeps improving. The renovated interior of South Station is reminiscent of the golden age of train travel. Work has begun on the South Station Transportation Center, a multimodal hub for T-Buses, intercity buses, commuter rail, and rapid transit. Services for persons with disabilities, including escalators and elevators, have increased. Future plans include: restoration of the Old Colony commuter rail line to Middleborough and Plymouth and extensions of commuter rail to Newburyport, Worcester, and New Bedford.

Our goal remains the same as when the first edition of *Car-Free* was published in 1977: to provide a guide to Boston's extensive public transit system, including MBTA subway routes, commuter rail, bus, and ferry lines. In this book you can discover how to get to over one thousand New England destinations without a car, and you can find out about every train, bus, and ferry route in eastern Massachusetts.

The Association for Public Transportation, which publishes *Car-Free in Boston,* is a non-profit corporation that promotes better public transportation and increased ridership (for more information about our organization, see page 169). We urge readers to become involved in the transit issues that affect their lives. In these troubled times, transit funding levels—and service levels—are subject to frequent change. If you use transit, be sure to let your elected officials know how important a good public transit system is to you.

The Association for
Public Transportation

Part I
Using Transit

Orange Line, Back Bay Station, Boston

HELPFUL TIPS FOR SUBWAY RIDERS

- The MBTA Information Booth is located at Park Street (on the Green Line outbound platform).

- **"Inbound"** is always toward downtown Boston—Park Street, State, Downtown Crossing, or Government Center. **"Outbound"** *means away from downtown.*

- Outside central Boston, both the Red Line and the Green Line have **branches**. (See the map on the back cover.) Check the sign on the *front* of an approaching train to see if it is going to your destination.

- **Green Line** trains (also called "streetcars" or "trolleys") have letters for different branches: B—Boston College; C—Cleveland Circle; D—Riverside; E—Heath St. or Arborway (Forest Hills). A red line through the letter on a sign means that the train goes only part way on that branch. All trains stop at Park Street, Boylston, Arlington, and Copley. All trains except "E" also stop at Hynes Convention Center/ICA and Kenmore. Only "E" trains stop at Prudential and Symphony.

  Not all doors are opened at every Green Line stop. When in doubt, you should sit near the middle doors when the train is in the subway, and near the front of the car when it is above ground.

  There is no free transfer between inbound and outbound at Copley; use Arlington instead.

- Bowdoin on the **Blue Line** closes at 6:30 pm Mon.–Fri. and is closed on Saturdays and Sundays.

- Most **Red Line** trains stop at all stations between Alewife and Andrew, including Harvard and Park Street. During rush hours, some trains may terminate at Park Street.

  The last transfer point southbound on the Red Line is at JFK/UMass.

- Finally, a rainy-day tip for the **Orange Line.** At Back Bay Station, you can go, via the Dartmouth Street underpass, through the Copley Place shopping area, to the Huntington Avenue bridge to the Prudential Center.

Chapter 1

The T (MBTA System)

Many Bostonians, especially those who give directions to tourists, refer to their public transit system as "the T," after the Ⓣ symbol that flags subway entrances. "Take the T to Park Street," they will instruct an inquiring tourist. "Then grab any Green Line car that goes to Kenmore for Fenway Park."

The official name of the public transit agency is the Massachusetts Bay Transportation Authority (MBTA). In addition to its four rapid transit lines, the MBTA also operates buses, commuter trains, and commuter boats in Boston and surrounding communities.

Rapid Transit (Subway)

The four transit lines—Red, Green, Orange, and Blue—that radiate out from downtown Boston are often called "the subway," even though every line comes above ground for much of its route.

There are over 75 transit stations, usually named for a nearby square, street, or landmark. In addition, Green Line trains stop at many street corners along the surface portions of their routes. (Some helpful hints for subway riders are listed on the facing page.)

A simplified, color-coded rapid transit map can be found in most subway stations, and one is printed on the back cover of this book. Detailed maps of each of the four lines, showing all MBTA stations, their street addresses, and bus connections, are on pages 119-129.

All four lines intersect in downtown Boston. You can transfer between lines, *at no extra charge*, at the following stations:

- **Park Street**—Red Line and Green Line (with underground walkway to the Orange Line at Downtown Crossing). You can transfer to the Blue Line by taking the Green Line to Government Center.
- **Downtown Crossing** (formerly "Washington")—Red Line and Orange Line (with underground walkway to the Green Line at Park Street).
- **Government Center**—Blue Line and Green Line.
- **State**—Blue Line and Orange Line.
- **Haymarket** and **North Station**—Green Line and Orange Line.

Fares

All fares in this book are those in effect at press time (summer of 1992). The MBTA's basic rapid transit fare is 85¢. At some outlying stations, however, a different fare is charged. Under the T's zone fare system, the fare you pay is determined by where you get on the train. Once you have paid, you can ride as far as you want (except to Quincy Adams or Braintree) without paying anything extra.

In some cases, then, a trip in one direction costs more than the return trip. For example, the fare from Riverside to Park Street on the Green Line is $2.00, while from Park Street to Riverside is just 85¢. A different fare is charged at the following stations:

- **Green Line surface streetcars**—stops west of Kenmore ("B" and "C" trains) or west of Symphony ("E" trains): regular fare, 85¢, when boarding inbound. *No fare when boarding outbound at these stops.*
- **Green Line-D (Riverside)**—stops from Reservoir to Fenway , inclusive: $1.00 when boarding inbound. *No fare when boarding outbound.*
- **Green Line-D (Riverside)**—stops from Riverside to Chestnut Hill inclusive: $2.00 when boarding inbound; or $1.00 plus a Newton Local Coupon. (Coupons are issued when you get off an inbound train between Woodland and Chestnut Hill, inclusive; they are good for a discount on your next trip.) *No fare when boarding outbound*
- **Red Line**—Quincy Center, Quincy Adams, and Braintree: two tokens ($1.70) when boarding at these stations. At Quincy Adams and Braintree, an additional token is also charged when you leave the station. (The local fare between North Quincy and Braintree is 85¢; ask the token seller for instructions before you pay your fare.)
- **Red Line**—Mattapan Line: The local fare between Mattapan and Cedar Grove is 60¢, on inbound trains only. *No fare on outbound trains.*

Turnstiles in subway stations accept only tokens and passes. Tokens are sold (and change for buses is available) at the collector's booth in most subway stations.

Exact change, in coins and tokens only, is required on all street-cars. Dollar bills are not accepted. Exact change is also required at Science Park and, sometimes, at Lechmere. *For special fares, see page 8.*

Buses

Most of the MBTA's bus routes operate *feeder service*, linking subway stations to neighborhoods not directly served by rapid transit. Some *crosstown* routes connect stations on different subway lines without going into downtown. Only a few MBTA buses actually enter downtown Boston, and most of these are express buses from outlying areas. Maps showing downtown Boston bus stops are on pages 22-23 and crosstown bus routes are on page 131. For cities, towns, and neighborhoods served by MBTA buses, see Chapter 16; for routes and schedules, see Chapter 17.

Buses stop only at designated stops, marked in most areas by white or yellow signs with the "T" logo, a picture of a bus, and a "no parking" symbol. In some places, such as Cambridge, bus stop signs are simply "No Parking" signs with the words "Bus Stop" added. The MBTA has begun installing new signs, which include bus schedules, throughout its system.

Fares

The basic bus fare is 60¢. On a few very long routes, a zone fare—40¢ extra for travel in three zones—is charged. Express bus fares range from $1.50 to $2.25, depending on the length of the route.

As on streetcars, **exact change** is required on buses; no dollar bills are accepted. MBTA tokens are accepted but no change is returned.

In general, there is **no free transfer** between buses, or between buses and the subway. Unless you have a monthly pass, you must pay the full fare on each bus. There are two exceptions, however:

- There is a free transfer between **T-Bus 39** (Forest Hills-Back Bay Sta.), which substitutes for the Green Line-E (Arborway) streetcar, and the Green Line at Copley or the Orange Line at Back Bay Station.
- There is a free transfer between **T-Bus 1** (Harvard-Dudley), to or from Dudley Sq. only, and the Orange Line at Mass. Ave. station.

In either case, riders should pay 85¢ on the bus and ask the driver for a subway transfer. Free transfer coupons to the buses are issued inside subway stations at Copley, Back Bay Station, and Mass. Ave. *For special fares, see page 8.*

Commuter Rail

MBTA Commuter Rail, shown in purple on MBTA maps and sometimes called the "Purple Line," extends from downtown Boston to as far as 60 miles away. Most routes have midday, night, and weekend service, making them more than just rush-hour "commuter rail." A map of all nine commuter rail lines is on the inside back cover of this book.

Commuter trains to suburbs north and northwest of Boston depart from North Station, on the Green and Orange lines.

Commuter trains to points south and west of the city leave from South Station, on the Red Line. All southside commuter trains, except the Fairmount Line, also stop at Back Bay Station, on the Orange Line.

Connections between rapid transit and commuter rail can also be made at Porter (Red Line), and at Malden Center, Ruggles, and Forest Hills (Orange Line).

For cities, towns, and neighborhoods served by commuter rail, see Chapter 16; for routes and schedules, see Chapter 18.

Fares

Commuter rail fares are zoned from a minimum of 85¢ to a maximum of $6.00. Zone fare prices are listed below under "Monthly Passes."

Commuter rail tickets are sold at North Station, South Station, and Back Bay Station, and at or near some suburban stations. You may also buy a ticket on the train. If a ticket office at your station is open at train time, there is a $2.00 extra charge for buying your ticket on the train during rush hours and a $1.00 extra charge during off-peak hours.

Twelve-ride commuter rail tickets, valid for 180 days, cost approximately the price of 10 one-way fares. *For special fares, see page 8.*

Commuter Boats

The Hingham commuter boat sails from Rowes Wharf, Monday through Friday; the one-way fare is $4.00. The Navy Yard Water Shuttle sails from Long Wharf to the Charlestown Navy Yard, daily; the fare is $1.00. *For special fares, see page 8.*

Information

Printed schedules are available for all MBTA rapid transit, bus, commuter rail, and commuter boat routes.

Rapid transit and bus schedules are issued four times a year, in early September, late December, late March, and mid June. Schedules are sometimes available at subway stations and from bus drivers. Schedules for all routes are available at the information booth in Park Street station, at the MBTA Operations Center at 45 High St. in downtown Boston, and at the Library in the State Transportation Building at 10 Park Plaza (near Boylston station; see the Downtown Boston/Back Bay map). Schedules are also distributed to over 400 community locations, including public libraries, city and town halls, stores, banks, and colleges. To have a schedule mailed to you, call 722-3200 or 800-392-6100.

Commuter rail schedules are updated less frequently, usually in April and October. Copies are available at North Station, South Station, and Back Bay Station, at the State Transportation Library, and from commuter rail ticket agents.

For schedule information you may also call the MBTA's Travel Information Line at 722-3200 or 800-392-6100.

Hours of Operation

MBTA rapid transit operates 20 hours each day—from shortly after 5:00 am until past 1:00 am. On Sunday, service begins about 40 minutes later than other days. The last trains leave downtown Boston at 12:45 am. Times of the first and last trains are on page 116.

Bus schedules vary greatly. Some routes have full 20-hour, 7-day service. Others operate weekdays only, daytime only, or even rush hours only.

Commuter rail from North Station operates seven days a week;

HOLIDAY SERVICE

MBTA service operates every day of the year. Bus and subway lines observe special holiday schedules, as follows:

- **Sunday schedule:** New Year's Day, Memorial Day, July 4th, Labor Day, Columbus Day, Thanksgiving, and Christmas.
- **Saturday schedule:** Martin Luther King Day, President's Day, Patriots Day, and Veterans Day.
- On **Patriots Day**, due to the Boston Marathon, Copley station (Green Line), at the finish line, is closed and some bus routes are rerouted or rescheduled.

Commuter rail lines follow slightly different holiday schedules:

- **Sunday schedule:** New Year's Day, Memorial Day, Labor Day, Thanksgiving, and Christmas.
- **Saturday schedule:** President's Day, July 4th, Columbus Day, Veterans Day.
- **Regular weekday schedule:** Martin Luther King Day and Patriots Day.

South Station commuter trains operate six days a week (except for the Framingham line, which operates only Mon. - Fri.). **Note:** in the summer of 1992 the MBTA began an experimental seven-day service on South Station commuter rail lines (except for Fairmont). For the latest information, call 800-392-6100.

On New Year's Eve (First Night), the last trip on all lines is approximately one hour later than normal.

See Chapters 17 and 18 for more specific information on all MBTA routes and hours of operation.

Monthly Passes

A monthly T pass is convenient and can also save you serious money. Monthly subway and local bus passes cost the same as 14 to 16 round trips; other passes are an even greater bargain. Besides getting you to work or school, a pass gives you unlimited free rides—at night, on weekends, anytime. *You can take a friend along on Sunday at no extra charge.*

Several museums and tourist attractions offer discounts to T passholders, as noted in Chapter 11; and special offers are featured on the back of each month's pass. If you own a car, you can save up to $75 a year on auto insurance, too; ask your agent for details.

Over 800 companies make passes available directly to their employees, and many even pay part of the cost as an employee benefit.

SPECIAL FARES

Senior citizens (over 65) with MBTA I.D. cards pay only 20¢ for all rapid transit lines and 15¢ for local buses. On zoned and express buses, and on commuter rail, senior citizens pay half the regular fare. A driver's license and other I.D. forms showing proof of age are accepted on commuter rail; but on buses and the subway you must have an MBTA senior citizen card.

Persons with disabilitieswho have an MBTA Transportation Access Pass (TAP) pay the same fares as senior citizens.TAPs from other regional transit authorities in Massachusetts are also accepted on the T. Blind persons ride the MBTA free at all times (they need a travel card from the Massachusetts Commission for the Blind).

Senior citizen cards and TAPs can be obtained at Downtown Crossing station on weekdays, 8:30 am-4:15 pm. Call 722-5438 (TDD 722-5854) for further information. Senior citizens' cards are 50¢; TAPs are $3.00 (valid for five years for persons with permanent disabilities; valid for one year for persons with a temporary disability). Riders with disabilities should call first to have an application mailed.

Children under five years ride the MBTA system free when they are accompanied by an adult. Children age 5-11 pay half fare.

Students through high school pay half fare for travel to and from classes on buses and boarding at Quincy Center, Quincy Adams, and Braintree on the Red Line and 40¢ on rapid transit with an MBTA student badge. A monthly student pass is available through some schools for $11.00. Students' fares and passes are not valid after 6:00 p.m.or on days when school is not in session. The MBTA also has special semester rates for participating colleges.

Commuter rail **family fares** allow a group of up to five people—one adult and four children or two adults and three children—to travel round-trip on off-peak trains for a special fare, usually the price of two adult round-trips. For the family fare, "children" are under age 18.

Note: The fares listed above were correct when this book went to press in the summer of 1992.

MBTA monthly passes are sold at Downtown Crossing, Government Center, and Harvard stations, on the last four and first four working days of each month (cash only at these outlets); at North Station, South Station, and Back Bay Station passes are sold during the last five and first ten days of the month and can be paid for by personal check or charged on Mastercard or Visa.

T passes are also sold at some neighborhood banks, stores, and at some colleges; and they are available by mail if you send in your order by the 10th of the preceding month. There is a $1.00 service charge for mail orders. An annual pass-by-mail is also available. Call 722-5218 for more information on monthly T passes, including a list of neighborhood pass outlets or a pass-by-mail order form.

There are four basic passes, which cover the entire MBTA subway and local bus system; plus passes for express buses, commuter rail, and commuter boats:

60¢ Local Bus — $20.00/month
- Valid for 60¢ fare on all local buses; additional zones payable in cash.
- Valid for 85¢ and $1.00 surface fares on the Green Line.
- Valid, with $1.00 cash or Newton Local Coupon, for $2.00 fare on the Green Line-D (Riverside).
- Valid on the Red Line between Ashmont and Mattapan only.
- *Not valid* on any other subway line or on any express bus.

85¢ Subway — $27.00/month
- Valid at all 85¢ rapid transit stations.
- Valid for 85¢ and $1.00 fares on the Green Line.
- Valid on the Red Line between Ashmont and Mattapan.
- *Not valid* at Green Line-D (Riverside) stops Chestnut Hill-Riverside, inclusive.
- *Not valid* on the Red Line at Quincy Center, Quincy Adams, or Braintree.
- Valid on T-Buses 1 (Harvard-Dudley, between Mass. Ave. station and Dudley *only*), 39 (Forest Hills-Back Bay Sta.), and 49 (Dudley-Downtown).
- *Not valid* on any other bus.
- Valid for commuter rail zones 1A (85¢) and 1B ($1.20).

$1.50 Combo — $46.00/month
- Valid at all rapid transit stations *except* Quincy Adams and Braintree.
- Valid at all Green Line stops.
- Valid for up to $1.50 fare on all buses; additional fare payable in cash.
- Valid for commuter rail zones 1A and 1B.

$1.70 Combo Plus — $48.00/month
- Valid at all rapid transit stations and Green Line stops.
- Valid for up to $1.70 fare on all buses; additional fare payable in cash.
- Valid for commuter rail zones 1A and 1B.

$2.00 Commuter Rail Zone 1 — $64.00/month
$2.25 Commuter Rail Zone 2 — $72.00/month
$2.50 Commuter Rail Zone 3 — $82.00/month
$3.00 Commuter Rail Zone 4 — $94.00/month

$3.25 Commuter Rail Zone 5 — $104.00/month
$3.50 Commuter Rail Zone 6 — $112.00/month
$3.75 Commuter Rail Zone 7 — $120.00/month
$4.00 Commuter Rail Zone 8— $128.00/month
$4.75 Commuter Rail Zone 9 — $136.00/month
$6.00 Commuter Rail Zone 11 — $150.00/month
  • Valid at all rapid transit stations and Green Line stops.
  • Valid for up to the indicated fare on all buses; additional fare
    payable in cash.
  • Valid for up to the indicated fare zone on all commuter rail lines.

$4.00 Commuter Boat — $136.00/month
  • Valid on MBTA commuter boats between Boston and Hingham.
  • Also valid for the same services as the Combo Plus pass.

Note: These pass prices and descriptions were correct when this
book went to press in the summer of 1992.

Boston Passport Visitor Pass

Although the Boston Passport is aimed at tourists, anyone can
buy and use it. A three-day Passport costs $9.00; a seven-day Pass-
port is $18.00. Each Passport allows unlimited use of all subway
lines, including surface Green Line branches, plus MBTA buses up
to $1.50 fare (additional fare, if any, payable in cash), and commuter
rail zones 1A and 1B—the same as a Combo Plus monthly pass. With
the Passport you can also get discounts at some tourist attractions
and restaurants. It is a good way to test-ride the T.

Boston Passports are sold at North Station, South Station, and
Back Bay Station; at Airport and Harvard subway stations; at visitor
information centers on Boston Common, in Quincy Market, and at
several hotels. They are also available by mail. Call 722-5218 for more
information.

Commendations, Complaints, and Suggestions

To comment about MBTA service, or to suggest improvements,
call MBTA Customer Relations at 722-5215. Or write: MBTA Customer Relations, 120 Boylston St., 3rd floor, Boston, MA 02116.

If you are commenting—good or bad—about an MBTA employee, try to get the employee's number or name. The exact time
and place, bus route number, and vehicle number will also help
identify the employee. If there is a problem with equipment, please
provide the vehicle number as well as the bus route number.

All MBTA services rely on financial assistance from federal, state,
and local governments. If you use transit, you should let your elected
officials know how important the T is to you. These officials may also
be able to help get better service in your community. If you have a
question or comment about the level or quality of service, or a
suggestion for improving service, you can contact your senator or
representative in the state legislature, or your city or town's repre-

sentative on the MBTA Advisory Board. Call 426-6054 for the name of your Advisory Board representative.

The Association for Public Transportation, the private, non-profit group that publishes this book, is also interested in your comments on transit service. Send them to APT, P.O. Box 1029, Boston, MA 02205.

Chapter 2
Not The T

A number of other carriers, besides the MBTA, operate public transit services in and near Boston.

Buses

Several intercity bus companies serve Boston. The two largest, Greyhound and Peter Pan, both have frequent daily buses to New York City and to Albany, as well as service to points within New England. Greyhound serves the entire United States and parts of Canada; its "Ameripass" is available for 7-, 15-, or 30-day periods.

There are three intercity bus terminals in Boston—the Greyhound terminal on St. James Ave., the Peter Pan terminal across from South Station, and the Bonanza Bus Lines terminal, located in Back Bay Station. The Greyhound and Peter Pan terminals are used by other companies; see Chapter 5 for details.

Both Greyhound and Peter Pan also have terminals at Riverside in Newton, on the "D" branch of the Green Line.

Commuter buses connect downtown Boston with nearby towns and suburbs. Some routes operate only during rush hours, while others have midday, night, and weekend service. Most commuter buses leave from Park Plaza (formerly called "Park Square"), Copley Square, Haymarket, or South Station. For more details, see Chapters 5 and 19, or call the bus company.

Local bus service in some communities is operated by private companies, or by the local city or town government.

Boston-area bus services are listed in Chapter 16, "Cities, Towns, and Neighborhoods," and in Part V, "Routes and Schedules."

Railroads

Amtrak, the United States' nationwide passenger rail system, has frequent daily trains to New York, NY, and Washington, DC, via Providence, RI. There are also daily trains to New York, NY, via Springfield, and to Chicago via Springfield and Albany.

Amtrak trains depart from South Station (on the Red Line); they also stop at Back Bay Station (Orange Line). Trains via Providence stop at Route 128 Station (Rt. 128/I-95, exit 13), and trains via Springfield make stops in Framingham and Worcester.

In summer, Amtrak also operates direct trains from New York to Cape Cod. These trains do not go through Boston.

Ferries

In addition to ferries operated by the T (see page 146), there are other boats serving Boston Harbor. For example, the Airport Water Shuttle links downtown Boston with Logan Airport, and there is commuter boat service to Hull.

The Airport Water Shuttle links downtown Boston with Logan Airport, and connects with boats from Hingham. (See Chapter 6.)

In summer, there are boats to Boston's harbor islands and to Gloucester, Nantasket, and Provincetown, plus a variety of harbor cruises.

Sightseeing cruises are listed in Chapter 8, and service to the Boston Harbor Islands is described in Chapter 9. For route-by-route listings, see Chapter 19.

Regional Transit Authorities

In many Massachusetts cities and towns, Regional Transit Authorities operate local buses. A complete list of these authorities is in Chapter 20. Many cities and towns which do not have regular public transit offer special services for senior citizens and the handicapped. Contact your local town hall or council on aging for information.

Tours and Charters

A wide variety of sightseeing tours are available in the Boston area, from 1-hour "trolley" tours of downtown to weekend or week-long tours of New England. For information on local tours, see Chapters 8 and 9; for escorted tours of New England, see a travel agent or the travel section of the Sunday newspaper.

If your club or group is planning an outing, you can obtain group rates on many carriers, including MBTA Commuter Rail. If you have enough people, you can charter a bus or a boat, or even rent a whole train.

Chapter 3

Other Transportation Options

Ridesharing—Carpools, Vanpools, Subscription Buses

CARAVAN for Commuters, Inc., is a private, non-profit organization that helps commuters in Massachusetts find alternatives to driving alone. Their Commuter Information Line, 227-7665 (CAR-POOL) or 800-248-5009, provides free information on transportation options, including train, bus, and ferry routes, carpools, vanpools, and park-and-ride lots.

CARAVAN can also help you join or organize a vanpool (groups of 12 to 15 persons who share the ride to work). Everyone who joins pays a monthly fee except for the volunteer driver. Vanpools are designed for people who work in locations where public transit is limited. Some vanpools accept part-time riders.

Many employers offer special buses or vans to their workers, leaving from subway or commuter rail stations. Some apartment and condominium developments also offer special buses to transit stations or to downtown Boston. If your employer or management office does not already offer this service, they may be interested in starting it. Have them call CARAVAN at 227-7665 for a free consultation.

Taxicabs

All Boston-area cabs charge on a meter basis. In the City of Boston, for example, the current fare is $1.50 minimum charge, plus $1.60 per mile. Tolls for bridges and tunnels must be paid by the passenger. There is no extra fare for additional passengers.

If you have trunks, bikes, or other unusual cargo, the driver can charge extra. If you are moving a *lot* of stuff, ask for a "wagon" (an extra charge). And for trips over 12 miles from downtown Boston, flat rates are charged—currently $2.10 per mile, plus tolls.

Many communities offer special discounts or "eldercab" services for senior citizens. In Boston, for example, residents over age 65 or with special needs can receive a 40 percent discount by purchasing tickets in advance. For more information, call your city or town Elderly Commission or Council on Aging for details.

If you have a complaint about taxi service, get the cab company's name and the medallion number, which is posted inside the cab and painted on the side and rear of the car. Then call your local licensing commission or police department; in Boston, call 536-TAXI.

For a complete list of cab companies, check your local yellow pages under "Taxicabs."

Car Rentals

A rental car gives you the convenience of a car when you need it without having to own one.

Prices are usually quoted as dollars per day, plus cents per mile, although a few firms include unlimited free mileage.

The "collision damage waiver" (or "CDW") is similar to insurance. It is usually an "extra" charge, not included in the base price—but it is often required. Some credit card companies offer CDW at no extra charge.

Most, but not all, firms require you to have a major credit card before they will rent to you. Others may require a large cash deposit or proof of your credit standing. Some do not rent to those below 25 years of age.

It is also wise to check the condition of the vehicle which you are renting before you accept it.

See the Yellow Pages under "Automobile Rental & Leasing" for a list of rental companies.

Bicycles

Many Bostonians ride bikes to work or school, and more and more employers are providing facilities for cyclists. New, more secure bicycle racks have been installed at many T stations. With a permit, which costs $5.00 for four years, you can take your bike on the T (see box).

Bus and boat companies and Amtrak allow you to take your bike on board or ship it as luggage. Many ferries and intercity buses will accept a bike (on a space-available basis) "as is," ready to ride when you get off. They usually require that you take the same boat or bus as your bike. Many bus companies charge from $5.00 to $15.00; some are free. On Amtrak and Greyhound, you must pack the bike in a box, available from Amtrak or bike shops, and since few trains have baggage cars you should ship the bike a day in advance so it will be there when you arrive. Consult the carrier for details.

Bicycles can also be rented in many towns. See Chapter 9 in this book or look under "Bicycles—Renting" in the Boston Yellow Pages.

There are several commuter bikepaths in the Boston area that either bring you downtown or lead to a rapid transit station where you can board the train. They are:

- **Paul Dudley White Bikepath** runs along the Charles River from Watertown Sq. to the Museum of Science.
- **The Southwest Corridor linear park** includes a bikepath from Forest Hills to Copley Place.
- **Bikepaths at Alewife station** (Red Line) link Belmont and Somerville.
- **Jamaicaway Bikepath** goes from Jamaica Pond to Brookline Village
- **Muddy River Bikepath** runs along the Muddy River bordering the Longwood Medical Area and on to Fenway station.
- **Minuteman Commuter Bikeway**, an 11-mile route from Arlington to Bedford, will be completed in late 1992.

BIKES ON THE T PROGRAM

- **Red, Orange, Blue lines:** weeknights after 8:00 p.m.; Saturdays before 8:30 a.m. and after 8:00 p.m.; Sundays all day.

- **Green Line, T buses:** bikes not allowed.

- **Commuter Rail:** Non-rush hours: 9:30 a.m. to 3:00 p.m. Rush hours: (reverse commute only): outbound from start of service until 3:00 p.m. and inbound from 9:30 a.m. to 6:30 p.m.

The program operates year-round except for the weeks between Thanksgiving and Christmas, and bikes are not allowed on days or nights of Boston Garden events and games at Fenway Park and at Aquarium, Park Street, Downtown Crossing, and Government Ctr. All cyclists must have a permit ($5.00 for four years) from the Senior and Access Pass Office at Downtown Crossing, open 8:30 a.m. to 4:15 p.m. Call 722-5799 for information.

The following resources may be of help to cyclists:
- **Boston Area Bicycle Coalition**, PO Box 1015, Cambridge 02142; phone 491-RIDE. The BABC publishes pamphlets, available at many bike shops and by mail, on a variety of topics related to biking.
- **Charles River Wheelmen** , 19 Chase Ave., W. Newton 02165; phone 325-BIKE. The CRW sponsors group rides of varying lengths and difficulties, every weekend of the year.
- **Boston's Bikemap** —available at bookstores, bike shops.
- **Explorer Map and Guide**—available at bookstores, bike shops.

Chapter 4
Services for Persons With Disabilities

The Americans with Disabilities Act (ADA), which became effective in July 1992, requires all public carriers to provide services for persons with disabilities. During the initial period of compliance it is best to call the individual train, bus, or ferry line for the latest information on these services.

An increasing number of MBTA services are accessible to persons who use mobility aids, including wheelchairs. For example, 26 rapid transit stations on the Red, Orange, and Blue lines now have either ramps or elevators to their train platforms; on commuter rail, 43 stations are now accessible, including North Station, South Station, and Back Bay Station. Many more accessible stations are under construction or planned for construction. Stations that are presently accessible are shown with an accessible symbol on pages 119-129 and on the inside back cover of this book. For an update on MBTA elevator service, call 451-0027 (TDD 722-5415).

Buses with wheelchair lifts and kneelers are now available on all MBTA routes. Some routes are fully accessible all of the time; on others, you must schedule your trip a day in advance. For more information or to schedule a trip, call 1-800-LIFT-BUS (1-800-543-8287) on the day before you wish to travel.

THE RIDE is the MBTA's door-to-door lift-equipped van service. It now operates, by advance reservation, in 44 cities and towns. Expansion is planned to seven more communities by May 1993; a total of 62 communities will be served by May 1996.

MBTA Access, a free booklet available from the MBTA, describes all of the T's services and programs for persons with disabilities. For a copy, or for more information on any of these services, including THE RIDE, call the MBTA Office for Transportation Access at 722-5123 (TDD 722-5415).

All Regional Transit Authorities (RTAs) in Massachusetts operate accessible services, including lift-equipped vans; some RTAs also have lift buses on their regular routes. If you are eligible for accessible services in your area, you are also eligible to receive such services from the MBTA and any other RTA; your MBTA or RTA Transportation Access Pass will allow you reduced fares across the state (see page 8).

For information on accessible intercity bus service, call the individual bus company (see phone list on pages 167-168).

All Amtrak trains departing Boston are wheelchair accessible at South Station, Ruggles, and Back Bay Station. Amtrak stations in most large cities are accessible. Advance reservation is required. Call 482-3660 (TDD 800-523-6590).

At Logan Airport, the Airport Handicapped Van (561-1771; 561-1990 for off-peak hours) provides transportation between terminals.

For information or advice on using accessible transportation services contact:

- **Information Center for Individuals with Disabilities,** 27-43 Wormwood, First Floor, Boston, MA 02210. Call 727-5540 or 800-462-5015 (Voice or TDD).
- **Massachusetts Coalition for Citizens with Disabilities,** 80 Boylston St., Suite 339, Boston, MA 02116. Call 482-1335 or 1-800-TRY-MCCD (Voice or TDD).

Part II
Getting Around

South Station, Boston

Boston Terminals

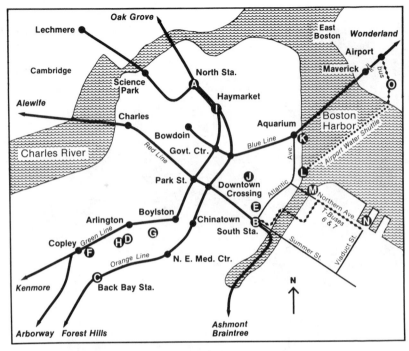

A North Station
126 Causeway St.
T-Commuter Rail

B South Station
Summer St. & Atlantic Ave.
T-Commuter Rail
Amtrak
See Downtown Boston map for commuter bus stops:
Brush Hill
Carey's
Hudson Bus *to Salem NH*
Interstate
Logan Link
Plymouth & Brockton
Trombly
Yankee Line

C Back Bay Station
145 Dartmouth St.
T-Commuter Rail
Amtrak
Bonanza

D Greyhound Terminal
10 St. James Ave.
Greyhound
Vermont Transit

E Peter Pan Terminal
555 Atlantic Ave.
American Eagle
Bloom Bus
C & J Trailways
Concord Trailways
Peter Pan
Plymouth & Brockton

F Copley Square
See Back Bay map for commuter bus stops:
Big W
Gulbankian's
Peter Pan *(some trips)*
Yankee Line
T-Buses to Newton, Watertown,
& Burlington

G Park Plaza
See Back Bay map for commuter bus stops:
Big W
Gulbankian's
Hudson Bus *to Lexington &*
Stoneham
Interstate
Plymouth & Brockton
Trombly

H St. James Ave.
See Back Bay map for commuter bus stops:
Hudson Bus *to Peabody*
Peter Pan
The Coach Co.

I Haymarket
See Downtown Boston map for commuter bus stops:
Big W
Hudson Bus *(all routes)*
The Coach Co.
T-Buses to Lynn, Salem,
Marblehead, Medford,
Woburn, & Burlington

J Federal St.
@ Franklin St.
See Downtown Boston map
T-Buses to Newton, Watertown,
& Waltham

K Long Wharf
T-Commuter Boat
to Charlestown
Bay State Cruise Co.
Boston Harbor Cruises

L Rowes Wharf
T-Commuter Boat *to Hingham*
Airport Water Shuttle

M Pier One
A. C. Cruise Line

N Commonwealth Pier
Bay State Cruise Co. *to*
Provincetown

O Logan Airport

Chapter 5

Downtown Boston and Cambridge

While driving anywhere in Boston can be difficult, taking a car downtown is guaranteed to be frustrating. Streets and highways are crowded and poorly marked, and parking—if you can find it—is expensive. Even experienced Boston drivers agree that public transit is the best way to go downtown.

In the heart of the city is "Downtown Crossing," a pedestrian zone where private cars are banned. In this shopping area are Jordan Marsh and Filene's department stores, shopping malls, and many smaller stores. Another downtown shopping area, also closed to cars, is Faneuil Hall Marketplace (or "Quincy Market"). Nearby are Boston's financial district and Government Center.

Back Bay is the area west of downtown, from the Public Garden to Massachusetts Ave. It includes the Newbury St. and Copley Place shopping areas, as well as offices of several insurance companies and other firms.

Cambridge, across the Charles River, is easily accessible by public transportation. Many Boston workers live in this area, famous for its colleges, bookstores, and cosmopolitan ambience (reflected by the international publications available at Out of Town News, alongside the Harvard T entrance).

Sightseers can sample all three areas in a few hours. A tourist staying at the Parker House on Tremont St., for example, could cut through Boston Common and the Public Garden to Newbury St., stroll its length, hop a Cambridge-bound bus at Massachusetts Ave., check out the bookstores in Harvard Sq., purchase a hometown newspaper near the subway entrance, and take the Red Line to Park Street station, a short walk back to the hotel.

Maps of downtown Boston , the Back Bay, and Cambridge are on pages 22-24 and 27.

Rapid Transit

All four subway lines serve **Downtown Boston**. The stops are close together—in some places only a block or two apart. The following subway stations serve downtown:

- **Park Street**, Park and Tremont Sts. *Red and Green lines.* The hub of the MBTA system, where the T's information booth is located. Serves Boston Common, State House, Beacon Hill; near Downtown Crossing shopping area.
- **Downtown Crossing** (formerly "Washington"), Washington and Summer Sts. *Red and Orange lines.* Downtown Crossing

shopping area (Filene's, Jordan Marsh, etc.), financial district.

- **Charles/MGH**, Charles and Cambridge Sts. *Red Line.* Borders Beacon Hill and the downtown area. If you walk down Cambridge St. toward Government Center, you will pass the Phillips all-night drugstore, Massachusetts General Hospital, Holiday Inn, Charles Cinema, the Massachusetts Department of Employment and Training in the Charles F. Hurley Building, and Suffolk University.
- **South Station**, Atlantic Ave. and Summer St. *Red Line.* Financial district, Children's Museum, Fort Point Channel area, "Leather District," Amtrak, commuter rail, Logan Link, Peter Pan Terminal, commuter buses, Rowes Wharf ferries.
- **Government Center**, Court and Tremont Sts. *Blue and Green lines.* Boston City Hall, state and federal offices, Faneuil Hall, Quincy Market.
- **State**, Washington and State Sts. *Blue and Orange lines.* Financial district, Faneuil Hall, Quincy Market; near Government Center, Old State House.
- **Aquarium** , Atlantic Ave. and State St. *Blue Line.* Waterfront, ferry docks, New England Aquarium, Quincy Market, North End.
- **Bowdoin**, Cambridge and New Chardon Sts. *Blue Line.* State offices, Beacon Hill.
- **Haymarket**, Congress and New Sudbury Sts. *Green and Orange lines.* North End, MBTA buses to North Shore points; near Government Center, weekend open-area markets.
- **Boylston**, Boylston and Tremont Sts. *Green Line.* Theatre district, Park Plaza, commuter buses; near Chinatown and New England Medical Center.
- **Chinatown** (formerly "Essex"), Washington and Boylston Sts. *Orange Line.* Chinatown; near theatre district and Park Plaza.
- **New England Medical Center** , Washington St. south of Stuart St. *Orange Line.* New England Medical Center, theatre district; near Park Plaza and Chinatown.

Back Bay is served by the Green Line and the Orange Line:

- **Arlington**, Boylston and Arlington Sts. *Green Line.* Public Garden, Park Plaza, insurance district, Newbury St. shopping, commuter buses, Greyhound Terminal.
- **Copley**, Boylston and Dartmouth Sts. *Green Line.* Insurance district, several hotels, Boston Public Library, Copley Place, Newbury St. shopping, Prudential Center; two- block walk to Back Bay Station (Amtrak and commuter rail).
- **Hynes Convention Center/ICA**, Massachusetts Ave. between Newbury and Boylston Sts. Green Line-B, C, and D. This station takes its name from nearby Hynes Convention Center and the Institute of Contemporary Art; also near Prudential

Center, Christian Science Center, Newbury St. shopping, Berklee Performance Center.

- **Prudential** , Huntington Ave. and W. Newton St. *Green Line-E.* Prudential Center, Christian Science Center, Copley Place, South End.
- **Symphony**, Huntington and Massachusetts Aves. *Green Line-E.* Symphony Hall, YMCA, Huntington Theatre, Horticultural Hall.
- **Back Bay Station** , Dartmouth St. south of Stuart St. *Orange Line.* Copley Place, Copley Square, John Hancock Building, Prudential Center, insurance district, Amtrak, commuter rail, Bonanza terminal, South End.

Cambridge is served by the Green Line and the Red Line.

- **Lechmere,** Cambridge St. and O'Brien Highway. *Green Line.* CambridgeSide Galleria shopping, Lechmere Sales, Riverfront Park.
- **Kendall,** Main St. at Carleton St. and 3 Cambridge Center. *Red Line.* East end of MIT, MIT Press bookstore, MIT Coop, free shuttle to CambridgeSide Galleria, John A. Volpe National Transportation Systems Center.
- **Central,** Massachusetts Ave. at Prospect St. *Red Line.* Cambridge City Hall, United States Post Office. Ethnic restaurants, discount clothing, furniture, and record shops highlight this area.
- **Harvard,** Massachusetts Ave. at Harvard Square. *Red Line.* In addition to Harvard University, Radcliffe College, and Lesley College, this area is known for its book and record stores, lively street music, the Loeb Drama Center and the American Repertory Theatre, the Hasty Pudding Theatre, and the Harvard Coop.
- **Porter,** Massachusetts Ave. at Somerville Ave. *Red Line..* Porter Square Shopping Center, commuter rail.
- **Davis,** College Ave. and Holland St., Somerville. *Red Line.* Tufts University, Somerville Theatre, Boston Baked Theatre, and the Seven Hills Park on the bikepath to Cambridge are features of this area.
- **Alewife,** Alewife Brook Pkwy. at Rindge Ave. and Rt. 2. *Red Line.* The Fresh Pond Shopping Center is a 1/4 mile walk from this station. Bikepaths to Somerville and the Minuteman Bikeway originate here.

Back Bay/Downtown

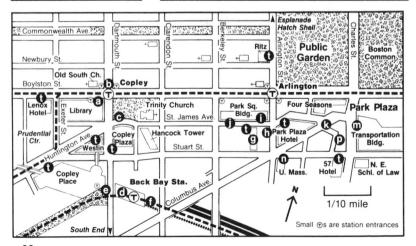

Downtown Boston

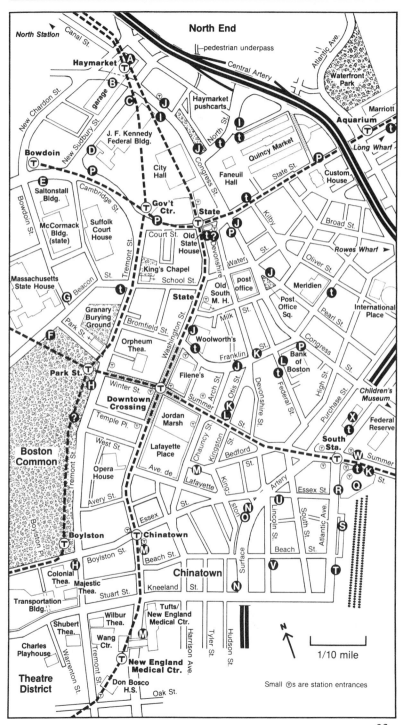

North Station

North End

pedestrian underpass

Canal St.

Central Artery

Atlantic Ave.

Waterfront Park

Haymarket

Marriott

New Chardon St.

garage

Haymarket pushcarts

North St.

Aquarium

Long Wharf

J. F. Kennedy Federal Bldg.

New Sudbury St.

Quincy Market

Bowdoin

City Hall

Congress St.

Faneuil Hall

State St.

Custom House

Saltonstall Bldg.

Cambridge St.

Gov't Ctr.

State

Kilby St.

Broad St.

Rowes Wharf

McCormack Bldg. (state)

Suffolk Court House

Court St.

Old State House

Devonshire

Water St.

Oliver St.

Bowdoin St.

Tremont St.

King's Chapel

School St.

post office

Post Office Sq.

Meridien

Massachusetts State House

Beacon St.

Old South M. H.

State

Pearl St.

International Place

Granary Burying Ground

Bromfield St.

Washington St.

Milk St.

Franklin St.

Congress St.

High St.

Children's Museum

Park St.

Orpheum Thea.

Woolworth's

Park St.

Winter St.

Filene's

Summer St.

Arch St.

Otis St.

Bank of Boston

Devonshire St.

Federal St.

Purchase St.

Federal Reserve

Boston Common

Downtown Crossing

Temple Pl.

Jordan Marsh

Chauncy St.

Kingston St.

Bedford St.

South Sta.

Summer St.

West St.

Lafayette Place

Opera House

Ave. de Lafayette

King St.

Artery

Essex St.

Lincoln St.

South St.

Atlantic Ave.

Beach St.

Boylston St.

Avery St.

Essex St.

Boylston

Chinatown

Beach St.

Chinatown

Surface

Colonial Thea.

Boylston St.

Kneeland St.

Majestic Thea.

Stuart St.

Transportation Bldg.

Wilbur Thea.

Tufts/ New England Medical Ctr.

Harrison Ave.

Tyler St.

Hudson St.

Shubert Thea.

Wang Ctr.

Charles Playhouse

New England Medical Ctr.

Theatre District

Warrenton St.

Don Bosco H.S.

Tremont St.

Oak St.

N

1/10 mile

Small Ⓣs are station entrances

23

Brookline Village

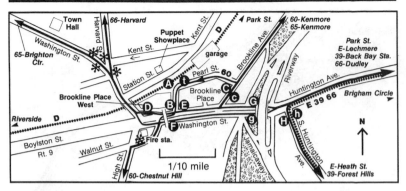

Ⓐ Brookline Village station
Green Line-D (Riverside)

Ⓑ Pearl St.
60-Chestnut Hill

Brookline Ave.

Ⓒ 65-Brighton Ctr.

ⓒ 60-Kenmore
65-Kenmore

Washington St.

Ⓓ 65-Brighton Ctr.
66-Harvard

Ⓔ Peter Pan to Framingham & Worcester (Rt. 9 local)

Ⓕ 60-Kenmore
65-Kenmore
66-Dudley

Ⓖ 66-Harvard

ⓖ 66-Dudley

S. Huntington Ave.

Ⓗ Green Line-E to Heath St.
39-Forest Hills

ⓗ Green Line-E to Lechmere
39-Back Bay Sta.

✱ Other bus stops

Ⓣ Taxi stand

Central Sq. Cambridge

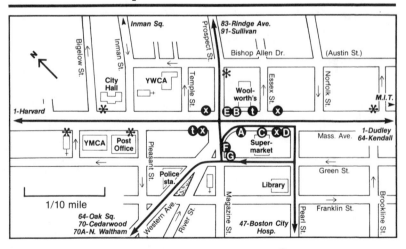

Massachusetts Ave.

Ⓐ Red Line *inbound*

Ⓑ Red Line *outbound*

Ⓒ 70-Cedarwood (Waltham)
70A-N. Waltham

Ⓓ 1-Dudley
47-Albany St.
64-Kendall *(rush hours)*
Metrobus to Longwood Ave.

Ⓔ 1-Harvard

Ⓕ Magazine St.
64-Oak Sq.
83-Rindge Ave.
91-Sullivan

Ⓖ Green St.
47-Albany St.

Ⓧ Other subway exits

✱ Other bus stops

Ⓣ Taxi stand

24

Boston **Cleveland Circle**

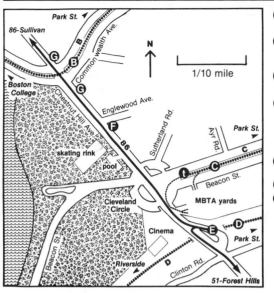

Ⓑ Commonwealth Ave.
Green Line-B (Boston College)

Ⓒ Cleveland Circle
Green Line-C (Cleveland Circle)

Ⓓ Reservoir station
Green Line-D (Riverside)

Ⓔ Reservoir busway
51-Forest Hills
86-Sullivan
Newbury College shuttle

Chestnut Hill Ave.

Ⓕ 86-Sullivan
Boston College buses

Ⓖ 86-Sullivan

ⓣ Taxi stand

Somerville **Davis Square**

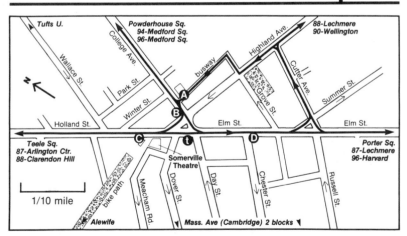

Ⓐ Davis Station and Busway
Red Line entrance
87-Arlington Ctr.
88-Clarendon Hill
90-Wellington
94-Medford Sq.
96-Medford Sq.

Ⓑ College Ave.
96-Harvard

Ⓒ Holland St.
Red Line entrance
87-Lechmere
88-Lechmere

Ⓓ Elm St.
87-Lechmere
88-Lechmere
90-Wellington
96-Harvard

ⓣ Taxi stand

Fenway/Longwood Area

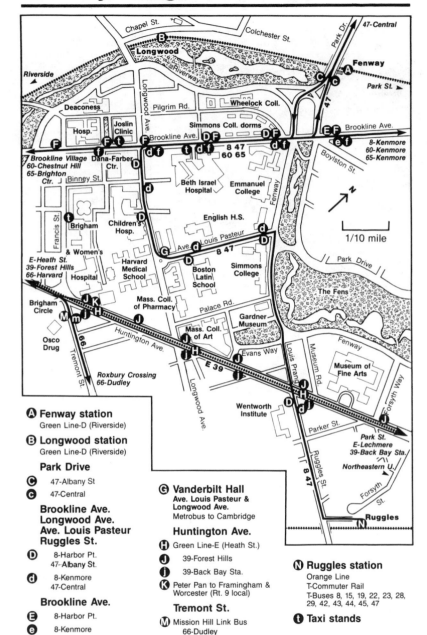

Ⓐ Fenway station
Green Line-D (Riverside)

Ⓑ Longwood station
Green Line-D (Riverside)

Park Drive

Ⓒ   47-Albany St

ⓒ   47-Central

**Brookline Ave.
Longwood Ave.
Ave. Louis Pasteur
Ruggles St.**

Ⓓ   8-Harbor Pt.
       47-Albany St.

ⓓ   8-Kenmore
       47-Central

Brookline Ave.

Ⓔ   8-Harbor Pt.

ⓔ   8-Kenmore

Ⓕ   60-Chestnut Hill
       65-Brighton Ctr.

ⓕ   60-Kenmore
       65-Kenmore

Ⓖ Vanderbilt Hall
Ave. Louis Pasteur &
Longwood Ave.
Metrobus to Cambridge

Huntington Ave.

Ⓗ   Green Line-E (Heath St.)

Ⓙ   39-Forest Hills

Ⓙ   39-Back Bay Sta.

Ⓚ   Peter Pan to Framingham &
     Worcester (Rt. 9 local)

Tremont St.

Ⓜ Mission Hill Link Bus
     66-Dudley

ⓜ   66-Harvard

Ⓝ Ruggles station
Orange Line
T-Commuter Rail
T-Buses 8, 15, 19, 22, 23, 28,
29, 42, 43, 44, 45, 47

ⓣ Taxi stands

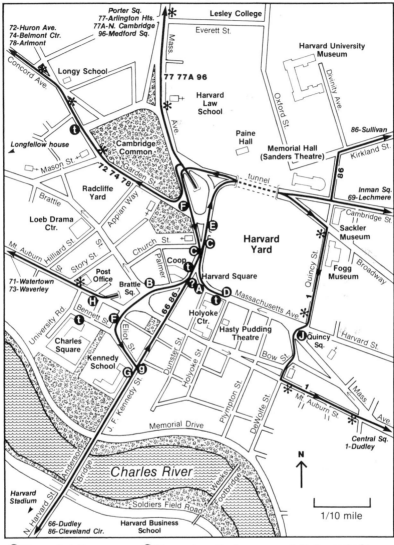

A Harvard station
Red Line
Upper level busway:
  72-Huron Ave.
  74-Belmont Ctr.
  77-Arlington Hts.
  77A-N. Cambridge
  78-Arlmont
Lower level busway Mon.-Sat.
(upper level busway on Sun.):
  71-Watertown
  73-Waverley

B Brattle Sq. entrance
Red Line and buses (see **A**)

C Church St./Johnston Gate
entrances
Red Line

D Massachusetts Ave.
  1-Dudley
  69-Lechmere

E Johnston Gate
  1-Dudley
  69-Lechmere
  86-Sullivan
  Wellesley Senate bus

F Dawes Island
  Mass. Ave. & Garden St.

Eliot Square
  Eliot & Mt. Auburn Sts.
  66-Dudley
  86-Cleveland Cir.

J. F. Kennedy St.
G 66-Dudley
     86-Cleveland Cir.
g 86-Sullivan

H Mt. Auburn St.
Bentley College bus

J Quincy Square
Mass. Ave. & Quincy St.
Metrobus to Longwood Ave.

* Other bus stops

t Taxi stands

? Information booth

27

Watertown Sq./Newton Corner

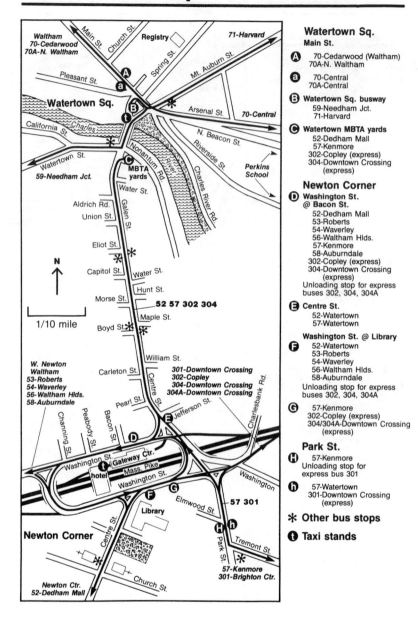

Watertown Sq.
Main St.

Ⓐ 70-Cedarwood (Waltham)
70A-N. Waltham

ⓐ 70-Central
70A-Central

Ⓑ **Watertown Sq. busway**
59-Needham Jct.
71-Harvard

Ⓒ **Watertown MBTA yards**
52-Dedham Mall
57-Kenmore
302-Copley (express)
304-Downtown Crossing
(express)

Newton Corner

Ⓓ **Washington St.
@ Bacon St.**
52-Dedham Mall
53-Roberts
54-Waverley
56-Waltham Hlds.
57-Kenmore
58-Auburndale
302-Copley (express)
304-Downtown Crossing
(express)
Unloading stop for express
buses 302, 304, 304A

Ⓔ **Centre St.**
52-Watertown
57-Watertown

Washington St. @ Library
Ⓕ 52-Watertown
53-Roberts
54-Waverley
56-Waltham Hlds.
58-Auburndale
Unloading stop for express
buses 302, 304, 304A

Ⓖ 57-Kenmore
302-Copley (express)
304/304A-Downtown Crossing
(express)

Park St.
Ⓗ 57-Kenmore
Unloading stop for
express bus 301

ⓗ 57-Watertown
301-Downtown Crossing
(express)

✳ **Other bus stops**

🅣 **Taxi stands**

MBTA Buses

The following MBTA buses serve downtown Boston:

7—City Point-Franklin/D'shire St. (via Summer St.)
11—City Point-Downtown (via Bayview)
43—Ruggles-Park St. (via Tremont St.)
49—Dudley-Downtown (via Washington St.)
53—Roberts-Downtown (via Newton Corner and Waltham)
54—Waverley-Downtown (via Newton Corner and Waltham)
55—Queensberry St.-Park St.
56—WalthamHlnds/Cedarwood-Downtown (rush hour trips only)
58—Auburndale-Downtown (certain trips only)
92—Assembly Sq. Mall-Downtown (via Main St. and Sullivan)
93—Sullivan-Downtown (via Bunker Hill St.)
300—Riverside-Downtown (express)
301—Brighton Center-Downtown (express)
304/304A—Watertown or Newton Corner-Downtown (express)
305—Waltham-Downtown (express)

Back Bay is served by the following bus routes:

1—Harvard-Dudley (via Massachusetts Ave.)
9—City Point-Copley (via Broadway)
10—City Point-Copley (via Boston City Hospital and Andrew)
39—Forest Hills-Back Bay Station
55—Queensberry St.-Park St.
302—Watertown-Copley (express)
352—Burlington-Boston (express) (certain trips only)

Cambridge is served by the following bus lines:

1—Harvard-Dudley, via Massachusetts Ave.
47—Central-Albany St.
64—Oak Sq.-Central
66—Harvard-Dudley, via Brookline
69—Harvard-Lechmere
70—Cedarwood-Central
71—Watertown-Harvard
72—Huron Ave.-Harvard
73—Waverly-Harvard
74—Belmont Ctr.-Harvard
77—Arlington Hts.-Harvard
77A—N. Cambridge-Harvard
78—Arlmont-Harvard
79—Arlington Hts.-Alewife
80—Arlington Ctr.-Lechmere
83—Rindge Ave.-Central
85—Spring Hill-Kendall

87—Arlington Ctr.-Lechmere
86—Sullivan-Cleveland Cir.
88—Clarendon Hill-Lechmere
91—Sullivan-Central
96—Medford Sq.-Harvard

The "Downtown Boston," "Back Bay," and "Cambridge" maps on pages 22-24 and 27 show the exact locations of most bus stops.

Railroad Stations

North Station, 126 Causeway St., Boston, under the Boston Garden sports arena. *Green and Orange lines.* Serves northside MBTA Commuter Rail.

South Station, Atlantic Ave. and Summer St., Boston. *Red Line.* Serves Amtrak and southside MBTA Commuter Rail. In the spring of 1992 Massport began Logan Link, a rush-hour shuttle service to Logan Airport from South Station. This station has been extensively renovated and now features a comfortable waiting room and several eateries.

Back Bay Station, 145 Dartmouth St., two blocks south of Copley Square. *Orange Line.* Serves Amtrak and south side MBTA Commuter Rail (except Fairmount Line). Bonanza bus terminal.

Porter Square Station, 1900 Massachusetts Ave., Cambridge. *Red Line* . Serves Fitchburg Line Commuter Rail.

Bus Terminals

Greyhound Terminal , 10 St. James Ave. *Green Line to Arlington;* walk 1 block south on Arlington St. (away from the Public Garden); turn right on St. James Ave. Serves Greyhound and Vermont Transit.

Peter Pan Terminal , 555 Atlantic Ave. *Red Line to South Station.* Serves American Eagle, Bloom Bus, C & J Trailways, Concord Trailways, Peter Pan, Plymouth & Brockton. (This was formerly the Trailways terminal.)

Bonanza Bus Terminal. See **Back Bay Station** above.

Commuter Bus Stops

Listed below are some of the major commuter bus stops in downtown Boston and the Back Bay. Different companies may stop at slightly different locations; and some buses make other stops besides those listed here. See the maps in this book or call the bus company for information.

Park Plaza. (formerly called "Park Square"). *Green Line to Boylston or Arlington.* Serves Gulbankian's, Hudson, Interstate, Plymouth & Brockton, Trombly.

St. James Ave. *Green Line to Arlington.* Serves Hudson, The Coach Co., Peter Pan, Big W.

Copley Square. *Green Line to Copley or Orange Line to Back Bay*

Station. Serves Big W, Gulbankian's, Peter Pan, Trombly (rush hour only), Yankee Line.

South Station. *Red Line.* Serves Brush Hill, Carey's, Hudson, Plymouth & Brockton. Nearby stops include Essex St. : Trombly, Yankee Line; Lincoln St. : Interstate; and Surface Artery : Big W.

Haymarket. *Green and Orange lines.* Serves Big W, Hudson, The Coach Co. MBTA buses to North Shore points.

Ferry Docks

Long Wharf, Atlantic Ave. at State St. Blue Line to Aquarium. Serves Bay State Cruise Co., Boston Harbor Cruises, MBTA Commuter Boat to Charlestown.

Rowes Wharf, 350 Atlantic Ave. behind the Boston Harbor Hotel. *Blue Line to Aquarium, follow Atlantic Ave. two blocks south. Or: Red Line to South Station, follow Atlantic Ave. three blocks north.* Serves Airport Water Shuttle, MBTA Commuter Boat to Hingham.

Pier 1 , 28 Northern Ave. at Sleeper St. *Red Line to South Station, walk north on Atlantic Ave. two blocks (past Peter Pan Terminal); turn right on Northern Ave. one block and cross the bridge.* Serves AC Cruise Line.

Commonwealth Pier, 164 Northern Ave. at Viaduct St. *Red Line to South Station; then T-Bus 6 (Marine Industrial Park) or 7 (City Point), or walk 3/4 mile east on Summer St. (away from downtown), and turn left on Viaduct St. Or: shuttle boat from Long Wharf.* Serves Bay State Cruise Co. to Provincetown.

Chapter 6

Logan Airport

Logan International Airport, in East Boston, is served by the MBTA Blue Line and the Airport Water Shuttle from downtown Boston, as well as buses, limousines, and taxis.

Although the airport is just two miles from downtown, it can seem like an eternity away when you're stuck in traffic. Traffic tie-ups are now common, not just at rush hours, but also at other times such as Sunday afternoons and major holidays.

For up-to-date information on ground transportation to Logan Airport, call 800-23-LOGAN.

Rapid Transit

The Blue Line goes to Airport station; from there, free Massport shuttle buses leave for all airline terminals every 8–12 minutes, 365 days a year, 5:30 am to 1:00 am. There are three shuttle bus routes:

- Airport bus 22 stops at Airport station, Terminals A and B, and the airport tower.
- Airport bus 33 stops at Airport station and Terminals C, D, and E.
- Airport bus 11 stops at all terminals (A, B, C, D, and E) and the airport tower; it does *not* go to Airport station.
- Late at night and early in the morning, these three routes are sometimes combined into a single route stopping at all terminals *and* Airport station.
- Massport employee shuttle bus stops at Airport station, *all* terminals, and can be used by persons with bicycles to arrive and depart via the Maverick Gate area.

Ferries

The Airport Water Shuttle links Logan Airport with Rowes Wharf in downtown Boston. Free shuttle buses operate between the airport ferry dock and all airline terminals.

The Airport Water Shuttle operates every 15 minutes on week-days (6:00 am-8:00 pm) and every half hour on Sundays and holidays (12:00 noon-8:00 pm). The trip from dock to dock takes about seven minutes. There is no service on Saturdays, July 4, Thanksgiving, or Christmas. The Water Shuttle transports bicycles at no extra charge.

At Rowes Wharf, the Water Shuttle connects with MBTA commuter boats from Hingham.

Buses and Limousines

Several bus and scheduled limousine companies go to Logan Airport. Service is available from most Boston hotels, plus the

Logan Airport Terminal Guide

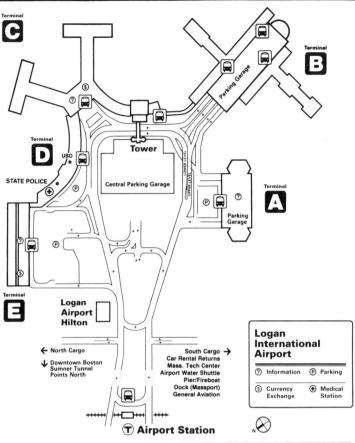

Terminal A
Continental	800-525-0280
Continental Express	569-8400
Key Air	561-6248
USAir Shuttle	482-3160

Terminal B
America West	800-247-5692
American	800-433-7300
American Eagle	800-433-7300
Cape Air	800-352-0714
Delta Shuttle	800-221-1212
Midwest Express	800-452-2022
Mohawk Airlines	800-252-2144
Quantas	800-227-4500
Sabena*	800-955-2000
Skymaster	800-553-9021
USAir/USAir Express	800-428-4322
Virgin	800-862-8621

Terminal C
Delta	800-221-1212
TWA*/TW Express	800-221-2000
United/United Express	800-241-6522

Terminal D
Charters
Alitalia*	800-223-5730

Terminal E
Aer Lingus	800-223-6537
Air Alliance	800-776-3000
Air Atlantic	800-426-7000
Air Canada	800-776-3000
Air France	800-237-2747
Air Nova	800-776-3000
British Airways	800-247-9297
El Al Israel Airlines	800-223-6700
Lufthansa	800-645-3880
Northeast Express	800-225-2525
Northwest	800-225-2525
Olympic	800-223-1226
Precision/NW Airlink	800-225-2525
Swissair	800-221-4750
TAP Air Portugal	800-221-7370

*International arrivals on Alitalia, Sabena, TWA, and Virgin use Terminal E. All other flights use the terminal indicated above.

Greyhound and Peter Pan terminals, and from many outlying sub-urbs and distant cities. Massport initiated a rush-hour shuttle-bus service from South Station to Logan, the Logan Link, in May 1992. Several shuttle buses a day are coordinated with peak-hour com-muter rail service. For complete listings of buses and limousines, look in Chapter 16, "Cities and Towns"; or check listings for the following carriers in Chapter 19:

Airways Transportation	Logan Express
Bonanza	Logan Link
C & J Trailways	M & L Transportation
City Transportation	Mass Limousine
Concord Trailways	Peter Pan
Hudson Airporter	Plymouth & Brockton
Green Harbor Transportation	Vermont Transit

Besides the Park and Ride locations listed in Chapter 16, over-night parking is permitted at Logan Express lots in Braintree and Framingham, with seven consecutive parking days discounted to the six-day rate.

Taxis

Taxi fares between downtown and Logan average about $12.00, depending on traffic, plus tolls. Passengers boarding at the airport must also pay a 50¢ surcharge. Taxis are available at all terminals at all times.

Flat-rate fares are in effect to points beyond a 12-mile radius from downtown Boston. You should confirm the fare in advance with the driver or the Logan taxi dispatcher.

Airport Telephone Numbers

Public Information Office	561-1800
State Police	567-2233
Medical Station	569-8652
Fire Emergency/First Aid	567-2020
Airport Handicap Van	561-1769
Foreign Language Translators	561-1803

Chapter 7

Transit in New England

You don't need a car to travel around New England. Buses and trains serve major cities and small towns throughout the region. The map in this chapter shows some of the places where you can go.

Connecticut

Connecticut is served by two different Amtrak routes from Boston, as well as Peter Pan (617-426-7838), Greyhound (617-423-5810), and Bonanza (617-720-4110) buses.

Amtrak's scenic "Shore Line" has nine trains daily, via Mystic, New London, and Old Saybrook. At Mystic, the Mystic Seaport museum village is just a few blocks from the train station. A second Amtrak route, with two trains daily, operates via Hartford. Both routes converge at New Haven, the home of Yale University, before continuing to Bridgeport and Stamford.

New Haven, Bridgeport, and Stamford are transfer points from Amtrak to Metro-North Commuter Railroad (800-638-7646) for local trains to Westport, Norwalk, New Canaan, Greenwich, and other towns.

Hartford, the state capital and the site of Mark Twain's house, has frequent bus service from Boston via Peter Pan, Greyhound and Bonanza. Greyhound also serves New Haven.

Other towns and cities you can reach from Boston by public transportation include Canaan, Danbury, Danielson, Fairfield, Kent, Meriden, Middletown, Milford, New Britain, Southbury, Storrs, Stratford, Wallingford, Willimantic, and Waterbury.

There are ferries across Long Island Sound from New London and Bridgeport. The ferry docks are adjacent to the Amtrak station:

New London—Block Island, RI (summer only): 203-442-7891
New London—Fishers Island, NY (year-round): 203-443-6851
New London—Orient Point, NY (year-round): 203-443-5281
New London—Montauk, NY (May-October): 800-MONTAUK
Bridgeport—Port Jefferson, NY (year-round): 203-367-3043

The following Connecticut cities have local bus service:

Bridgeport 203-333-3031
Danbury 203-748-203
New London 203-886-2631
Meriden 203-235-6851
Middletown 203-346-0212
Milford 203-783-3258
New Britain 203-828-0511

New Haven 203-624-0151
Hartford 203-525-9181
Norwalk 203-852-0000
Stamford 203-327-RIDE
Wallingford 203-294-2160
Waterbury 203-753-2538
Westport 203-226-7171

New England

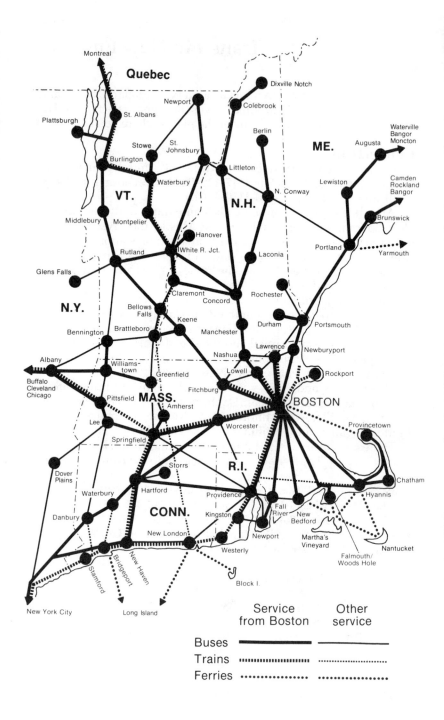

Maine

Portland, Maine's largest city, is served by Greyhound (617-423-5810) and Concord Trailways (1-800-639-5150) buses from Boston.

Greyhound buses then continue north from Portland, following either the inland route via Lewiston, Augusta, and Waterville, or the coastal route via Brunswick, Rockland, and Camden. Both routes meet at Bangor, where you can connect to buses for northern Maine and "down East" points, including Bar Harbor, the gateway to Acadia National Park. Concord Trailways buses continue nonstop to Bangor.

Vinalhaven, North Haven, and Matinicus islands are reached by ferry from Rockland. Call 207-596-2202.

Other towns and cities you can reach from Boston by public transportation include Bar Harbor, Bath, Bellfast, Berwick, Biddeford, Calais, Caribou, Ellsworth, Freeport, Houlton, Machias, Orono, Presque Isle, Saco, Waterville, and Wiscasset.

The following Maine cities have local bus service:

Augusta 207-622-4761	Lewiston/Auburn 207-783-2033
Bangor 207-947-0536	Portland 207-774-0351
Berwick 603-862-2328	S. Portland 207-767-5556
Biddeford/Saco 207-282-5408	

For Maine tourist information, call 800-533-9595 or 207-289-2423.

New Hampshire

Central New Hampshire is served by Concord Trailways (603-238-3300) and Vermont Transit (617-292-4700) buses from Boston. Both companies have several trips daily to Manchester and to Concord, the state capital.

Concord Trailways buses then continue north into the Lake Winnipesaukee and White Mountains regions. Hiking trails are accessible at many of the stops along the route. Several ski areas are also near bus stops such as Lincoln (North Woodstock), Conway, and Jackson.

One of Concord Trailways' stops is at the Appalachian Mountain Club camp in Pinkham Notch. In summer, the AMC has a "hiker's shuttle service" which connects the camp with several nearby trailheads. Call 603-466-2727 for details and reservations.

Vermont Transit goes to Lebanon and Hanover (site of Dartmouth College), with one bus daily to Newport, Claremont, and Mt. Sunapee. Another Vermont Transit route stops at Keene.

Portsmouth, on the seacoast, is served by C & J Trailways (617-426-7838) and Greyhound (617-423-5810). C & J Trailways also serves the University of New Hampshire at Durham.

Peter Pan (617-426-7838) has daily summer buses from Boston to Hampton Beach. C & J Trailways, Concord Trailways, Hudson Bus (617-395-8080), The Coach Co. (1-800-225-4846), and Vermont Transit operate commuter schedules to Boston from several southern New Hampshire cities.

All C & J Trailways, Concord Trailways, and Vermont Transit buses from Boston also serve Logan Airport. For additional airport service, see Chapter 18 listings for Hudson Airporter (617-395-8080) and M & L Transportation (1-800-225-4846).

The following New Hampshire cities have local bus service:

Dover/Durham 603-862-2328   Nashua 603-880-0100
Hampton Beach 603-926-8717   Portsmouth 603-862-2328
Hanover/Lebanon 603-448-2815   Rochester 603-862-2328
Manchester 603-623-8801

For New Hampshire tourist information, call 603-271-2666.

Rhode Island

Rhode Island is served by Bonanza buses (617-720-4110) and Amtrak (617-482-3660) trains from Boston. Bonanza has frequent service to Providence, Pawtucket, and Newport from both downtown Boston and Logan Airport; and Amtrak stops at Providence, Kingston, and Westerly. In addition, MBTA Commuter Rail (617-227-5070) serves Providence, the state capital.

Block Island can be reached by ferry from Providence and Newport, and from New London, CT (Amtrak).

All bus service within Rhode Island is operated by Rhode Island Public Transit Authority (RIPTA); see Chapter 20, "Regional Transit Authorities," for details.

For Rhode Island tourist information, call 800-556-2484.

Downtown Providence as seen from South Water St.

Vermont

Most intercity buses in Vermont are operated by Vermont Transit, a private company. Virtually all points in the state can be reached directly from Boston or by connections at White River Jct. or Rutland.

Bennington, in the southwestern part of the state, is served by Bonanza buses (617-720-4110) from Boston.

Peter Pan has winter service to the Mount Snow ski area.

The following Vermont cities have local bus service:

Barre/Montpelier 802-479-1071   Rutland 802-773-3244
Burlington 802-864-0211   White River Jct. 603-448-2815
    For Vermont tourist information, call 802-828-3236.

Beyond New England

New York

Amtrak (617-482-3660), Peter Pan (617-426-7838), Greyhound (617-423-5810), and Bonanza (617-720-4110) all have frequent daily service from Boston to New York City. Many Amtrak trains also stop at New Rochelle, and connecting Metro-North commuter trains are available from Stamford, CT, to Rye, Mt. Vernon, and other towns.

Long Island Railroad trains depart from Amtrak's Pennsylvania Station in New York City; ferries to Long Island are described above, in the Connecticut listing.

If you are flying to New York, call 800-AIR-RIDE for information on bus, train, limousine, and ferry service from LaGuardia, Kennedy, and Newark airports.

Albany, the state capital, is served by Peter Pan and Greyhound buses from Boston and Amtrak's daily "Lake Shore Limited." All have through or connecting service across New York state to Utica, Syracuse, Rochester, and Buffalo. Connections may also be made at the Albany bus terminal for other New York state points.

Fishers Island can be reached by two ferries from New London, CT.

Other areas that can be reached from Boston by public transportation include Dover Plains, Long Island, Plattsburgh, Port Chester, White Plains, and Yonkers.

Here are transit information numbers for major New York cities:

Albany 518-482-8822   New Rochelle 914-682-2020
Buffalo 716-855-7211   New York City 718-330-1234
Long I. (Nassau) 516-222-1000   Rochester 716-288-1700
Long I. (Suffolk) 516-360-5700   Syracuse 315-442-3400

Three different commuter railroads serve New York City:

Long Island Railroad 718-217-LIRR
Metro-North Commuter Railroad 800-638-7646
New Jersey Transit 201-460-8444
    For New York state tourist information, call 800-I-LOVE-NY.

Canada

Bus service is available from Boston to several Canadian cities. Vermont Transit has a daily bus to Montreal, with connections to Quebec city. Buses to Toronto leave from Buffalo, NY, and Montreal.

Amtrak's overnight "Montrealer" goes from Washington, DC, to Montreal; connections from Boston can be made at New Haven or New London, CT.

In summer, Prince of Fundy Cruises operates an overnight ferry from Portland, ME, to Yarmouth, Nova Scotia, with connecting bus service to Halifax. Call 800-341-7540 for reservations. Concord Trailways has seven buses to Amherst, Truro, Halifax, Antigonish, and Sydney, Nova Scotia.

For Canadian tourist information, call 536-1730 in Boston; for passenger train information, call VIA Rail Canada at 800-561-3949.

Part III
Places to See, Things to Do

Skating in the Public Garden

VISITOR INFORMATION

Following are the city's major tourist information centers. The centers marked with * sell Boston Passport MBTA visitor passes.

- **Boston Visitor Information Line** Call 536-4100 weekdays.

- **Boston Common Information Booth***—Tremont St. near Park Street station. Red Line or Green Line to Park Street.

- **Boston National Historical Park Visitor Center** (242-5642)—15 State St., corner of Devonshire St., across from the Old State House. Freedom Trail information and tours; public restrooms; wheelchair accessible. Orange Line or Blue Line to State; Green Line to Government Center.

- **Bostix***—adjacent to Faneuil Hall, off Congress St. Information on cultural events and organizations; ticket sales, including some half-price, same-day tickets. (Closed Mondays.) Orange Line or Blue Line to State; Green Line to Government Center.

- **Faneuil Hall Marketplace Information Center***—South Market St., adjacent to Quincy Market. Orange Line or Blue Line to State; Green Line to Government Center.

- **Cambridge Discovery Information Booth** (497-1630)—Harvard Square. Cambridge information and tours. Red Line to Harvard.

- **The Travelers Aid Society** (542-7286)—offices at 17 East St., Boston (near South Station); booths at the Greyhound Bus Terminal and Logan Airport, Terminals A and E.

In and Near Bo

Historic, Cultural, and Other Attractions

Boston's crooked streets may be an annoyance to motorists, but they are a delight to walkers, whether they are following the famous Freedom Trail, shopping, or just taking a stroll. By an adroit mix of walking and using the transit system, you can cover a lot of territory.

All the places in this section are served by the MBTA's four rapid transit lines. Destinations in **bold type** have detailed listings in Chapter 11.

Guidebooks to the Freedom Trail and other Boston neighborhoods are available at visitor information centers and at local bookstores.

The Freedom Trail

The Freedom Trail is a self-guided walking tour of sites associated with this nation's early history. It wends its way from Boston Common, past **Faneuil Hall** and through the North End to Charlestown. Along the way are the **Old South Meeting-House**, the **Old State House**, the **Paul Revere House** and the **Old North Church**, "Old Ironsides" (**U.S.S. *Constitution***) and the **Bunker Hill Monument**. Several of these sites are now part of the Boston National Historical Park.

To start the trail, take the *Red* or *Green Line* to Park Street. The trail, which is marked by a red line on the sidewalk, begins at the Visitor Information Booth about 100 feet south of the station on Tremont St. Maps of the trail can be bought at this booth. The National Park Visitor Center at 15 State St. (242-5642), across from the Old State House, offers free maps, a free slide show, and (from April to November) free ranger-guided tours.

The Freedom Trail has provided inspiration for two other trails: The Black Heritage Trail (discussed below under "Beacon Hill") and the Women's Heritage Trail. Featuring walks in downtown, the North End, Chinatown, and Beacon Hill, the Women's Heritage Trail, visits sites associated with Amelia Earhart, Rose Kennedy, Phillis Wheatley, Mary Baker Eddy, Louisa May Alcott, Julia Ward Howe, and many other noted women. For information, call 248-9828

Sightseeing Tours and Cruises

Guided walking tours allow you to visit many Boston neighborhoods—including Beacon Hill and the North End—where narrow streets prevent buses from entering. Many different groups offer tours in warm weather months, catering to diverse interests including architectural sites, historical areas (one such tour is led by

"Benjamin Franklin"), and murder and mystery locations (Boston, after all, is the birthplace of Edgar Allan Poe). There's even an annual midnight-to-dawn bicycle tour of architectural and historic sites. Check newspaper calendar listings under "Walking Tours."

Several firms offer bus and "trolley" tours of the city. On so-called *trolley tours,* you can usually get off at any stop and then board a later trolley to complete the tour. *Motorcoach (bus) tours* do not allow reboarding. The following tours all include Boston and Charlestown; motorcoach tours also include Cambridge.

- **Boston Trolley Tours** (427-TOUR)—Boston/Charlestown tour (The "Blue Trolley").
- **Brush Hill Tours** (236-2148)—"Beantown Trolley" and motorcoach tours. ~ *disconnected*
- **Gray Line** (426-8805)—motorcoach tours.
- **Old Town Trolley** (269-7010)—Boston/Charlestown tour and Cambridge tour.

These companies offer sightseeing cruises of Boston Harbor:

- **Bay State Cruise Co.** (723-7800)—from Long Wharf (Blue Line to Aquarium): sightseeing; Nantasket Beach; lunch and dinner cruises; whalewatch cruises. Also, from Commonwealth Pier: Provincetown (Cape Cod) day trip.
- **Boston Harbor Cruises** (227-4321)—from Long Wharf (Blue Line to Aquarium): sightseeing; lunch cruises.
- **New England Aquarium** (973-5277)—from Central Wharf (Blue Line to Aquarium): whalewatch cruises.
- **Spirit of Boston** (569-4449)—from Rowes Wharf (Blue Line to Aquarium, or Red Line to South Station): lunch and dinner cruises.
- **A. C. Cruise Line** (426-8419)—from Pier 1, Northern Ave. (Red Line to South Station, or Blue Line to Aquarium): Gloucester day trip; whalewatch cruises.

Check newspaper ads and listings for other cruises such as music cruises; and see Chapter 19 for ferries to the Boston Harbor Islands State Park.

The Back Bay

This neighborhood of 19th-century townhouses, churches, and shopping areas is served by the *Green Line,* with stops at *Arlington, Copley, Prudential, Symphony,* and *Hynes Convention Ctr./ICA;* and by the *Orange Line* at *Back Bay Station.* (See map, page 22.)

Among the Back Bay's museums and attractions are the Public Garden with its famed Swan Boats, the **Gibson House Museum, Trinity Church,** the **Boston Public Library,** the **Institute of Contemporary Art (ICA),** and the **Christian Science Center** and **Mapparium.**

Boston's two tallest buildings, the **John Hancock** and **Prudential** towers, both have public observation decks.

Two fictional creations have attracted visitors to the area. The duckling statues in the Public Garden are based on the Mallard family of ducks in Robert McCloskey's children's classic *Make Way for Ducklings*. The nearby Bull & Finch pub, at 84 Beacon St., is usually crowded with fans of "Cheers," the television show it inspired.

Beacon Hill

Beacon Hill remains a quiet enclave in the middle of the busy city. Since its one-way streets have been purposely designed to frustrate drivers, it is an excellent place for walking. Atop the hill is the **Massachusetts State House**, and below are some of the city's finest houses. *Take the Red Line or Green Line to Park St.* Louisburg Square, with its patrician homes, is the centerpiece of Beacon Hill.

The Black Heritage Trail winds its way across Beacon Hill; the **Boston African-American National Historic Site** (also known as the "African Meeting House") and the **Museum of Afro American History** are on the hill's north slope. For information about the trail, call 742-5415; or pick up a free brochure at one of the city's visitor centers. At the foot of Beacon Hill, Charles Street, with its many restaurants and antique shops, is a popular shopping area. *Take the Red Line to Charles/MGH.*

Beacon Hill, Boston

Cambridge

Harvard Square in Cambridge is known for its many bookstores, restaurants, and shops, as well as the nation's oldest college. From Boston, take the Red Line to Harvard. Cambridge Discovery's information booth (497-1630) is next to the subway entrance. Harvard University's information office is in Holyoke Center, a modern building behind an outdoor cafe, a block from the subway station. The university has several museums, including the **Busch-Reisinger**, **Fogg**, and **Sackler** art museums, the **Semitic Museum**, and the **Harvard University Museums of Natural History** complex with the Glass Flowers. (See map, page 27.)

On Brattle St. is the **Longfellow National Historic Site,** which was Gen. George Washington's headquarters during the American Revolution.

On Massachusetts Ave., facing the Back Bay across the river, is the Massachusetts Institute of Technology (M.I.T.), which also has a **museum**. *Take T-Bus 1 (Harvard-Dudley) or the Red Line to Kendall to the campus.*

Both colleges offer tours of their campuses, and in summer, tours of historic Cambridge and Brattle St. start at the Cambridge Discovery booth.

Charlestown

The granite obelisk of the **Bunker Hill Monument** towers over Charlestown's 18th- and 19th-century houses. On the waterfront below is the **Charlestown Navy Yard**, home of the U.S.S. *Constitution*, nicknamed "Old Ironsides." You can take a *T-Commuter Boat* from Long Wharf to the Navy Yard (free connecting shuttle bus within the Navy Yard); or take *T-Bus 92 or 93*, which you can board either at Haymarket *(Green or Orange lines)* or in front of Woolworth's on Washington St. in Boston*(Red Line to Downtown Crossing).*

Chinatown

Boston's Chinatown is one of the largest Asian neighborhoods in the United States. To get there, take the *Orange Line to Chinatown* station. Or take the *Green Line to Boylston* and walk one block east on Boylston St. to Chinatown station. From there, walk one block south on Washington St., and turn left on Beach St. into the heart of Chinatown's retail district. This route will take you through what remains of Boston's adult-entertainment area, the Combat Zone. (See map, page 23.)

An alternate route is the *Red Line to South Station,* then walk south along the "Surface Artery" to Beach St., where you will see a large ceremonial Chinese gate at the entrance to Chinatown.

Downtown Crossing

The streets of Boston's downtown shopping area are now a pedestrian mall lined with pushcart vendors. *Take the Red Line or*

Orange Line to Downtown Crossing. You can walk from the subway station directly into Filene's or Jordan Marsh department stores without going outside. Or see Chapter 5 for a list of T-Buses serving downtown. (See map, pages 22-23.)

Faneuil Hall and Quincy Market

These 19th-century markets, reincarnated as a modern shopping center, have become one of the nation's most popular tourist attractions. *Take the Orange Line or Blue Line to State;* or *the Green Line to Government Center* and walk across City Hall Plaza.

The North End

The North End, Boston's oldest neighborhood, is the heart of the city's Italian-American community. It is known for its festivals on summer weekends, and its restaurants and bakeries, as well as for the **Paul Revere House** and the **Old North Church**. *Take the Green Line or Orange Line to Haymarket* and walk through the pedestrian underpass beneath the Central Artery Expressway.

The horse-and-carriage tours, located in Quincy Market (across from the Bostonian Hotel), go into the North End, adding to its romantic atmosphere.

Quincy

Quincy, the "Presidents' City," was the hometown of Presidents John Adams and John Quincy Adams. Their mansion, now the **Adams National Historic Site**, is open from April to November. It and several other historic sites may be visited by taking the *Red Line (Braintree) to Quincy Center.* For information call the Quincy Historical Society at 773-1144.

For information on tours of Quincy's historic granite industry, including America's first commercial railroad, call 698-1802. The quarries are off of Ricciuti Drive; take *T-Bus 215 (Quincy Ctr.-Ashmont)* to Willard and Copeland Sts., and follow Willard St. under the highway.

Note: Quincy **Market** is in downtown Boston, not in Quincy **Center**, which is 10 miles south of downtown.

The Waterfront

Take the *Blue Line to Aquarium*, and you will be in the center of Boston's historic waterfront. At Long Wharf and Rowes Wharf, you can board cruise boats to explore the harbor; nearby are Waterfront Park and the **New England Aquarium**. If you're downtown, you can walk out State St. to the waterfront; the "Harborwalk" self-guided tour pamphlet is available at the National Park Visitor Center at 15 State St.

On the Fort Point Channel, near South Station *(Red Line)* is the "Museum Wharf" complex: the **Children's Museum**, the **Computer Museum**, and the replica **Boston Tea Party Ship**.

Parks and Recreation

Many of Boston's parks, beaches, and other recreation areas are accessible by public transit. This section covers sites which are close to the city; more distant parks and beaches are in the next chapter.

Parks marked "BP&R" are operated by Boston Parks and Recreation; call 635-4505 for information on special programs in these and other city parks.

Boston's Emerald Necklace is a seven-mile string of parks, most of which were designed by Frederick Law Olmsted. With a few short interruptions, you can hike in parkland from Boston Common to Franklin Park in Dorchester. All of the BP&R parks listed here are part of the necklace. For information on Boston Park Rangers tours, call 522-2639.

Parks marked "MDC" are operated by the Metropolitan District Commission. Maps of individual MDC parks, showing hiking trails, are available by sending a stamped self-addressed envelope to Metro Parks, 20 Somerset St., Boston MA 02108; specify the park(s) for which you want maps. Or call 727-5250 for information. For a list of MDC skating rinks and swimming pools, call 727-9547.

For information on a specific activity, see the following listings:

Beaches: Dorchester; East Boston; Revere; Quincy; South Boston; Winthrop.
Canoeing: Newton (Charles River).
Golf: Cambridge (Fresh Pond, T-Bus 72); Dorchester (Franklin Park); also Putterham Meadows in Brookline (T-Bus 51, Cleveland Circle-Forest Hills); and George Wright Golf Course in Hyde Park (T-Bus 50, Cleary Sq.-Forest Hills via Roslindale).
Ice Skating: Boston (Public Garden); Brookline (Chestnut Hill); Waltham (Beaver Brook); or call the MDC.
Rowboats: Jamaica Pond.
Sailing: Boston (Community Boating); Somerville (Blessing of the Bay); Jamaica Pond.
Skiing, cross-country: Rentals in Weston; other parks offer trails.
Swimming Pools: Boston (Charles River); Brookline (Chestnut Hill); or call the MDC.

Boston: Downtown and the Back Bay

Boston Common is the oldest public park in America. *Red Line to Park St., or Green Line to Park Street or Boylston.* (BP&R)

Public Garden—Stroll around the lagoon, feed the ducks, or take a ride on the Swan Boats (Apr.-Sept.). You can rent ice skates in winter. *Green Line to Arlington.* (BP&R)

Charles River Esplanade —A popular spot for jogging, bike riding on the Paul Dudley White Bikepath, roller skating, and sunning. *Take the Red Line to Charles/MGH* and cross the overpass to the river; or take the *Green Line to Arlington, Copley, Hynes Convention Ctr./ICA, or Kenmore* and walk two to four blocks north to the river. There is a public swimming pool near the Science Museum *(Green Line to Science Park, or Red Line to Charles/MGH.)* You can hike or bike on both sides of the river for six miles, from the Science Museum to Watertown Sq. (MDC)

Community Boating, Inc.—Learn to sail and enjoy inexpensive sailing on the Charles (523-1038). *Red Line to Charles/MGH.*

Back Bay Fens—Tree-lined lagoons make this one of Boston's most beautiful parks. Be sure to visit the Rose Garden on Park Drive, near Jersey St. *Take the Green Line-E (Heath St.) or T-Bus 39* (Forest Hills-Back Bay Sta.) to the Museum stop and cross behind the Museum of Fine Arts. Or: *Green Line-(B, C, or D) to Hynes Convention Ctr./ICA* and walk two blocks west on Boylston St. to the Fenway. (BP&R)

Southwest Corridor Park—see listing under "Jamaica Plain."

Boston Harbor Islands. See Chapter 9.

Brookline and Brighton

Riverway —Half in Boston and half in Brookline, this park is a pleasant oasis in the middle of the city. *Green Line-D (Riverside) to Fenway or Longwood.* (BP&R)

Chestnut Hill Reservoir —The 1.7-mile track around the reservoir is popular with joggers; there is also a picnic area and a public swimming pool. *Green Line-B to Chestnut Hill Ave., Green Line-C to Cleveland Circle, or Green Line-C (Riverside) to Reservoir;* walk out Beacon St. past the Ground Round restaurant. (MDC)

Christian Herter Park —This park on the Charles River has a playground, wading pool, and picnic tables. *Take T-Bus 70 (Cedarwood-Central), 70A (N. Waltham-Central), or 86 (Sullivan-Cleveland Circle)* to Everett St.; walk one block north to the river. (MDC)

Cambridge

Charles River Basin —*Red Line to Harvard*, then walk along J. F. Kennedy St. to the river. On Sundays from April to November, Memorial Drive becomes "Riverbend Park," and cars are banned between Western Ave. and the Eliot Bridge. (MDC)

Fresh Pond —*Red Line to Harvard, then T-Bus 72 (Huron Ave.)* to Fresh Pond Pkwy. The footpath around the pond is popular for joggers. No swimming. (MDC)

Mount Auburn Cemetery—The cemetery is also a botanical garden and a birdwatcher's paradise. *Red Line to Harvard, then T-Bus 71 (Watertown), 72 (Huron Ave.), or 73 (Waverley).*

Dorchester

Franklin Park —This is Boston's largest park and one of landscape architect Frederick Law Olmsted's masterpieces. *Take the Orange Line to Green station* and walk four blocks east (to the right) into the park. To reach the park's eastern side, near the zoo and the golf course, *take the Orange Line to Ruggles, then T-Bus 22 (Ashmont via Jackson Sq.), 28 (Mattapan), or 45 (Franklin Park). Or: T-Bus 16 from either JFK/UMass (Red Line) or Forest Hills (Orange Line).* For more information and a map, send a self-addressed stamped envelope to the Franklin Park Coalition, 170 Morton St., Jamaica Plain, MA 02130. (BP&R)

   Malibu and Savin Hill Beaches *—Red Line (Ashmont) to Savin Hill.* Walk east on Savin Hill Ave. to Playstead St. and turn right. (MDC)

East Boston
   Constitution Beach *—Blue Line to Orient Heights.* Walk one block east on Saratoga St. to Barnes Ave. and turn right past the library. (MDC)

Jamaica Plain
   Arnold Arboretum *—Green Line-E/T-Bus 39 to The Monument,* then walk west on Centre St. to the Arboretum's main gate. Or: *Orange Line to Forest Hills* and walk north into the Arboretum. (BP&R)

   Jamaica Pond *—Green Line-E/T-Bus 39 to Pond St.;* walk one block west on Pond St. You can rent a rowboat or sailboat, and the pond is stocked with fish. No swimming. (BP&R)

   Olmsted Park *—*This quiet park is part of the Emerald Necklace. *Green Line-E/T-Bus 39 to Bynner St.;* walk one block west on Bynner St. You can walk north in the park to Brookline Village *(Green Line-D)* or south to Jamaica Pond. (BP&R)

   Southwest Corridor Park *—*A 52-acre park has been built along the route of the MBTA Orange Line, including a three-mile bike path from Forest Hills to Copley Place. *Take the Orange Line to any station from Back Bay Station to Forest Hills.* (MDC)

   Franklin Park *—*See listing under "Dorchester."

Malden and Melrose
   Pine Banks Park *—*This park has hiking and skiing trails, and a picnic area with a duck pond and a small zoo. *Take the Orange Line to Oak Grove;* follow signs "To Buses," then walk along the driveway to the left. Near the end of the parking lot, go through the opening in the fence on your right, and cross a footbridge. Walk one block to the end of Fairlawn St.; turn left on Main St. One block to the park entrance.

Medford and Stoneham
   Mystic River *—Orange Line to Wellington.* Make two right turns leaving the station; walk through the parking lot, toward Boston, then through a gate and past a gravel storage area. When you reach the river's edge, turn right under the tracks. The park extends 3 miles upriver, past Medford Sq. (served by T-Buses 94, 95, 96, 101, and 134). (MDC)

Middlesex Fells —This 2,000-acre park can be reached by several MBTA routes. *Take the Orange Line to Oak Grove,* make two right turns leaving the station, and walk north on Washington St. 1/2 mile, then left up Goodyear Ave. to a trailhead. Or take the *Orange Line to Malden Ctr.,* then *T-Bus 99 (Upper Highland)* to the end.

The western half of the park can be reached by the *Orange Line to Wellington, then T-Bus 100 (Elm St.).* Get off at the rotary and cross over the highway to Pine Hill and a lookout tower; or stay on the bus to the end of the line and walk 1 1/2 blocks north on the Fellsway to a trailhead.

Hudson Bus (Boston-Stoneham) has early morning and afternoon buses, Mon.-Fri., to the northern part of the park, including the Stone Zoo.

Newton

Charles River —*Green Line-D to Riverside;* walk behind the car barns and cross an unused railroad bridge to the park. A three-mile walk along the river is possible. (MDC)

The Charles River Canoe and Kayak Center , canoe and kayak rentals, is a 20-minute walk from *Riverside (Green Line-D),* call 965-5110 for directions; or take *T-Bus 58 (Auburndale)* from Newton Corner (Mon.-Fri.).

Hemlock Gorge and Echo Bridge —*Green Line-D (Riverside)* to Waban. Turn left on Beacon St. over the tracks, then left on Waban Ave. after the church, and left again on Annawan Rd. to the river (about 1/2 mile). Follow the river to the left. (MDC)

Charles River, Newton

Hammond Pond Woods—Green Line-D (Riverside) to Chestnut Hill. Turn left on Hammond St., then right before the shopping center to the park entrance on your right. No swimming. (MDC)

Quincy

Wollaston Beach —Red Line to Braintree to Wollaston; walk east on Beale and Beach Sts. (one mile). Or take *T-Bus 217 (Wollaston Beach),* Mon.-Sat., from Wollaston or Ashmont (Red Line). (MDC)

Neponset Marshes—Red Line to Ashmont, then T-Bus 217 (Wollaston Beach), Mon.-Sat., to Adams and Squantum Sts. This is an excellent spot for birdwatching. (MDC)

Revere

Revere Beach—Blue Line to either Revere Beach or Wonderland; walk one block east to the beach. (MDC)

Somerville

"Blessing of the Bay"—Inexpensive sailing and lessons on the Mystic River (628-9610). *Orange Line to Sullivan, then T-Bus 95 (West Medford)* to Shore Drive and walk under the highway.

South Boston

Castle Island —Linked to the mainland, Castle Island is a good fishing spot, and there is a small, sheltered beach. Historic Fort Independence is also located here. *Red Line to Broadway, then T-Bus 9 (City Point) or 11 (Bayview)* to the end of the line. From the bus stop at 1st and P Sts., walk mile east along Pleasure Bay. Less frequent buses to City Point leave from South Station *(T-Bus 7)* and Copley *(T-Buses 9 and 10).* (MDC)

Carson Beach—Red Line (Ashmont) to JFK/UMass, then walk north along Day Blvd. to the beach. (MDC)

M St. Beach —Red Line to Broadway, then T-Bus 11 (Bayview). Get off anywhere along E. 8th St. and walk two blocks south to the beach. (MDC)

Waltham and Belmont

Beaver Brook and Waverley Oaks —This small park has picnic tables, wildflowers, and a duck pond where you can ice skate in winter. *Red Line to Harvard, then T-Bus 73 (Waverley)* to the end of the line; walk 1/4 mile up Trapelo Rd. to the park. (MDC)

Watertown

Charles River—There is a nice park on the north bank of the river, and you can bike or walk along the river all the way to downtown Boston—six miles. *Take any of the following T-Buses to Watertown Sq.: 57 (Watertown-Kenmore); 70 (Cedarwood-Central); 70A (N. Waltham-Central); or 71 (Watertown-Harvard).* (MDC)

Weston

Weston Ski Track —Cross-country skiing and rentals (891-6575). Green Line-D to Riverside, then a one-mile walk; call for directions.

West Roxbury

Stony Brook Reservation—This 600-acre wooded park has miles of hiking and skiing trails and scenic views from hilltops. *Orange Line* or *Green Line-E/T-Bus 39 to Forest Hills; then T-Bus 34 (Dedham Line), 34E (East Walpole), or 40 (Georgetowne).* Get off at Washington and LaGrange Sts. (MDC)

Winthrop

Winthrop Beach — *Blue Line to Orient Heights,* then take any Paul Revere "Winthrop Beach" or "Point Shirley" bus. (MDC)

Chapter 9
Day and Weekend Trips

Historic Areas

One-day sightseeing tours to many of the places listed in this section—including Lexington and Concord, Salem, Plymouth, and Newport—are offered by Brush Hill (236-2148) and Gray Line (426-8805). See page 36 for transit map of New England.

Amherst, Northampton, and South Hadley

These three western Massachusetts towns are home to the "Five Colleges." In Amherst are Amherst College, Hampshire College, and the University of Massachusetts. On the Amherst College campus are the Mead Art Building and the Pratt Museum of Natural History, and just across the street is the home of poet Emily Dickinson. Northampton is the site of Smith College, which has a renowned art museum, and the town has many crafts galleries. Mt. Holyoke College, which also has an art museum, is in S. Hadley.

Peter Pan has regular buses from Boston to Amherst and Northampton via Springfield; three trips a day stop in S. Hadley. PVTA operates local buses from Northampton to Amherst and from Amherst to S. Hadley; during the school year there is also service from Northampton to S. Hadley. For visitor information call 413-549-7555 in Amherst, 413-253-0700 in Northampton, and 413-532-6451 in S. Hadley.

The Berkshires

There are cultural attractions and elegant inns throughout this scenic region. From Boston, take Peter Pan or Greyhound to Lee, Lenox, and Pittsfield. BRTA operates local buses between the towns Mon.-Sat.

Lenox is the summer home of the Boston Symphony Orchestra. Tanglewood, where the concerts are held, is a 25-minute walk from the Lenox bus stop.

In Pittsfield, there are several fine historical museums:

Arrowhead (home of Herman Melville), 780 Holmes Rd., Pittsfield.
•BRTA Orange Bus (Chapman Corner).
Berkshire Museum, 39 South St., Pittsfield.
•One block from Park Sq.; three blocks from Pittsfield Bus Terminal.
Hancock Shaker Village, Albany Rd. (Rt. 20), Hancock.
•BRTA Brown Bus (W. Pittsfield) to end of line; walk one mile farther.

The towns of Stockbridge and Great Barrington can be reached by BRTA or Bonanza buses from Lee, Lenox, and Pittsfield. For tourist information, call Berkshire Visitors Bureau at 413-443-9186.

Concord

Concord was the site of the American Revolution's second battle, the "shot heard 'round the world;" and, later, home to the country's 19th-century literary flowering. *Take a Fitchburg Line commuter train* from North Station or from Porter Sq./Cambridge (Red Line). From the Concord train station turn right on Thoreau St., then left on Sudbury St. (Friendly's at the corner) to the town center. The Old North Bridge is a 20-minute walk from the train station, as is the Concord Museum. The homes of Ralph Waldo Emerson and Louisa May Alcott may also be visited; directions to Thoreau's Walden Pond are on page 61. For information call the Chamber of Commerce at 508-369-3120 or the National Park Service at 484-6156.

Fall River

Once the home of a thriving textile industry, Fall River today features two important maritime museums and an excellent local historical museum. *Bonanza* buses leave from Boston's Back Bay Station; local buses are operated by SRTA Mon.-Sat. Visitor information is available at 72 Bank St. (508-679-0922) or at the Heritage State Park (508-675-5759).

Battleship Cove, Water St.
Marine Museum, 70 Water St.
Fall River Heritage State Park, 100 Davol St.
•SRTA Bus 7 (Bay St.) to Columbia and Eagle Sts., walk north on Eagle St.
•Or walk north from the bus terminal on Main St., across I-195;

turn left on Central St. parallel to the highway (mile).
Fall River Historical Society, 451 Rock St.
•From the bus terminal walk 7 blocks north on Main St., then right on Walnut St. 2 blocks to Rock St.

Framingham

Shoppers World, the second oldest shopping mall in the country, attracts visitors to Framingham. *Take Peter Pan from Boston; Massport Logan Express.*. The Danforth Museum is another tourist attraction (See map, page 66).

Gloucester and Rockport

These two towns form Cape Ann, on Massachusetts' scenic North Shore. They are served by *Rockport Line commuter trains* from Boston's North Station; CATA local buses operate Mon.-Sat.

The ancient fishing village of Gloucester has grown into a city, but it still retains much of its 18th- and 19th-century ambience. From the commuter rail station, walk 1/2 mile south on Washington St. to the center of town, or take CATA's Business Express bus. (See map, page 67.)

To get to the Rocky Neck artist's colony, take CATA's Red Line (Thatcher Rd.) bus, or *A. C. Cruise Line* direct from Pier One in Boston.

Virtually everything in Rockport, including the Bearskin Neck artist's colony, is a short walk from the train station. The town is full of crafts shops, galleries, restaurants, and inns. (See map, page 68.) CATA's Blue Line (Lanesville) and Red Line (Thatcher Rd.) buses— both of which operate between Gloucester and Rockport—offer spectacular ocean views and are good alternatives to more expensive tours.

For information, call the Cape Ann Chamber of Commerce at (508-283-1601) or the Rockport Board of Trade (508-546-5997).

Lexington

Lexington's Battle Green is where the first shots of the American Revolution were fired. *Take the Red Line to Alewife, then T-Bus 62 (Bedford) or 76 (Hanscom Field)* to Lexington Center, Mon.-Sat. The Battle Green, Munroe Tavern, Hancock House, and Old Belfry are all within a short walk of the town center. The Buckman Tavern and the Museum of Our National Heritage are located a few bus stops before Lexington Center. For information call the Chamber of Commerce at 862-1450.

Lowell

Lowell was the first planned city of the American industrial revolution. Today many of its early 19th-century mills are being restored, and the National Park Service leads popular Mill and Canal Tours of the city.

Lowell Line commuter trains depart from Boston's North Station.

Local buses are operated by LRTA, Mon.-Sat.; and an all-new, old-fashioned electric trolley links many of the historic sites.

The Boott Cotton Mills Museum, the first major National Park Service museum on industrial history, recently opened in Lowell National Historical Park, featuring a re-created 1920s weave room with 88 operating power looms. Visitors experience the clatter, heat, and smell of the factories.

Beat writer Jack Kerouac was born in Lowell, and each October there is a three-day celebration in his honor, with poetry readings and other events.

The National Park Visitor Center is at 246 Market St. From the Lowell train station, take LRTA's downtown shuttle bus; or walk 5 blocks north on Thorndike St., then right 4 blocks on Dutton St. to Market St. Sidewalks are on the *west* (left) side of both Thorndike and Dutton Sts.; and go over the underpass at Appleton St. (See map, page 68.) For information and tour reservations (required!), call 508-459-1000.

Marblehead

This seaside town, with its twisting, narrow streets, is much as it was 200 years ago. Today it is also one of the world's sailing capitals. There are shops and restaurants, and two historic house museums. Take T-Bus 441 or 442 from Haymarket. For visitor information, call 1-631-2868.

New Bedford

A hundred years ago, New Bedford prospered as a great whaling port. The Seamen's Bethel described in *Moby Dick* still stands, and across the street is a fine Whaling Museum. A Glass Museum is also in the restored historic waterfront just a few blocks from the bus terminal. Visitor information is at 47 N. Second St., or call 508-991-6200. (See map, page 68.)

American Eagle buses to New Bedford leave from the Peter Pan terminal in Boston, and SRTA operates local buses.

Newport, RI

A century ago, Newport was a summer resort for wealthy families. Seven of their extravagant mansions are now open for tours. The city also has the Tennis Hall of Fame, and many surviving colonial-era buildings, including America's first synagogue. Sightseeing tours by "trolley," train, and boat are available, and bikes can be rented. Tours depart from the Gateway Visitor Center, which is also the stop for *Bonanza* buses from Boston and local RIPTA buses. The mansions are on Bellevue Ave., on RIPTA's Red and Yellow routes. For visitor information call 800-326-6030.

Old Sturbridge Village

Located 50 miles west of Boston, Old Sturbridge Village is a re-creation of an early 19th-century New England rural town. Visitors learn about life in the United States when it was a young nation. Peter Pan has daily buses to this museum from Boston. For information, call 508-347-3362.

Plymouth

Here the Pilgrims established the first English colony in New England. You can see Plymouth Rock and board a full-scale replica of the *Mayflower*. Take Plymouth & Brockton from either Park Plaza or Boston/South Station. The North Plymouth bus station is a three-mile taxi ride from Plymouth Center, where most of the town's historic sites and museums are located.

Plimoth Plantation, a stockaded living-history re-creation of Plymouth in 1627, is three miles south of the town center. The Plymouth Rock Trolley Co. (508-747-3419) runs shuttles between the center of Plymouth, Plimoth Plantation, and other visitor attractions.

For information call the Chamber of Commerce at 508-746-3377. Most sites are open from April to November.

Portland, ME

Portland's Old Port Exchange is several city blocks of restored 19th-century buildings, housing restaurants and galleries, next to the working waterfront. The downtown area also has an excellent art museum and two historic house museums, and several firms offer cruises of Casco Bay.

Portland is served by *C & J Trailways and Greyhound buses* from Boston. C & J Trailways stops downtown on Forest Ave. The Greyhound station, one mile west of downtown on Congress St., is served by Portland Metro Bus 1, daily except certain holidays.

For visitor information call 207-772-5800. Local transit is operated by Portland Metro, 207-774-0531, daily except certain holidays.

Portsmouth, NH

This New Hampshire seacoast city is noted for its 18th- and 19th-century architecture. The Strawbery Banke museum (open May-October) has preserved 10 acres of historic buildings, and there are 6 other house museums open for tours. Prescott Park, on the waterfront, is the site of a six-week summer arts festival; cruises to the Isles of Shoals and the Piscataqua River are also available.

Portsmouth is served by *C & J Trailways* (at the Pease International Trade Port entrance) and by *Greyhound* buses that stop in Market Sq. in the heart of the historic district. For visitor information call 603-436-1118.

Providence, RI

Rhode Island's capital is served by *Bonanza buses, Amtrak trains,* and *MBTA Commuter Rail* from Boston. Among its many attractions is Brown University, 1/2 mile east of the Kennedy Plaza bus stop, and the new train station. Nearby is Benefit Street's "mile of history," featuring over 100 preserved houses, and the Rhode Island School of

Design with its renowned art museum. Local buses are operated by RIPTA; for visitor information call 401-274-1636. (See map, page 70.)

Museum of Rhode Island History, Aldrich House, 110 Benevolent St.
- •RIPTA Bus 38 (Rumford/Tunnel), 40 (Butler/Tunnel), or 41 (Elmgrove/Tunnel) to Waterman and Cooke Sts.; walk one block south.

Roger Williams Park, Museum of Natural History, and Zoo, Elmwood Ave.
- •RIPTA Bus 20 (Elmwood).

Slater Mill Historic Site, Roosevelt Ave. at Main St., Pawtucket.
- •RIPTA Bus 98-99 (Providence-Pawtucket) to Roosevelt Ave. and Main St.

Rockport. See **Gloucester and Rockport.**

Salem

Salem, site of the witch trials of the 1690s and a prosperous port in the early 1800s, is served by *Rockport/Ipswich Line commuter trains* from North Station and by *T-Buses 450 and 455* from Haymarket.

Among the city's many attractions are the Peabody Museum of Salem, the Essex Museum, the House of Seven Gables, the old Custom House (now part of the Salem Maritime National Historic Site), and the Salem Witch Museum multi-media show. All are within a 15-minute walk of the train station. From spring through fall, the Salem Trolley (508-744-5463) links these sites and others such as Salem Willows. For more information call the Chamber of Commerce at 508-744-0004 or the National Park Service at 508-741-3648. (See map, page 69.)

Springfield and Holyoke

Springfield is Western Massachusetts' largest cultural and commercial center. Its downtown museum complex, the Quadrangle, contains extensive art, history, and science collections; the Basketball Hall of Fame is downtown at 1150 W. Columbus Ave. Both museums are just a few blocks from the bus and train stations. Also on Columbus Ave. is Stage West, which presents several plays each year. Symphony Hall, home of the Springfield Symphony, is next to City Hall on Court St. (See map, page 69.)

Springfield is served by *Peter Pan, Greyhound, and Amtrak* from Boston. Local buses are operated by Pioneer Valley Transit Authority (PVTA), Mon.-Sat. For visitor information call 413-787-1548.

Eastern States Exposition and **Storrowtown Village Museum**, 1305 Memorial Ave., West Springfield.
- •During Exposition week in Sept., special Peter Pan buses leave from the Springfield Bus Terminal, connecting with buses from Boston.

•PVTA Bus 704 (Feeding Hills Ctr.) or 705 (Main St./Agawam).

The Holyoke Heritage State Park includes a Children's Museum and the Volleyball Hall of Fame. The nearby Holyoke City Museum ("Wistariahurst") is in an elegant Victorian mansion. Take *PVTA Bus 217 or 221 from Springfield.*For visitor information call ʰthe State Park at 413-534-0909.

Williamstown
Williamstown is home to Williams College and its summer theatre festival; the Sterling and Francine Clark Art Institute is famous for its collection of European and American paintings.

The Hoosac Tunnel near North Adams was once one of the longest railroad tunnels in the nation; today the tunnel and North Adams' textile industry is the focus of the Western Gateway Heritage State Park.

For information, call 413-458-9077 in Williamstown or 413-663-6312 in North Adams.

Worcester
New England's second-largest city is known for its colleges and universities. Its excellent Art Museum, the scholarly collections of the American Antiquarian Society, and the Salisbury Mansion (restored to its 1830s splendor) are near Lincoln Square, one-half mile north of downtown Worcester. The city's historical museum is at 30 Elm St., one block from City Hall.

Worcester is served by *Peter Pan, Greyhound, and Amtrak* from Boston; local buses are operated by WRTA. For information call the Visitors Bureau at 508-753-2920. (See map, page 70.)

New England Science Center, 222 Harrington Way.
•WRTA Bus 12 (Plantation/Lake View) to Plantation and Franklin Sts. or WRTA Bus 18 (Hamilton/Edgemere).

Higgins Armory Museum (medieval arms and suits of armor), 100 Barber Ave.
•WRTA Bus 30N (Summit/W. Boylston or Summit/Holden) to Barber Ave.

Parks and Recreation

This section lists parks, beaches, and other recreation areas which are suitable for a day or weekend trip from Boston.

The Appalachian Mountain Club (AMC) often sponsors group hikes near Boston and throughout New England; hike leaders can help arrange car pools or other transportation. Schedules are published in the AMC's monthly members' magazine. For membership information, call 523-0636.

For information on a specific activity, see the following listings:
Beaches: Boston Harbor (Lovells I.); Cape Cod; Gloucester; Hampton Beach; Lynn; Manchester; Marblehead; Nantasket; Rockport.
Beaches (fresh water): Concord (Walden Pond); Milton (Blue Hills, west); Winchester.
Bicycle rentals: Cape Cod; Gloucester; Ipswich; Lincoln; Manchester; Marblehead; Martha's Vineyard; Nantucket.
Camping: Boston Harbor Islands; Hingham (Wompatuck).
Canoeing: Concord.
Golf: Lynn (Lynn Woods); Milton (Ponkapoag).
Horseback riding: Milton (Blue Hills).
Skiing, cross-country: Rentals at Lincoln and Lynn Woods; many other parks offer trails.
Skiing, downhill: Milton (Blue Hills, west).

The Appalachian and Long Trails

Bus service is available from Boston to the following communities near the Appalachian Trail:

- Lee and Pittsfield, MA—*Peter Pan, Greyhound.*
- North Adams and Williamstown, MA; Bennington, VT—*Peter Pan*
- Falls Village, Cornwall Bridge, and Kent, CT—*Bonanza from Lee, MA*
- Cuttingsville, Rutland, Long Trail Lodge, Sherburne, Woodstock, White River Jct., VT; Hanover, NH—*Vermont Transit.*
- Lincoln, Pinkham Notch, and Gorham, NH—*Concord Trailways.*

Concord Trailways' stops at the Appalachian Mountain Club camp in Pinkham Notch, NH. In summer, the AMC has a "hiker's shuttle service" which connects the camp with several nearby trailheads. Call 603-466-2727 for details and reservations.

These towns near Vermont's Long Trail are served by *Vermont Transit.*: Westfield, Eden, Johnson, Richmond, Middlebury, and Waterbury, VT.

Boston Harbor and its Islands

There are eight islands in the **Boston Harbor Islands State Park:**
Georges Island is the park's gateway. It is the departure point for free water taxis to the other islands, and the site of historic Fort Warren. The *Bay State Cruise Co.* sails to Georges Island, from Long Wharf in Boston, mid-May through mid-October.

In summer, daily ferries to Georges Island also depart from Hingham (*Mass. Bay Lines*) and there is limited service from Nantasket (weekdays, *Bay State Cruise Co.*) and Lynn (weekends and Wed., call 598-0260).

Bumpkin, Gallops, Grape, Lovells and **Peddocks islands** are reached by free water taxi from Georges Island. You can camp on Bumpkin, Grape, Lovells, and Peddocks. Permits are required; for Bumpkin and Grape, call 740-1605; Lovells and Peddocks, 727-5290.

Non-profit groups and persons 62 or older can get free ferry tickets to the islands on weekdays; call 740-1605 for an application form or for more information about the Harbor Islands State Park.

The Friends of the Boston Harbor Islands (523-8386) organize special cruises to the islands, including trips to Boston Light on Little Brewster.

Thompson Island is privately owned and open to visitors twice a week in summer. For information call 328-3900.

Cape Cod

Plymouth & Brockton (P&B) buses to Hyannis depart from Park Plaza and the Peter Pan terminal in Boston. *Bonanza* buses to Falmouth and Woods Hole leave from Back Bay Station. (See maps, pages 66 and 67.) And the *Bay State Cruise Co.* has a daily summer ferry to Provincetown, at the tip of the Cape, from Boston's Commonwealth Pier.

Bonanza also has daily buses to the Cape from New York, NY, and Providence, RI; and Amtrak runs trains from New York to Hyannis in summer. Peter Pan has buses to the Cape from Worcester, Springfield, and Amherst.

The Cape Cod Regional Transit Authority operates year-round buses, Mon.-Sat., along the Cape's southern shore between Hyannis and Woods Hole. Bicycles can be rented in Hyannis, Falmouth, and Provincetown. The Cape Cod Scenic Railroad (508-771-3788) operates sightseeing trains from Hyannis, June–October, four days a week.

Kalmus Beach—From the Hyannis bus station, a 30-minute walk south on Ocean Ave.

Chatham, Harwich Port, and **South Yarmouth**—served by *P&B buses from Hyannis* (change buses in Hyannis.)

Provincetown—The *Bay State Cruise Co.* offers a three-hour ferry trip from Boston. Or take a P&B bus to "P-town" via Hyannis (change buses in Hyannis). In summer, Lower Cape Bus runs local buses in Provincetown.

Orleans, Eastham, Wellfleet, and **Truro**—served by *P&B buses from Hyannis and Provincetown.* Go to Hyannis and change buses there or take the ferry to Provincetown and catch the bus at the end of the dock.

For visitor information, call the Cape Cod Chamber of Commerce in Hyannis (508-362-3225) or the Provincetown Chamber of Commerce (508-487-3424).

Concord

To reach this historically important town, take a *Fitchburg Line commuter train* from North Station or from Porter Sq. (Red Line) in Cambridge.

Walden Pond—The pond where Thoreau lived is a 30-minute walk from the train station. Leaving the depot, turn right on Thoreau St. to its end, then right on Walden St. After you cross Route 2, take any of the trails on the right to the pond, or continue straight on Walden St. to a small beach. Alternatively, you can take the train to Lincoln and rent a bike from Lincoln Guide Service (259-9204).

Great Meadows Wildlife Refuge—a two-mile walk from the train station; for directions call 508-443-4661. Or rent a canoe at South Bridge.

South Bridge Boat House—Canoe rentals (508-369-9438). From the depot, turn left on Thoreau St. to its end, then left on Main Street (1/2 mile).

Gloucester

Take a *Rockport Line commuter train* from North Station; connecting local buses are operated by Cape Ann Transportation Authority (CATA), Mon.-Sat. Bikes can be rented at Giles of Gloucester (508-283-3603), near the train station. (See map, page 67.)

Pavilion Beach, Half Moon Beach, and **Stage Fort Park**—A one-mile walk from the Gloucester train station. Go south on Washington St., then right on Middle St. (at the equestrian statue) and right again on Western Ave. (Rte. 127). The park entrance is on the left at the end of the causeway. These beaches are on the harbor and are somewhat rocky.

Good Harbor Beach—Take *CATA Red Line (Thatcher Rd.) bus* (Mon.-Sat.) from Gloucester. This is one of Cape Ann's finest beaches.

Hampton Beach, NH

Peter Pan has daily summer buses to this popular resort from Boston. The beach is in an urban setting with amusement arcades and motels. For visitor information call 800-438-2826 (brochures only) or 603-926-8717.

Hingham

World's End—This 250-acre peninsula was landscaped by Frederick Law Olmsted. Take the *Red Line (Braintree) to Quincy Ctr.; then T-Bus 220 (Hingham).* Get off at Otis and North Sts., by Hingham Harbor; walk down Summer St. past the traffic circle, then turn left on Martin's Lane (about 1 mile). Or take *People Care-iers' "Hull" bus* from Hingham to Martin's Lane. The reservation is at the end of the street.

Wompatuck State Park—*Red Line (Braintree) to Quincy Ctr., then T-Bus 220A (Hingham Loop)* to Main and Union Sts.; walk up Union St. slightly over one mile to the park. Or take *T-Bus 220 (Hingham)* to the end of the line and walk one mile up Main St. to Union St.

Ipswich

Crane's Beach—*Take an Ipswich Line commuter train* from North Station, Mon.-Sat. It is four miles from the train station to the beach; bikes can be rented at the Skol Shop (508-356-5872). Taxis are also available.

Lincoln

This town has hundreds of acres of conservation land for hiking or cross-country skiing. Also located here are the Mass. Audubon Society's Drumlin Farm and the DeCordova Museum and Park. Take a *Fitchburg Line commuter train* from North Station or Porter Sq. (Red Line) in Cambridge. The Lincoln Guide Service (259-9204), near the train station, rents bikes and skis.

Lynn

Take T-Bus 441 or 442 (Marblehead), or 455 (Salem via Loring Ave.) from Haymarket, or *T-Commuter Rail (Rockport/Ipswich Lines)* from North Station to downtown Lynn.

Lynn Beach and Nahant Beach—From the new Lynn train/bus station, walk 1/2 mile east on Carroll Pkwy. to the rotary and cross the parkway to the beach. Lynn Beach is to the left; Nahant Beach to the right. Both beaches are wide and sandy.

King's Beach—*T-Bus 442 (Marblehead-Haymarket via Humphrey St.)* stops 1/2 block from the beach.

Lynn Woods—This 2,200-acre park has nearly 30 miles of trails. From downtown Lynn *take T-Bus 436 (Goodwins Circle)* to Great Woods Rd. by the golf course (592-8238), or *take T-Bus 429 (North Saugus)* to Penny Brook Rd. (Both buses operate Mon.-Sat.) Park maps are available and skis can be rented (598-4212) at the headquarters on Great Woods Rd.

Manchester-by-the-Sea

Take *Rockport Line Commuter Rail* from North Station to this Cape Ann town. Bicycles can be rented at Seaside Cycle (508-526-1200).

Singing Beach—This small but excellent beach, 1/2 mile from the station, is very popular with transit riders. You cannot get closer to the beach by driving; people with cars must park at the railroad station.

Marblehead

Take T-Bus 441 or 442 (Marblehead) from Haymarket. Bike rentals are available at Marblehead Cycle (1-631-1570) on Bessom St., downtown.

Devereux Beach—Get off the bus at Ocean Ave. in Marblehead; (*not* Ocean Ave. in Swampscott); walk 1/2 mile east on Ocean Ave.

Martha's Vineyard

The easiest way to the Vineyard is *Bonanza* bus from Back Bay Station in Boston to Woods Hole, then a *Steamship Authority* ferry to Vineyard Haven (year-round) or Oak Bluffs (summer only). Other ferries sail from Falmouth (Island Queen), Hyannis (Hy-Line), and New Bedford (Cape Island Express).

Summer buses on the island are operated by Island Transport and Martha's Vineyard Transit Authority; bicycles can be rented at all of

the island's ferry docks.
For visitor information, call 508-693-0085.

Milton and Canton

The Blue Hills have over 500 miles of trails; Great Blue Hill, at 635 feet, is higher than the John Hancock Tower. For park information call 698-1802. There are several nearby stables for horseback riding. (MDC)

Blue Hills Reservation, west—*Red Line to Mattapan, then Hudson Bus to Canton*, Mon.-Sat. Get off at the Trailside Museum. The Skyline Trail extends eight miles to Willard St. (see "Blue Hills, east"). The **Blue Hills Ski Area** (828-5070), has a chair lift and three slopes for downhill skiing.

From the Hillside St. bus stop, it is a one-mile hike to Houghton's Pond, where you can swim, fish, and have a cookout (a fire permit is necessary).

Blue Hills, central—*Red Line to Ashmont, then T-Bus 240 (Avon Line) or 240A (Crawford Sq.)*. The bus goes right through the park.

Blue Hills, east—*Red Line (Braintree) to Quincy Ctr., then T-Bus 238 (Crawford Sq.)*. Get off at West and Willard Sts., by the skating rink. Or: *T-Bus 215 (Quincy Ctr.-Ashmont)* to Copeland and West Sts. (Boyd Sq.); follow West St. 1/2 mile.

Fowl Meadow—*Orange Line or Green Line-E/T-Bus 39 to Forest Hills; then T-Bus 32 (Wolcott Sq.)* to the end of the line. Walk 1/2 mile east on the Neponset Valley Pkwy. The trail begins just across the river on the right. Or hike from the Trailside Museum (see "Blue Hills, west"). (MDC)

Ponkapoag Pond—*Red Line to Mattapan, then Hudson Bus to Canton*. (Mon.-Sat.). Get off at the Ponkapoag Golf Course and hike east around the golf course. No swimming. (MDC)

Nantasket

The big amusement park is gone, but the wide beach and some small arcades remain. The *Bay State Cruise Co.* has daily ferries from Long Wharf in summer. Or: *Red Line (Braintree) to Quincy Ctr., then T-Bus 220 to Hingham, then People Care-iers' "Hull" bus*. (MDC)

Nantucket

Ferries to Nantucket sail from Hyannis, where the docks are a 1/2-mile walk from the bus station. (See map, page 67.) The *Steamship Authority* has year-round ferries, and Hy-Line sails from May to October.

Barrett's Tours operates summer buses on the island. Bikes can be also rented near the ferry docks.

For visitor information, call 508-228-1700 or 508-228-0925.

Rockport

Take a *Rockport Line commuter train* from North Station to this North Shore town. (See map, page 68.)

Rockport Beach—This small, rocky beach is just north of the town center, 1/2 mile from the Rockport train station.

Halibut Point—You can walk on huge slabs of granite which lead down to the crashing surf. Take *CATA Blue Line (Lanesville) bus* (Mon.-Sat.) from the train station in either Rockport or Gloucester to Gott Ave.; the park is at the end of Gott Ave. Or walk a little over two miles from Rockport; go north from town on Granite Ave., then turn right on Gott Ave. No swimming.

Weymouth

Great Esker Park—This high gravel ridge was deposited along the shores of the Back River by glaciers in the last Ice Age. Take the *Red Line to Quincy Ctr., then T-Bus 220 (Hingham)*. Get off at Harborlight Mall and enter the park behind the shopping center.

Winchester

Mystic Lakes—*Lowell Line commuter rail* to Wedgemere; walk left on Mystic Valley Parkway 1/2 mile to a small fresh-water beach and park. (MDC)

Falmouth/Woods Hole

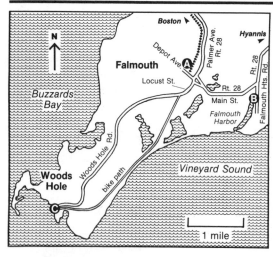

A **Falmouth Station**
Depot Ave.
508-548-7588
Bonanza to Boston &
New York
Peter Pan to Springfield
CCRTA (Hyannis-Woods Hole)

B **Falmouth Harbor**
Falmouth Heights Rd.
508-548-4800
Island Queen to Martha's
Vineyard *(May-Oct.)*

C **Woods Hole Terminal**
508-548-3788 (ferry)
Steamship Authority to
Martha's Vineyard *(year-round)*
Bonanza to Boston &
New York
Peter Pan to Springfield
CCRTA (Hyannis-Woods Hole)

Framingham

* to/from Boston
** to/from Logan Airport

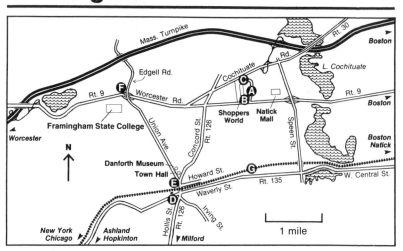

Shoppers World

A **Commuter Lot** **P**
("On the hill")
Peter Pan:
— Boston-Framingham
express*
LIFT 1, 2, 3, & 4
Natick Neighborhood Bus

B **Bus Shelter-Rt. 9**
(South side of mall)
Peter Pan:
— Boston-Worcester,
Rt. 9 local*
— Boston-Framingham
express* *(some trips)*
— Boston-Worcester
express* *(some trips)*
LIFT 1, 2, 3, & 4
Natick Neighborhood Bus
Crystal Transport to Milford

C **Massport Terminal** **P**
(North side of mall)
Logan Express**
Natick Neighborhood Bus

Downtown Framingham

D **Railroad station** **P**
443 Waverly St.
T-Commuter Rail*
(Framingham Line)
Amtrak to New York & Chicago
LIFT 5 to Hopkinton

E **Concord & Howard Sts.**
All LIFT routes
Crystal Transport to Milford

F **Framingham Center**
Rt. 9 & Edgell Rd.
Peter Pan:
— Boston-Worcester,
Rt. 9 local*
— Boston-Framingham
express* *(some trips)*
— Boston-Worcester
express* *(some trips)*
LIFT 2, 2X, & 3

G **West Natick station** **P**
Rt. 135 @ Boden Lane
T-Commuter Rail*
(Framingham Line)

P **Park & ride lots**

66

Gloucester

to/from Boston

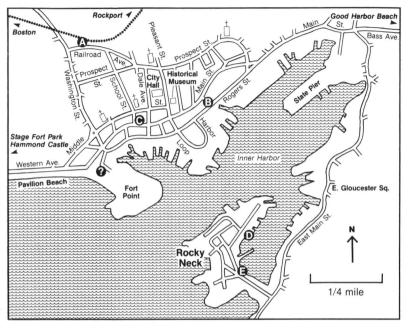

Ⓐ Railroad station
Railroad Ave.
T-Commuter Rail*
(Rockport Line)
CATA bus stop *on Railroad Ave.*

Ⓑ Manuel Lewis Drive
@ Rogers St.
(Dunkin Donuts)
All CATA buses

Ⓒ CATA Waiting Station
118 Main St. @ Centre St.
All CATA buses

Rocky Neck

Ⓓ 51 Rocky Neck Ave.
A. C. Cruise Line* *(May-Sept.)*

Ⓔ 1 Wonson St.
CATA Red Line bus

❓ Visitor Information
33 Commercial St.

Hyannis

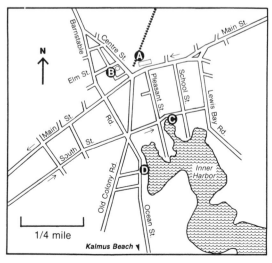

Ⓐ Railroad Station
252 Main St.
Amtrak to New York
(June-Sept.)
Cape Cod Scenic RR
excursions *(June-Oct.)*

Ⓑ Bus Terminal
Elm & Centre Sts.
508-775-5524
Plymouth & Brockton to
Boston, Chatham, &
Provincetown
Bonanza to New York
Peter Pan to Springfield
CCRTA (Hyannis-Woods Hole)

Ⓒ South St. Dock
508-771-4000
Steamship Authority to
Nantucket *(year-round)*
CCRTA (Hyannis-Woods Hole)

Ⓓ Ocean St. Dock
508-778-2600
Hy-Line to Nantucket &
Martha's Vineyard *(May-Oct.)*

Lowell

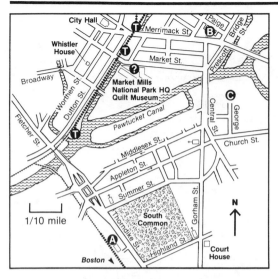

Ⓐ Gallagher Terminal
145 Thorndike St.
508-459-7101
T-Commuter Rail* (Lowell Line)
Vermont Transit* **
Greyhound
Peter Pan
LRTA Downtown Shuttle

Ⓑ LRTA Transit Center
Paige & Merrimack Sts.
All LRTA buses
MVRTA to Lawrence

Ⓒ Lowell Sheraton
Hudson Airporter**
M & L Transportation**
LRTA Downtown Shuttle

Ⓣ Lowell Natl. Park trolley stops

❓ Visitor Information
246 Market St.
National Park Service tours

New Bedford

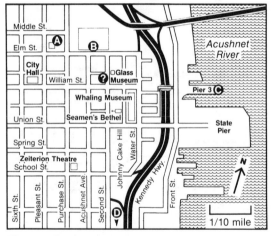

Ⓐ SRTA Bus Terminal
Elm & Pleasant Sts.
508-990-0000
American Eagle*
Bonanza
All SRTA buses

Ⓑ Elm St. Garage
Shuttle bus to
Billy Woods Wharf

Ⓒ Pier 3
Cuttyhunk Boat

Ⓓ Billy Woods Wharf
Cove Rd.
1¼ miles south of downtown
Cape Island Express to
Martha's Vineyard (May-Oct.)
Shuttle bus from
Elm St. Garage

❓ Visitor Information
47 N. Second St.

Rockport

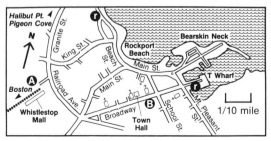

Ⓐ Railroad Station
T-Commuter Rail*
(Rockport Line)
CATA Blue Line bus on
Railroad Ave.

Ⓑ Richdale store
21 Broadway
All CATA buses

ⓡ Public rest rooms

Salem

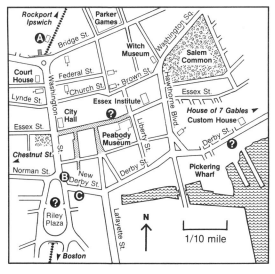

Ⓐ Railroad station
Washington & Bridge Sts.
T-Commuter Rail*
(Rockport/Ipswich Lines)
    450-Haymarket*
    451-N. Beverly
    455-Haymarket*
    458-Danvers

Ⓑ Riley Plaza
@ New Derby St.
Michaud Bus

Ⓒ New Derby St.
    450-Haymarket*
    451-N. Beverly
    455-Haymarket*
    458-Danvers

❓ Visitor Information
National Park Service
Museum Place (Essex St.)
Central Wharf (Derby St.)
Chamber of Commerce
Riley Plaza

Springfield

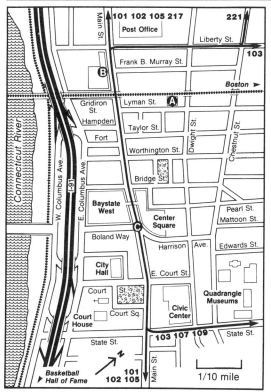

Ⓐ Railroad Station
66 Lyman St.
413-788-4772
Amtrak*

Ⓑ Bus Terminal
1776 Main St.
413-781-3320
    Peter Pan/Bonanza
413-781-1500
    Greyhound/Vt. Transit
Peter Pan* **
Greyhound*
Bonanza
Vermont Transit
PVTA Buses 101, 102, 103,
105, 107, 109, 217, 221 (on
Main St.)

Ⓒ Baystate West
Main St. & Boland Way
All PVTA buses

*Not all PVTA routes are
shown on this map*

69

Worcester

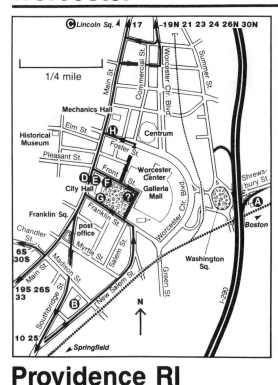

Ⓐ Railroad Station
45 Shrewsbury St.
508-755-0356
Amtrak*

Ⓑ Bus Terminal
75 Madison St.
508-754-4600 Peter Pan
508-754-3247 Greyhound
Peter Pan* **
Greyhound*

Ⓒ Lincoln Sq.
Peter Pan** *from Marriott Hotel*
WRTA Buses 17, 19N, 21, 23, 24, 26N, 30N

City Hall Plaza

Ⓓ Main St.
WRTA Buses 19S, 25, 26S, 30S

Ⓔ WRTA Buses 1, 6N, 11, 15, 17, 19N, 22, 24, 26N, 30N, 33

Ⓕ Front St.
WRTA Buses 4, 5E, 18, 21, 23, 28, 32, 40

Ⓖ Franklin St.
WRTA Buses 6S, 10, 30N, 33

Ⓗ Foster St.
WRTA Buses 2, 5W, 21, 23, 32

❓ Visitor Information

Not all WRTA routes are shown on this map

Providence RI

Ⓐ Railroad Station
100 Gaspee St.
401-727-7382
T-Commuter Rail*
(Attleboro Line)
Amtrak*
RIPTA Buses 56, 57
(on Gaspee St.)

Ⓑ Bonanza Terminal
1 Bonanza Way
2 miles north of downtown
401-751-8800
Bonanza* **
RIPTA Buses 98, 99 *(on N. Main St., 4 blocks from Bonanza terminal)*

Ⓒ Kennedy Plaza
All RIPTA buses
Bonanza* to Bonanza terminal & Boston
GATRA to Taunton, MA

Ⓓ Greyhound Terminal

❓ Visitor Information
Visitors Bureau
30 Exchange Terrace
National Park Service
N. Main St. @ Smith St.

Not all RIPTA routes are shown on this map

Chapter 10

Major Spectator Sports

Baseball

Boston Red Sox, Fenway Park, Boston. Green Line-(B, C, or D) to Kenmore. Or: Green Line-D (Riverside) to Fenway. Or: special T-Commuter Rail trains to all *weekend* home games from the following stations:

- **Attleboro/Fairmount Lines**: Attleboro, Mansfield, Sharon, Canton Jct., Rt. 128 Sta., Fairmount, Morton St., Uphams Corner.
- **Franklin Line**: Forge Park/495, Franklin, Norfolk, Walpole, Windsor Gardens, Norwood Central, Norwood Depot, Readville.
- **Framingham Line**: *Framingham, *W. Natick, *Natick, *Wellesley Sq., *Wellesley Hills, *Wellesley Farms, Auburndale, W. Newton, Newtonville.

Framingham Line stations marked with an asterisk (*) also have service to *weeknight* home games.

Basketball and Hockey

Boston Celtics and Boston Bruins, Boston Garden, 150 Causeway St., Boston. Green Line, Orange Line, or T-Commuter Rail to North Station.

Football

New England Patriots, Foxboro Stadium, Foxboro. Special T-Commuter Rail trains to all Patriots home games from South Station, Back Bay Station, Hyde Park, Rt. 128 Station, Canton Jct., Sharon, and Mansfield.

Hockey. See **Basketball and Hockey.**

Dog Racing

Wonderland Park, Revere. Blue Line to Wonderland. Or: T-Bus 440 (Lynn-Haymarket via Lynnway).

Raynham/Taunton Greyhound Park, Raynham, MA. Bloom Bus (Boston-Taunton) stops at the park for afternoon races.

Horse Racing

Rockingham Park, Salem, NH. Hudson Bus runs special buses on all days Rockingham is open, from 5 Boston-area locations including

St. James Ave., Government Center (Green and Blue lines), Haymarket (Green and Orange lines), Sullivan (Orange Line), and Medford Sq.

Suffolk Downs, Revere. Blue Line to Suffolk Downs. Free shuttle bus to entrances.

Annual Events

The Boston Marathon is on Patriots Day in April. The finish line is at Copley Sq., but *Copley station is closed on Marathon day*. For the final stretch, take the Orange Line to Back Bay Station; the Green Line to Hynes Convention Ctr./ICA, Arlington, or Kenmore; or the Green Line-C (Cleveland Circle) to any stop on Beacon St. To see the race earlier, take the Green Line-B (Boston College) to the end of the line for "Heartbreak Hill"; the Green Line-D (Riverside) to Woodland; or T-Commuter Rail (Framingham Line) to any stop in Wellesley, Natick, or Framingham. (Commuter Rail follows regular weekday schedule on Patriots Day.)

The Head of the Charles Regatta, in which hundreds of college crews row, occurs in October. Take the Red Line to Harvard and walk south on J. F. Kennedy St. to the Charles River. Or take the Green Line-B (Boston College) to B. U. Central and walk across the B. U. Bridge.

U.S.. Tennis Championship at Longwood. Green Line-D (Riverside) to Chestnut Hill (*not* Longwood). The Longwood Cricket Club is next to the station.

Part IV
Destination
Listings

Museum of Fine Arts, Boston

WHY PAY MORE?

➤ MBTA Monthly Pass holders are entitled to discounts at some institutions listed in this chapter (indicated by *). The Pass Program also includes discounts for participating restaurants and retail outlets. For more information, call 722-5218.

➤ If you are planning to purchase tickets for a production at one of the theaters listed in Chapter 12, check out Bostix in Faneuil Hall (723-5181) where half-price, same-day tickets are sold for some local shows.

➤ Many attractions offer discounts for members and special rates for families, senior citizens, and those who visit during off-peak hours. Inquire with the institution for details.

Chapter 11

Museums and Tourist Attractions

This chapter includes primarily museums and tourist attractions in the Metropolitan Boston area. For additional listings, see Chapter 9, "Day and Weekend Trips—Historic, Cultural, and Scenic Attractions."

Adams National Historic Site
135 Adams St., Quincy.
- Red Line (Braintree) to Quincy Ctr.; 1/2-mile walk N on Burgin Pkwy. to Adams St.

African Meeting House
8 Smith Ct. (behind 46 Joy St.), Boston.
See "Boston African-American National Historic Site."

American Jewish Historical Society
2 Thornton Rd., Waltham.
- T-Bus 70 (Cedarwood-Central) to end of line; walk up Cedarwood Ave. to Thornton Rd.

Blue Hills Trailside Museum
1904 Canton Ave., Milton.
- Hudson Bus (Mattapan-Canton), connects w/ Red Line at Mattapan.

Black Heritage Trail
Beacon Hill, Boston.
See "Boston African-American National Historic Site."

Boston African-American National Historic Site
46 Joy St., Boston.
- Blue Line to Bowdoin.
- Red line to Charles/MGH.
- Green Line to Government Ctr.

Boston National Historical Park
Visitor Center, 15 State St., Boston.
- Orange Line or Blue Line to State.
- Green Line to Government Ctr.

Boston Public Library
666 Boylston St., Boston.
- Green Line or T-Buses to Copley.
- Orange Line or T-Commuter Rail to Back Bay Sta.

Boston Tea Party Ship and Museum *
Congress Street Bridge, Boston.
- Red Line to South Sta.; walk NE on Atlantic Ave. 1 block (past Peter Pan), then right on Congress St. 1 block.

Bunker Hill Monument
Monument Sq., Charlestown.
- Orange Line to Community College; 1/2-mile walk.
- T-Commuter Boat from Long Wharf to Charlestown Navy Yard; 1/2-mile walk.
- T-Bus 92 (Assembly Sq.-Downtown) to Main and Winthrop Sts.
- T-Bus 93 (Sullivan-Downtown) to Bunker Hill and Lexington Sts.

Bunker Hill Pavilion *
"The Whites of Their Eyes"
55 Constitution Rd., Charlestown.
See "Charlestown Navy Yard."

Busch-Reisinger Museum
In same building with Fogg Art Museum
32 Quincy St., Cambridge.
- Red Line or T-Buses to Harvard.

Charles River Museum of Industry
154 Moody St., Waltham.
- T-Commuter Rail or any T-Bus to Central Sq., Waltham; walk 1 block S on Moody St.; turn left just before the river.

Charlestown Navy Yard
Charlestown.
- T-Commuter Boat from Long Wharf; 1/4 mile walk from Charlestown dock to U.S.S. *Constitution* (Navy Yard Shuttle Bus).
- T-Bus 92 (Assembly Sq.-Downtown) to City Sq.; 1/4 mile walk.
- T-Bus 93 (Sullivan-Downtown) to the Navy Yard.
- T-Bus 111 (Woodlawn-Haymarket) to

---

* discount offered to MBTA monthly passholders (as of June 1992)

City Sq.; 1/4 mile walk.
- Green Line, Orange Line, or T-Commuter Rail to North Sta.; 1/4 mile walk across the Charlestown Bridge.
- In summer, Bay State Cruise Co. and Boston Harbor Cruises from Long Wharf allow you to get off at the Navy Yard and return on a later boat.

Children's Museum*
300 Congress St., Boston.
- Red Line to South Sta.; walk NE on Atlantic Ave. one block (past Peter Pan), then right on Congress St. two blocks, past the Tea Party Ship.

Christian Science Center
Massachusetts Ave. at Huntington Ave., Boston.
- Green Line-E to Symphony.
- T-Bus 1 (Harvard-Dudley).
- Green Line-(B, C, or D) to Hynes Convention Ctr./ICA; walk S on Mass. Ave. 2 blocks.
- Orange Line to Mass. Ave.; walk N on Mass. Ave. two blocks.

The Commonwealth Museum
Columbia Point, Dorchester.
- Red Line to JFK/UMass; take Kennedy Library shuttle bus and walk from Kennedy Library to the museum.
- T-Bus 8 (Harbor Pt.-Kenmore) to U.Mass.; walk to museum.

Computer Museum *
300 Congress St., Boston.
Same directions as Children's Museum.

U.S.S. *Constitution* (Old Ironsides) U.S.S. Constitution Museum
Charlestown Navy Yard, Charlestown.
See "Charlestown Navy Yard."

Danforth Museum of Art
123 Union Ave., Framingham.
- T-Commuter Rail (Framingham Line) to Framingham; 1/4-mile walk.

The Discovery Museums
177 Main St., Acton.
- T-Commuter Rail (Fitchburg Line) to S. Acton; walk 1/2 mile N on Main St.

Faneuil Hall
Merchants Row, Boston.
- Orange Line or Blue Line to State.

- Green Line to Government Ctr.

Fogg Art Museum
32 Quincy St., Cambridge.
- Red Line or T-Buses to Harvard.

Franklin Park Zoo
Blue Hill Avenue, Dorchester.
- Orange Line/Green Line-E to Forest Hills; free shuttle bus to zoo, weekends & holidays, every 12 min.
- T-Bus 16 (Forest Hills-JFK/UMass).
- T-Bus 22 (Ashmont-Ruggles).
- T-Bus 28 (Mattapan-Ruggles).
- T-Bus 29 (Mattapan-Jackson Square).
- T-Bus 45 (Franklin Park Zoo-Ruggles).

Freedom Trail
Boston.
The trail begins at Boston Common; see Ch. 8.
- Red Line or Green Line to Park St.

Fuller Museum of Art
455 Oak St., Brockton.
- From Ashmont (Red Line) take BAT Bus 12 (Brockton); transfer to BAT Bus 4A (Westgate via N. Warren).

Isabella Stewart Gardner Museum
280 the Fenway, Boston.
- Green Line-E to Museum.
- T-Bus 8 (Harbor Pt.-Kenmore).
- T-Bus 39 (Forest Hills-Back Bay Sta.).
- T-Bus 47 (Central-Albany St.).
Get off at Museum and Huntington Ave.; walk N on Louis Prang St. (Texaco station at corner) 1-1/2 blocks to the museum.

Gibson House Museum
137 Beacon St., Boston.
- Green Line to Arlington.

Glass Flowers
See "Harvard University Museum."

Gore Place
52 Gore St., Waltham.
- T-Bus 70 (Cedarwood-Central).
- T-Bus 70A (N. Waltham-Central).

John Hancock Observatory *
St. James Ave., Copley Sq., Boston.
- Green Line or T-Buses to Copley.
- Orange Line or T-Commuter Rail to Back Bay Sta.

Musicians at the Gardner.

Harvard University Museum of Natural History
24 Oxford St., Cambridge.
- Red Line or T-Buses to Harvard.

Institute of Contemporary Art (ICA)
955 Boylston St., Boston.
- Green Line-(B, C, or D) to Hynes Convention Ctr./ICA.
- T-Bus 1 (Harvard-Dudley).

Jackson Homestead Newton City Museum
527 Washington St., Newton.
- Any T-Bus or Express Bus to Newton Corner; walk 1/2 mile W on Washington St.
- T-Bus 53, 54, 56, or 58 from Newton Corner or Downtown Crossing.

Kendall Whaling Museum
27 Everett St., Sharon.
- T-Commuter Rail (Attleboro Line) to Sharon; walk E on Rt. 27, left at fork onto Upland Rd.; right on Everett St. (1/2 mile).

John F. Kennedy National Historic Site
Birthplace of the President
83 Beals St., Brookline.
- Green Line-C to Coolidge Corner; walk 4 blocks N on Harvard St., right 1 block on Beals St.
- T-Bus 66 (Harvard-Dudley) to Beals St.

John F. Kennedy Library And Museum
Columbia Point, Dorchester.
- Red Line to JFK/UMass; free shuttle bus to the library every 20 min. (wheelchair accessible).
- T-Bus 8 (Harbor Pt.-Kenmore) to U.Mass.; walk to library.
- T-Bus 16 (Forest Hills-JFK/UMass).
- T-Bus 17 (Fields Corner-JFK/UMass).
- Boston Harbor Cruises water shuttle from Long Wharf.

Longfellow National Historic Site
105 Brattle St., Cambridge.
- Red Line or T-Buses to Harvard; 6-block walk up to Brattle St.

Longyear Historical Society
(Mary Baker Eddy Museum)
120 Seaver St., Brookline.
- Green Line-D to Brookline Hills or Beaconsfield; 5-block walk from either stop to top of hill; call for directions.

Mapparium
1 Norway St., Boston.
See "Christian Science Center."

Massachusetts Historical Society
1154 Boylston St., Boston.
- Green Line-(B, C, or D) to Hynes Convention Ctr./ICA.
- T-Bus 1 (Harvard-Dudley).

Massachusetts State House
Beacon St., Boston.
- Red Line or Green Line to Park St.

Milton Art Museum
44 Edge Hill Rd., Milton.
- T-Bus 245 (Quincy Ctr.-Mattapan).

M.I.T. Museum
265 Massachusetts Ave., Cambridge.
- Red Line to Central; walk 5 blocks S on Mass. Ave. to the museum.
- T-Bus 1 (Harvard-Dudley) to Sidney St. or Windsor St.

Museum of Afro American History *
46 Joy St., Boston.
See "Boston African-American National Historic Site."

Museum of Fine Arts
465 Huntington Ave., Boston.
- Green Line-E to Museum.
- T-Bus 8 (Harbor Pt.-Kenmore).
- T-Bus 39 (Forest Hills-Back Bay Sta.).
- T-Bus 47 (Central-Albany St.).

Museum of Our National Heritage
33 Marrett Rd., Lexington.
- T-Bus 62 (Bedford-Alewife).
- T-Bus 76 (Hanscom Field-Alewife).
Get off at Mass. Ave. and Marrett Rd.

Museum of Science *
Science Park, Boston.
- Green Line (Lechmere) to Science Park.
- Red Line to Charles/MGH; walk E along the Charles River to the Museum.

Museum of the National Center of Afro-American Artists
300 Walnut Ave., Roxbury.
- T-Bus 22 (Ashmont-Ruggles)
- T-Bus 44 (Jackson Sq.-Ruggles)
Get off at Walnut Ave. and Seaver St.

Museum of Transportation *
Larz Anderson Park, 15 Newton St., Brookline.
- T-Bus 51 (Cleveland Cir.-Forest Hills) to Newton and Clyde Sts.; walk E on Newton St. 1/2 mile.
From Boston: Green Line-D to Reservoir, then T-Bus 51 as above.

New England Aquarium
Central Wharf, Boston.
- Blue Line to Aquarium.

Old North Church (Christ Church)
193 Salem St., Boston.
- Green Line, Orange Line, or T-Buses to Haymarket; cross under the Central Artery and walk up Salem St.

Old South Meeting-House
310 Washington St., Boston.
- Orange Line or Blue Line to State.
- Red Line to Downtown Crossing.

Old State House
206 Washington St., Boston.
- Orange Line or Blue Line to State.
- Green Line to Government Ctr.

Frederick Law Olmsted National Historic Site
99 Warren St., Brookline.
- Green Line-D to Brookline Hills; walk 2 blocks S on Cypress St., right 4 blocks on Walnut St., left 1 block on Warren St. (after the church).
- T-Bus 60 (Chestnut Hill-Kenmore) to Warren St.; cross Rt. 9 and walk 2 blocks S on Warren St.

Harrison Gray Otis House
141 Cambridge St., Boston.
- Blue Line to Bowdoin.
- Green Line to Government Ctr.
- Red Line to Charles/MGH.

Peabody Museum of Archeology
See "Harvard University Museum."

Prudential Skywalk *
Prudential Ctr., 800 Boylston St., Boston.
- Green Line-E to Prudential.

Quincy Historical Society
8 Adams St., Quincy.
- Red Line (Braintree) to Quincy Ctr.

Paul Revere House
19 North Sq., Boston.
- Green Line, Orange Line, or T-Buses to Haymarket; follow the Freedom Trail.

Arthur M. Sackler Art Museum
485 Broadway, Cambridge.
- Red Line or T-Buses to Harvard.

Saugus Ironworks National Historic Site
244 Central St., Saugus.
- T-Bus 430 (Saugus-Malden Ctr.).

Semitic Museum
6 Divinity Ave., Cambridge.
- Red Line or T-Buses to Harvard.

Somerville Museum
1 Westwood Rd., Somerville.
- T-Bus 88 (Clarendon Hill-Lechmere) to Highland Ave. and Central St.; walk 3 blocks S on Central St.

Sports Museum of New England
CambridgeSide Galleria.
- 100 CambridgeSide Place, Cambridge.
- Green Line or T-Buses to Lechmere.
- Free shuttle bus from Kendall or Lechmere.

Walter D. Stone Memorial Zoo
149 Pond St., Stoneham.

●Hudson Bus (Boston-Stoneham), *bus runs 7:00-10:00 am and 4:00-6:15 pm only.*

Swan Boats
Public Garden, Boston.
●Green Line to Arlington.

Trinity Church
Copley Sq., Boston.
●Green Line or T-Buses to Copley.
●Orange Line or T-Commuter Rail to Back Bay Sta.

Chapter 12

Theaters, Cinemas, and Auditoriums

Agassiz Theatre
10 Garden St., Cambridge.
●Red Line to Harvard.

American Repertory Theatre
See "Loeb Drama Center."

Back Alley Theatre
1253 Cambridge St., Inman Sq., Cambridge.
●T-Bus 69 (Harvard-Lechmere).
●T-Bus 83 (Rindge Ave.-Central).
●T-Bus 91 (Sullivan-Central).

Bayside Exposition Center
200 Mt. Vernon St., Dorchester.
●Red Line to JFK/UMass; 3-block walk.
●T-Bus 8 (Harbor Pt.-Kenmore).
●Special shuttle buses from JFK/UMass to some events.

Beacon Hill Cinemas 1-3
1 Beacon St., Boston.
●Red Line to Park St.
●Green Line to Govt. Center.

Beacon Hill Playhouse
54 Charles St., Boston
●Red Line to Charles/MGH.

Berklee Performance Center
136 Massachusetts Ave., Boston.
●Green Line-(B, C, or D) to Hynes Convention Ctr./ICA.
●T-Bus 1 (Harvard-Dudley).

Boston Baked Theatre
255 Elm St., Somerville
●Red Line or T-Buses to Davis.

Boston Center for the Arts
539 Tremont St., Boston.
●Orange Line to Back Bay Sta.; walk S

on Clarendon St. 5 blocks to Tremont St. and turn left.
●Green Line to Arlington; walk S on Berkeley St. 7 blocks to Tremont St. and turn right.
●T-Bus 39 (Forest Hills-Back Bay Sta.); walk S on Clarendon St. 5 blocks to Tremont St. and turn left.
●T-Bus 43 (Ruggles-Park St.).

Boston Garden
150 Causeway St., Boston.
●Green Line or Orange Line to North Sta.
●T-Commuter Rail to North Sta.

Boston University School for the Arts Concert Hall
855 Commonwealth Ave., Boston.
●Green Line-B to B.U. West.
See also "Tsai Performance Center."

Boston University Theatre
See "Huntington Theatre Co."

Brattle Theatre
40 Brattle St., Cambridge
●Red Line or T-Buses to Harvard.

Cabot Street Theatre
286 Cabot St., Beverly.
●T-Commuter Rail (Rockport/Ipswich Lines) to Beverly Depot; walk 3 blocks E on Railroad Ave. to Cabot St., then left 1/2 mile to the theater.

Cambridge Multicultural Arts Center
41 Second St., Cambridge.
●Green Line or T-Buses to Lechmere.

The Centrum at Worcester
50 Foster St., Worcester.
●Peter Pan from Boston to Worcester; 1/2

mile from the Worcester Bus Terminal.
See map page 70.

Charles Cinema 1-3
195 Cambridge St., Boston.
●Red Line to Charles/MGH.

Charles Playhouse
76 Warrenton St., Boston.
●Green Line to Boylston; walk S on
  Tremont to Stuart, right on Stuart, left
  on Warrenton.
●Orange Line to N. E. Medical Ctr.

Charlestown Working Theatre
442 Bunker Hill St., Charlestown.
●Orange Line or T-Buses to Sullivan; 4-
  block walk.
●T-Bus 93 (Sullivan-Downtown).

Cheri Complex 1-4
50 Dalton St., Boston.
●Green Line-(B, C, D) to Hynes
  Convention Ctr./ICA.
●Green Line-E to Prudential.
●T-Bus 39 (Forest Hills-Back Bay).

Cinema 57 1-2
200 Stuart St., Boston.
●Green Line to Boylston.
●Orange Line to N.E. Medical Ctr.
●T-Bus 43 (Ruggles-Park St.).

Colonial Theatre
106 Boylston St., Boston.
●Green Line to Boylston.
●Orange Line to Chinatown.

Converse Hall
Tremont Temple, 88 Tremont St., Boston.
●Red Line or Green Line to Park St.

Coolidge Corner Theatre
290 Harvard St., Brookline.
●Green Line-C to Coolidge Corner.
●T-Bus 66 (Harvard-Dudley).

Copley Place Cinema 1-11
100 Huntington Ave., Boston.
●Orange Line or T-Commuter Rail to
  Back Bay Sta.
●Green Line or T-Buses to Copley.

Cyclorama
See "Boston Center for the Arts."

Double Edge Theatre
5 St. Lukes Rd., Allston.
●Green Line-B to Fordham Rd.

Emerson Majestic Theatre
221 Tremont St., Boston.
●Green Line to Boylston.
●Orange Line to N. E. Medical Ctr.

Faneuil Hall
Merchants Row, Boston.
●Green Line to Govt. Ctr.
●Blue Line or Orange Line to State.

Firehouse Multicultural Arts Center
659 Centre St., Jamaica Plain.
●Green Line-E/T-Bus 39 (Forest Hills-
  Back Bay Sta.).

First Night
New Years Eve, Boston.
●On New Years Eve the last trip on all
  MBTA lines operates at least 1 hour later
  than normal; no fare is charged after
  10:00 pm.

Foxboro Stadium
Rt. 1, Foxborough
●Special T-Commuter Rail trains to
  some concerts and sporting events from
  South Sta. and Back Bay Sta.

Great Woods
S. Main St. (Rt. 140), Mansfield.
●T-Commuter Rail (Attleboro Line) to
  Mansfield; 3-mile walk/taxi ride S of
  station.

John Hancock Hall
180 Berkeley St., Boston.
●Green Line to Arlington.
●Orange Line to Back Bay Sta.

Harvard Square Cinema
10 Church St., Cambridge
●Red Line to T-Buses to Harvard.

Hasty Pudding Theatre
12 Holyoke St., Cambridge.
●Red Line or T-Buses to Harvard.

Hatch Shell Concerts on the Esplanade
Embankment Rd., Boston.
●Red Line to Charles/MGH.
●Green Line to Arlington; walk N on
  Arlington St. along the Public Garden
  to the Esplanade.

Huntington Theatre Co.
264 Huntington Ave., Boston.
●Green Line-E to Symphony.

●Orange Line to Mass. Ave.
●T-Bus 1 (Harvard-Dudley).
●T-Bus 39 (Forest Hills-Back Bay Sta.).

Hynes Convention Ctr.
900 Boylston St., Boston.
●Green Line-(B, C, or D) to Hynes
Convention Ctr./ICA.
●T-Bus 1 (Harvard-Dudley).
●T-Bus 39 (Forest Hills-Back Bay Sta.).

Janus Cinema
57 J.F. Kennedy St., Cambridge.
●Red Line or T-Buses to Harvard.

Jordan Hall
30 Gainsborough St., Boston.
●Green Line-E to Symphony.
●Orange Line to Mass. Ave.
●T-Bus 1 (Harvard-Dudley) to Symphony.
●T-Bus 39 (Forest Hills-Back Bay Sta.).

Jorge Hernandez Cultural Center at Villa Victoria
85 W. Newton St., Boston.
●T-Bus 43 (Ruggles-Park St.).
●Green Line-E to Prudential; walk 4
blocks S on W. Newton St.
●Orange Line to Back Bay Sta.; walk 4
blocks S on Dartmouth St.; turn right
on Tremont St. 2 blocks.
●T-Bus 39 (Forest Hills-Back Bay Sta.);
walk 4 blocks S on Dartmouth St.; turn
right on Tremont St. 2 blocks.

Killian Hall
Massachusetts Institute of Technology,
160 Memorial Drive.
●Red Line to Kendall.
●T-Bus 1 (Harvard-Dudley).

Kresge Auditorium
Massachusetts Institute of Technology,
Massachusetts Ave., Cambridge.
●T-Bus 1 (Harvard-Dudley).

Loeb Drama Center
64 Brattle St., Cambridge.
●Red Line or T-Buses to Harvard.

Longy School of Music
1 Follen St., Cambridge.
●Red Line and T-Buses to Harvard;
walk 3 blocks N on Garden St. past
Sheraton Commander Hotel.

Lyric Stage
140 Clarendon St., Boston.
●Orange Line or T-Commuter Rail to

Back Bay Sta.
●Green Line or T-Buses to Copley.

Mechanics Hall
321 Main St., Worcester.
●Peter Pan from Boston to Worcester; 1/2
mile from the Worcester Bus Terminal.
See map page 70.

Concert at Hatch Shell, Boston.

Mobius
354 Congress St., Boston.
●Red Line to South Sta.; 5-block walk.

National Ctr. of Afro-American Artists (Elma Lewis School)
300 Walnut Ave., Roxbury
●T-Bus 22 (Ashmont-Ruggles) to
Seaver St. and Elm Hill Ave.

Newbury St. Theatre
565 Boylston St., Boston.
●Green Line or T-Buses to Copley.

New Theater
565 Boylston St., Boston.
●Green Line or T-Buses to Copley.

New England Hall
225 Clarendon St., Boston.
●Green Line or T-Buses to Copley.

New Repertory Theatre
54 Lincoln St., Newton Highlands.
●Green Line-D to Newton Highlands.

Nickelodeon Cinemas
34 Cummington St., Boston.
●Green Line to first outbound stop after
Kenmore (Blandford St.).

Open Door Theatre
Pinebank Park, the Jamaicaway,
Jamaica Plain.
- Green Line-E/T-Bus 39 (Forest Hills-
  Back Bay Sta.) to Perkins St.; walk 3
  blocks W on Perkins to the
  Jamaicaway and turn left.

The Opera House
539 Washington St., Boston.
- Red Line or Orange Line to Downtown
  Crossing.
- Green Line to Park St.

Orpheum Theatre
Hamilton Place, off Tremont St. across
from Park St. Church, Boston.
- Red Line or Green Line to Park St.

Paris Cinema
841 Boylston St., Boston.
- Green Line to Hynes/Convention Ctr./
  ICA or Copley.

Park Plaza Castle
Arlington St., Boston.
- Green Line to Arlington; walk two
  blocks S on Arlington St.

The Performance Place
277 Broadway, Somerville.
- T-Bus 89 (Clarendon Hill-Sullivan).
- T-Bus 101 (Malden Ctr.-Sullivan, via
  Medford Sq.).

Providence Civic Center
1 LaSalle Sq., Providence, RI.
- Bonanza from Boston/Back Bay Sta.
  to Providence; 1/4-mile walk from
  Kennedy Plaza.
- Amtrak to Providence.
See map page 70.

Puppet Showplace
30 Station St., Brookline.
- Green Line-D or T-Buses to Brookline
  Village.

Sanders Theatre
Memorial Hall, Kirkland St., Cambridge.
- Red Line or T-Buses to Harvard.

Shubert Theatre
265 Tremont St., Boston.
- Orange Line to N. E. Medical Ctr.
- Green Line to Boylston.

Somerville Theatre
55 Davis Sq., Somerville.

- Red Line or T-Buses to Davis.

Strand Theatre
543 Columbia Rd., Uphams Corner,
Dorchester.
- T-Bus 15 (Kane Sq.-Ruggles).
- T-Bus 16 (Forest Hills-JFK/UMass).
- T-Bus 17 (Fields Corner-JFK/UMass).
- Red Line to JFK/UMass; 15-minute
  walk W on Columbia Rd., or special
  shuttle buses from JFK/UMass to
  some events.

Symphony Hall
301 Massachusetts Ave., Boston.
- Green Line-E to Symphony.
- Orange Line to Mass. Ave.
- T-Bus 1 (Harvard-Dudley) to Sym-
  phony.
- T-Bus 39 (Forest Hills-Back Bay Sta.).

Tanglewood
West St. (Rt. 183), Lenox.
*See Lenox listing in Ch. 16; a 25-min.
walk from the Lenox bus stop.*

Terrace Room, Boston Park Plaza Hotel
64 Arlington St., Boston.
- Green Line to Arlington.

Theatre Lobby
216 Hanover St., Boston.
- Green or Orange lines to Haymarket.

Triangle Theater
58 Berkeley St., Boston.
- Orange Line to Back Bay Sta.; walk S
  on Clarendon St. 2 blocks, left on
  Chandler St., right on Berkeley.
- Green Line to Arlington; walk S on
  Berkeley St. 6 blocks.
- T-Bus 39 (Forest Hills-Back Bay Sta.).

Trinity Repertory Co.
201 Washington St., Providence, RI.
- Bonanza from Boston/Back Bay Sta.
  to Providence; 1/4-mile walk from
  Kennedy Plaza.
- Amtrak to Providence.
See map page 70.

Tsai Performance Center
Boston University,
655 Commonwealth Ave., Boston.
- Green Line-B to B.U. Central or B.U.
  East.
- T-Bus 47 (Central-Albany St.).

Wang Center for the Performing Arts

268 Tremont St., Boston.
- Orange Line to N. E. Medical Ctr.
- Green Line to Boylston.

Wilbur Theatre

246 Tremont St., Boston.
- Orange Line to N. E. Medical Ctr.
- Green Line to Boylston.

World Trade Center Exhibition Hall

Commonwealth Pier, 164 Northern Ave., Boston.
- Red Line to South Sta.; 3/4-mile walk S on Summer St., left on Viaduct St.
- T-Bus 7 (City Pt–Franklin & Devonshire).
- Free shuttle buses from South Sta., 7:00 am-7:00 pm, every 10 min.

Chapter 13

Shopping Centers

The Arsenal Marketplace

485 Arsenal St., Watertown.
- T-Bus 70 (Cedarwood-Central).
- T-Bus 70A (N. Waltham-Central).

Assembly Square Mall

133 Middlesex Ave., Somerville.
- T-Bus 90 (Davis-Wellington).
- T-Bus 92 (Assembly Sq.-Downtown) *before 4:00 pm (6:20 pm Sat) only.*
- T-Bus 95 (W. Medford-Sullivan).

Burlington Mall

Rt. 128 & Middlesex Tpk., Burlington.
- T-Bus 350 (Burlington-Alewife).
- Burlington People Mover 1, 5, and 6.
- Lexpress (Lexington-Burlington Mall).

CambridgeSide Galleria

First St., Cambridge.
- Green Line or T-Buses to Lechmere.
- Free shuttle bus from Lechmere or Kendall.

Chestnut Hill Shopping Center

27 Boylston St. (Rt.9), Newton.
- T-Bus 60 (Chestnut Hill-Kenmore).
- Green Line-D to Chestnut Hill, walk S on Hammond St. and right on Boylston St. (1/2 mile).

The Mall at Chestnut Hill

199 Boylston St. (Rt.9), Newton.
- T-Bus 60 (Chestnut Hill-Kenmore) to end of line at Hammond Pond Pkwy.; 1 1/2-block walk. Look for stairs to the right to get up to parking lot.

Copley Place

100 Huntington Ave., Boston.
- Orange Line or T-Commuter Rail to Back Bay Sta.
- Green Line or T-Buses to Copley or Back Bay Sta.

Dedham Mall

300 V.F.W. Pkwy. (Rt. 1), Dedham.
- T-Bus 34E (Walpole Ctr.-Forest Hills).
- T-Bus 35 (Dedham Mall-Forest Hills, via Stimson).
- T-Bus 52 (Dedham Mall-Watertown).
- Dedham Local Bus.

Dedham Plaza

725 Providence Hwy. (Rt. 1), Dedham.
- T-Bus 34E (Walpole Ctr.-Forest Hills). Bus stops at back entrance to plaza.

Downtown Crossing

Summer and Washington Sts., Boston.
- Red Line or Orange Line to Downtown Crossing.
- Green Line to Park St.
- Blue Line to State.
See Ch. 5 for buses to Downtown Crossing.

Faneuil Hall Marketplace

Congress St., Boston.
- Green Line to Government Ctr.; walk across City Hall Plaza to the Market.
- Blue Line to State or Aquarium.
- Orange Line to State.

Quincy Market, Boston.

Fresh Pond Mall
186 Alewife Brook Pkwy., Cambridge.
●Red Line to Alewife; 1/4-mile walk.
●T-Bus 74 (Belmont Ctr.-Harvard), *trips "via Concord Ave." only.*
●T-Bus 78 (Arlmont-Harvard).

Liberty Tree Mall
Independence Way, Danvers.
●T-Bus 435 (Lynn-Danvers).
●T-Bus 458 (Salem-Danvers).

Marketplace Center
200 State St., Boston.
●Blue Line to State or Aquarium, across Surface Artery.
●Green Line to Government Ctr.; walk across City Hall Plaza past Faneuil Hall Market.

Meadow Glen Mall
3850 Mystic Valley Pkwy., Medford.
●Hudson Bus (Fulton St.-Meadow Glen Mall), via Medford Sq.
●T-Bus 134 (N. Woburn-Wellington) to Locust St.; 2 block walk.
●T-Bus 134M (Medford-Wellington) to Locust St.

Middlesex Mall
43 Middlesex Turnpike, Burlington.
●Burlington People Mover 1 and 5.
●Lexpress (Lexington-Burlington Mall).

Mystic Mall
166 Everett Ave., Chelsea.
●T-Bus 112 (Wellington-Maverick).
●T-Commuter Rail (Rockport/Ipswich Line) to Chelsea; 4-block walk.

Natick Mall and Sherwood Plaza
1345 Worcester St. (Rt. 9), Natick.
●Peter Pan (Boston-Worcester, Rt. 9 local).
●Natick Neighborhood Bus.
●LIFT 2, 3, and 4.

Newbury St. shopping area
Back Bay, Boston.
●Green Line to Arlington, Copley or Hynes Convention Ctr./ICA.
●Orange Line or T-Commuter Rail to Back Bay Sta.

New England Shopping Center
1205 Broadway (Rt. 1), Saugus.
●T-Bus 430 (Saugus-Malden Ctr.).

Northgate Shopping Center
Squire Rd., Revere.
●T-Bus 119 (Northgate-Beachmont).
●T-Bus 411 (Revere House-Malden Ctr.).

Northshore Shopping Center
Rt. 128 at Rt. 114, Peabody.
●T-Bus 435 (Lynn-Danvers).
●Michaud Bus (Lake Shore-Northshore Shopping Ctr.).
●Michaud Bus (Salem-Northshore Shopping Ctr.).

Porter Square
White St., Cambridge.
●Red Line to Porter.
●T-Bus 77 (Arlington Hts.-Harvard).
●T-Bus 77A (N. Cambridge-Harvard).
●T-Bus 87 (Arlington Ctr.-Lechmere)

Quincy Market
See "Faneuil Hall Marketplace."

Shoppers World
Rt. 9, Framingham.
●Peter Pan (Boston-Worcester, Rt. 9 local).
●Peter Pan (Boston-Framingham, express).
●Crystal Transport (Framingham-Milford).
●Gulbankian's (Framingham-Hudson), Sat. only.

- LIFT 1, 2, 3, and 4.
- Natick Neighborhood Bus.

Silver City Galleria
2 Galleria Drive, Taunton
- American Eagle bus from Boston
- Bloom Bus lines from Boston

South Shore Plaza
250 Granite St., Braintree.
- T-Bus 236 (Quincy Ctr.-South Shore Plaza).
- T-Bus 238 (Quincy Ctr.-Crawford Sq.).
- T-Bus 240A (Crawford Sq.-Ashmont): Some trips have through service to the mall from Ashmont, Milton, and N. Randolph.

Swampscott Mall
Paradise Rd., Swampscott.

- T-Bus 441 (Marblehead-Haymarket).
- T-Bus 455 (Salem-Haymarket, via Loring Ave.).

Twin City Mall
264 O'Brien Hwy., Cambridge.
- T-Bus 80 (Arlington Ctr.-Lechmere).
- T-Bus 87 (Arlington Ctr.-Lechmere).
- T-Bus 88 (Clarendon Hill-Lechmere).
- T-Bus 69 (Harvard-Lechmere) to Lambert St., 1 block walk.

Watertown Mall
550 Arsenal St., Watertown.
- T-Bus 70 (Cedarwood-Central).
- T-Bus 70A (N. Waltham-Central).

Woburn Mall
300 Mishawum Rd., Woburn.
- T-Commuter Rail (Lowell Line) to Mishawum.

Chapter 14

Educational Institutions

Amherst College
Amherst.
- Peter Pan (Boston-Amherst) to Amherst Ctr.; 1 block walk.
- PVTA/Five Colleges shuttle buses.

Andover-Newton Theological School
210 Herrick Rd., Newton Centre.
- Green Line-D (Riverside) to Newton Centre.
- T-Bus 52 (Dedham Mall-Watertown).

Aquinas Junior College
—Milton
303 Adams St., Milton.
- T-Bus 217 (Wollaston Beach-Ashmont).
—Newton
15 Walnut Park, Newton.
- Any T-Bus or Express Bus to Newton Corner; walk 1/2 mile W on Washington St. to Walnut Park.
- T-Buses 53, 54, 56, 58 from Newton Corner or Downtown Crossing to Washington St. and Walnut Park.

Art Institute of Boston
700 Boylston St., Boston
- Green Line (B, C, or D) or T-Buses to Kenmore.

Babson College
Forest St. and Wellesley Ave., Wellesley.
- T-Commuter Rail (Framingham Line) to Wellesley Hills; walk 1 mile S on Forest St.
- Babson College student government bus from Woodlawn *(Green Line-D)*, Fri-Sat-Sun; call 239-4330.

Bay State Junior College
122 Commonwealth Ave., Boston.
- Green Line to Copley.

Bentley College
Forest and Beaver Sts., Waltham.
- T-Bus 54 (Waverley-Newton Corner).
- T-Bus 73 (Waverley-Harvard) to Waverley, transfer to T-Bus 54.
- Bentley College shuttle bus from Harvard Sq., nights and weekends; call 891-2148.

Berklee College of Music
1140 Boylston St., Boston.
- Green Line-(B, C, or D) to Hynes Convention Ctr./ICA.
- T-Bus 1 (Harvard-Dudley).

Boston Architectural Center
320 Newbury St., Boston.
- Green Line-(B, C, or D) to Hynes Convention Ctr./ICA.
- T-Bus 1 (Harvard-Dudley).

Boston Center for Adult Education
5 Commonwealth Ave., Boston.
- Green Line or T-Buses to Arlington.

Boston College
140 Commonwealth Ave., Chestnut Hill (Newton).
- Green Line-B (Boston College) to end of line. Stop is at north edge of campus.
- Green Line-D (Riverside) to Chestnut Hill; mile 1/2 walk N on Hammond St. to south edge of campus.
- Boston College shuttle bus from Cleveland Cir. and Commonwealth Ave., daily; call 552-3060.

—Newton Campus
885 Centre St., Newton.
- T-Bus 52 (Dedham Mall-Watertown).
- Green Line-D (Riverside) to Newton Centre; then T-Bus 52 (Watertown).
- Any T-Bus to Watertown Sq. or Newton Corner; then T-Bus 52 (Dedham Mall).
- Boston College shuttle bus from main campus and Cleveland Cir., daily; call 552-3060.

Boston Conservatory of Music
8 the Fenway, Boston.
- Green Line-(B, C, or D) to Hynes Convention Ctr./ICA.
- T-Bus 1 (Harvard-Dudley).

Boston University
Charles River Campus
Commonwealth Ave., Boston.
- Green Line-B (Boston College) to Blandford St., B.U. East, B.U. Central, and B.U. West stops.
- T-Bus 47 (Central-Albany St.).
- T-Bus 57 (Watertown-Kenmore).

—Medical School
80 E. Concord St., Boston.
See "Boston University Medical Center" in Chapter 15.

Bradford College
320 S. Main St., Bradford (Haverhill).
- T-Commuter Rail (Haverhill) to Bradford.

Brandeis University
415 South St., Waltham.
- T-Commuter Rail (Fitchburg Line) to Brandeis/Roberts.
- T-Bus 53 (Roberts-Newton Corner-Downtown).
- T-Bus 70 (Cedarwood-Central) to end of line; walk up Cedarwood Ave., left on Thornton Rd. to campus.

Bridgewater State College
100 State St., Bridgewater.
- Interstate (Boston-Middleborough).

Brown University
45 Prospect St., Providence, RI.
- Amtrak, T-Commuter Rail, or Bonanza to Providence; 1/2-mile walk from train station or Kennedy Plaza, or take one of the following buses:
- RIPTA Bus 38 (Rumford/Tunnel).
- RIPTA Bus 40 (Butler/Tunnel).
- RIPTA Bus 41 (Elmgrove/Tunnel).
- RIPTA Bus 42 (Hope/Tunnel).

Bunker Hill Community College
Rutherford Ave., Charlestown.
- Orange Line to Community College.

Cambridge Center for Adult Education
42 Brattle St., Cambridge.
- Red Line or T-Buses to Harvard.

Cambridge College
44B Brattle St., Cambridge.
- Red Line or T-Buses to Harvard.

Clark University
950 Main St., Worcester.
- WRTA Bus 19S (Cherry Valley or Leicester Ctr.).
- WRTA Bus 26S (Auburn Mall).

Curry College
1071 Blue Hill Ave., Milton.
- Hudson Bus (Mattapan-Canton).

Eastern Nazarene College
23 E. Elm Ave., Wollaston (Quincy).
- Red Line (Braintree) to Wollaston; 1/2-mile walk.
- T-Bus 212 (Quincy Ctr.-N. Quincy, via Billings Rd.).
- T-Bus 217 (Wollaston Beach-Ashmont).

Emerson College
100 Beacon St., Boston.
- Green Line to Arlington.

Emmanuel College
400 the Fenway, Boston.
- Green Line-D (Riverside) to Fenway.
- T-Bus 8 (Harbor Pt.-Kenmore).
- T-Bus 47 (Central-Albany St.)
- T-Bus 60 (Chestnut Hill-Kenmore).
- T-Bus 65 (Brighton Ctr.-Kenmore).
- Metrobus (Cambridge-Longwood Med. Area).

Fisher Junior College
118 Beacon St., Boston.
- Green Line to Arlington.

Framingham State College
100 State St., Framingham.
- Peter Pan (Boston-Worcester, Rt. 9 local).
- Peter Pan (Boston-Framingham, express).
- LIFT 2, 2X, and 3.

Hampshire College
Route 116, Amherst.
- Peter Pan (Boston-Amherst), 3 trips daily stop at the college.
- Peter Pan (Boston-Amherst) to Amherst Ctr. or U.Mass., transfer to PVTA.
- PVTA/Amherst Bus 301 (Mt. Holyoke).
- PVTA/Five Colleges shuttle buses.

Harvard University
Harvard Sq., Cambridge.
- Red Line or T-Buses to Harvard.
- Metrobus (Cambridge-Longwood Med. Area).

Harvard University, Cambridge

—Business School
Soldiers Field Rd., Allston.
(Across the Charles River from Harvard Sq.).
- Red Line or T-Buses to Harvard; walk across river (1/2 mile) or T-Bus 66 or 86.
- T-Bus 66 (Harvard-Dudley, via Brookline).
- T-Bus 70 (Cedarwood-Central) to Western Ave.
- T-Bus 86 (Sullivan-Cleveland Cir.).

—Medical Area
25 Shattuck St., Boston.
- Green Line-E to Longwood Ave.
- T-Bus 8 (Harbor Pt.-Kenmore).
- T-Bus 39 (Forest Hills-Back Bay Sta.).
- T-Bus 47 (Central-Albany St.).
- T-Bus 66 (Harvard-Dudley, via Brookline).
- Metrobus (Cambridge-Longwood Med. Area).

Holy Cross College
College St., Worcester.
- WRTA Bus 10 (College Hill).
- WRTA Bus 4 (Millbury Line) to McKeon Rd., 1/2-mile walk.

Laboure College
2120 Dorchester Ave., Dorchester.
See "Carney Hospital" in Chapter 15

Lasell Junior College
1844 Commonwealth Ave., Newton.
- Green Line-D (Riverside) to Riverside, walk 1/2-mile E on Grove St., turn right on Woodland Rd. to back of campus.

Lesley College
29 Everett St., Cambridge.
- Red Line and T-Buses to Harvard; walk 3 blocks N on Mass. Ave. to Everett St.
- T-Bus 77 (Arlington Hts.-Harvard).
- T-Bus 77A (N. Cambridge-Harvard).

Longy School of Music
1 Follen St., Cambridge.
- Red Line and T-Buses to Harvard; walk 3 blocks N on Garden St. past the Sheraton Commander Hotel.

Massachusetts Bay Community College
50 Oakland St., Wellesley.
- Shuttle bus from Riverside *(Green Line-D)*, Mon-Fri, Sept-May.
- Peter Pan (Boston-Worcester, Rt. 9 local) to Oakland St., then 1 block walk.

Massachusetts College of Art
621 Huntington Ave., Boston.
- Green Line-E to Longwood Ave.
- T-Bus 8 (Harbor Pt.-Kenmore).
- T-Bus 39 (Forest Hills-Back Bay Sta.).
- T-Bus 47 (Central-Albany St.).
- T-Bus 66 (Allston-Dudley) to Brigham Cir., 2-block walk.

Massachusetts College of Pharmacy
179 Longwood Ave., Boston.
- Green Line-E to Longwood Ave.
- T-Bus 8 (Harbor Pt.-Kenmore).
- T-Bus 39 (Forest Hills-Back Bay Sta.).
- T-Bus 47 (Central-Albany St.).
- T-Bus 66 (Allston-Dudley) to Brigham Cir., 2-block walk.
- Metrobus (Cambridge-Longwood Med. Area).

Massachusetts Institute of Technology
77 Massachusetts Ave., Cambridge.
- Red Line to Kendall. Station is at east end of campus.
- T-Bus 1 (Harvard-Dudley). Bus stop is in middle of campus.
- Metrobus (Cambridge-Longwood Med. Area).

Middlesex Community College
Springs Rd., Bedford.
- T-Bus 62 (Bedford-Alewife), *before 7:00 pm only.*

Mount Holyoke College
South Hadley.
- Peter Pan (Boston-Amherst), 3 trips daily stop at the college.
- Peter Pan (Boston-Amherst) to Amherst Ctr. or UMass., transfer to PVTA.
- PVTA/Amherst Bus 301 (Mt. Holyoke).
- PVTA/Five Colleges shuttle buses.
- PVTA/Holyoke Bus 211 (S. Hadley Ctr.).

Mount Ida College
777 Dedham St., Newton Centre.
- T-Bus 52 (Dedham Mall-Watertown).
- Green Line-D (Riverside) to Newton Centre, then T-Bus 52 (Dedham Mall).

New England Conservatory of Music
290 Huntington Ave., Boston.
- Green Line-E to Symphony.
- Orange Line to Mass. Ave.
- T-Bus 1 (Harvard-Dudley).
- T-Bus 39 (Forest Hills-Back Bay Sta.).

New England School of Law
154 Stuart St., Park Plaza, Boston.
- Green Line to Boylston.
- Orange Line to N. E. Medical Ctr.
- T-Bus 43 (Ruggles-Park St.).

Newbury College
—Boston Campus
921 Boylston St., Boston.
- Green Line-(B, C, or D) to Hynes Convention Ctr./ICA.
- T-Bus 1 (Harvard-Dudley).
—Brookline Campus
129 Fisher Ave., Brookline.
- Green Line-D (Riverside) to Reservoir, 6-block walk.
- Shuttle van from Reservoir, Mon-Fri during the school year.

Northeastern University
360 Huntington Ave., Boston.
- Green Line-E to Northeastern.
- Orange Line or T-Buses to Ruggles.
- T-Bus 39 (Forest Hills-Back Bay Sta.).
- T-Commuter Rail (Needham, Franklin, Attleboro/Stoughton lines).

North Shore Community College
3 Essex St., Beverly
- College Annex, Sohier Rd., Beverly.
- T-Bus 451 (North Beverly-Salem).
—Lynn Campus
300 Broad St., Lynn
- T-Commuter Rail (Rockport/Ipswich Lines) and all T-Buses to Lynn/Central Sq.; 2-block walk.

Pine Manor College
400 Heath St., Chestnut Hill (Brookline).
- T-Bus 60 (Chestnut Hill-Kenmore) to Randolph Rd., walk up Randolph to Heath St.

Providence College
River Ave. at Eaton St., Providence .
- RIPTA Bus 50 (Douglas) to Admiral St. and River Ave.
- RIPTA Bus 57 (Smith) to Smith St. and River Ave.

Quincy Junior College
34 Coddington St., Quincy.
- Red Line (Braintree) or T-Buses to Quincy Ctr.

Radcliffe College
Garden St., Cambridge.
- Red Line or T-Buses to Harvard.

Regis College
235 Wellesley St., Weston.
●Daily shuttle buses from Riverside
(Green Line-D) during the school year.

Roxbury Community College
1234 Columbus Ave., Roxbury.
●Orange Line to Roxbury Crossing.
●T-Bus 66 (Allston-Dudley).
●Also served by T-Buses 15, 19, 22, 23,
28, 29, 42, 44, 45.

Salem State College
352 Lafayette St., Salem.
●T-Bus 455 (Salem-Haymarket, via
Loring Ave.).

Simmons College
300 the Fenway, Boston.
●Green Line-D to Fenway (for dormito-
ries).
●Green Line-E to Museum (for academic
buildings).
●T-Bus 8 (Harbor Pt.-Kenmore).
●T-Bus 47 (Central-Albany St.).
●T-Bus 60 (Chestnut Hill-Kenmore).
●T-Bus 65 (Brighton Ctr.-Kenmore).
●Metrobus (Cambridge-Longwood Med.
Area).

Smith College
Elm St., Northampton.
●Peter Pan (Boston-Amherst) to
Northampton; 3-block walk.
●PVTA/Five Colleges shuttle buses.

Stonehill College
320 Washington St., North Easton.
●BAT Bus 9 (Pearl St.).

Suffolk University
41 Temple St., Beacon Hill, Boston.
●Red Line and Green Line to Park St.
●Blue Line to Bowdoin.

Tufts University
Boston Ave., Medford.
●Red Line to Davis; 3/4-mile walk, or
take T-Bus 94 or 96 (Medford Sq.).
●T-Bus 80 (Arlington Ctr.-Lechmere, via
Medford Hillside).
●T-Bus 94 (Medford Sq.-Davis).
●T-Bus 96 (Medford Sq.-Harvard).
●T-Bus 89 (Clarendon Hill-Sullivan).
*This bus stops at the edge of the
campus; the others go through the
middle of the campus.*
—Medical School
136 Harrison Ave., Boston.

*See "Tufts-New England Medical
Center" in Chapter 15.*

University of Massachusetts
—Amherst
●Peter Pan (Boston-Amherst), stops at
the campus.
●PVTA/Five Colleges shuttle buses.
—Boston: Downtown Center
100 Arlington St., Park Plaza, Boston.
●Green Line to Arlington.
●UMass shuttle bus from Harbor
Campus, Mon-Fri.
—Boston: Harbor Campus
Dorchester.
●Red Line to JFK/UMass; then UMass
shuttle bus to the campus, daily.
Buses operate every 15 min. or less,
until at least 10:20pm Mon-Thurs,
7:00pm Fri, and 5:45pm weekends
and school vacations. Call 287-5040.
●T-Bus 8 (Harbor Pt.-Kenmore).
●T-Bus 16 (Forest Hills-JFK/UMass),
rush hours only.
●T-Bus 17 (Fields Corner-JFK/UMass)
●UMass shuttle bus from Park Plaza,
Mon-Fri; every 30 min. until 9:30 pm
(5:00 pm Fri).
—Dartmouth
Old Westport Rd., N. Dartmouth.
●SRTA (Fall River-New Bedford).
—Lowell: North Campus
1 University Ave., Lowell.
●LRTA Bus 11 (Pawtucketville).
—Lowell: South Campus
Broadway, Lowell.
●LRTA Bus 10 (U. of Lowell S.).
—Medical School
55 Lake Ave. N., Worcester.
●WRTA Bus 24 (Belmont St./Lake Ave.).
● Peter Pan (Boston-Worcester, Rt. 9
local)—from Boston/Peter Pan, Park
Plaza, Copley Sq., and Brigham Cir.

University of Rhode Island
Kingston, RI.
●Amtrak (Shore Line) to Kingston, RI;
then RIPTA Bus (Newport or Galilee),
Mon-Sat; or 2-mile walk or taxi.
●Bonanza to Providence (Kennedy
Plaza), then RIPTA Bus (Kingston), 4-
6 trips daily.

Wellesley College
106 Central St., Wellesley.
●T-Commuter Rail (Framingham Line)
to Wellesley Sq., 10-minute walk.
●Wellesley and MIT operate a bus
between the schools for cross-

registered students, Mon-Fri. If space
is available, others from the Wellesley
and MIT communities may ride. Call
253-1668.
●Wellesley Senate bus from Harvard
Sq., MIT, Mass. Ave. & Beacon St.,
and Woodland (Green Line-D), Fri
night-Sat-Sun. Tickets sold at
Wellesley, Harvard, MIT, and
Marlboro Market. Call 235-0320
x2670.

Wentworth Institute
550 Huntington Ave., Boston.
●Green Line-E to Museum
●Orange Line or T-Buses to Ruggles.
●T-Bus 8 (Harbor Pt.-Kenmore).
●T-Bus 39 (Forest Hills-Back Bay Sta.).
●T-Bus 47 (Central-Albany St.).

Wheaton College
E. Main St., Norton.
●GATRA (Attleboro-Taunton), *connects
w/T-Commuter Rail (Attleboro Line) at
Attleboro,* Mon-Fri.
●Wheaton College shuttle bus from
Mansfield and Attleboro, *connects w/
T-Commuter Rail (Attleboro Line),*
Mon-Thurs nights.
●Wheaton College shuttle bus from
Boston, Fri nights.

Wheelock College
200 the Riverway, Boston.
●Green Line-D to Fenway.
●T-Bus 8 (Harbor Pt.-Kenmore).
●T-Bus 47 (Central-Albany St.).
●T-Bus 60 (Chestnut Hill-Kenmore).
●T-Bus 65 (Brighton Ctr.-Kenmore).
●Metrobus (Cambridge-Longwood
Med. Area).

Williams College
●Peter Pan (Boston-Bennington, VT)
stops at the college

Women's Educational &
Industrial Union
356 Boylston St., Boston
●Green Line to Arlington or T-Buses to
Copley

Worcester Polytechnic
Institute
100 Institute Rd., Worcester.
●WRTA Bus 6N (Holden/Chaffins).
●WRTA Bus 32 (Holden/Jefferson).
●Or take any of these WRTA Buses to
Lincoln Sq. (1/2-mile walk): 17, 19N,
21, 23, 24, 26N, 30N.

Worcester State College
486 Chandler St., Worcester.
●WRTA Bus 6S (Chandler/Dawson Rd.).

Chapter 15

Hospitals

Atlanticare Medical Center
Lynn Hospital Division
212 Boston St., Lynn.
●T-Bus 429 (Lynn-N. Saugus).
●T-Bus 435 (Lynn-Danvers).
●T-Bus 450 (Salem-Haymarket)
●Lynn East/West Loop buses.

Beth Israel Hospital
330 Brookline Ave., Boston.
●Green Line-D to Longwood; 4-block walk.
●T-Bus 8 (Harbor Pt.-Kenmore).
●T-Bus 47 (Central-Albany St.).
●T-Bus 60 (Chestnut Hill-Kenmore).
●T-Bus 65 (Brighton Ctr.-Kenmore).

●Metrobus (Cambridge-Longwood Med.).

Boston City Hospital
818 Harrison Ave., Boston.
●T-Bus 1 (Harvard-Dudley).
●T-Bus 8 (Harbor Pt.-Kenmore).
●T-Bus 10 (City Pt.-Copley).
●T-Bus 47 (Central-Albany St.).
●T-Bus 49 (Dudley-Downtown) to
Mass. Ave., 1-block walk.

Boston Specialty and
Rehabilitation Hospital
249 River St., Mattapan.
●T-Bus 27 (Mattapan-Ashmont).

Boston University Medical Center
88 E. Concord St., Boston.
- T-Bus 8 (Harbor Pt.-Kenmore).
- T-Bus 10 (City Pt.-Copley).
- T-Bus 47 (Central-Albany St.).
- T-Bus 49 (Dudley-Downtown) to E. Newton St., 1-block walk.
- T-Bus 1 (Harvard-Dudley) to Boston City Hosp., 3-block walk.

Brigham & Women's Hospital
75 Francis St., Boston
- Green Line-E to Brigham Circle.
- T-Bus 39 (Forest Hills-Back Bay Sta.) to Brigham Circle.
- T-Bus 60 (Chestnut Hill-Kenmore) to Francis St.
- T-Bus 65 (Brighton Ctr.-Kenmore) to Francis St.
- T-Bus 66 (Harvard-Dudley) to Brigham Circle.
- Metrobus (Cambridge-Longwood Med. Area).

Cambridge Hospital
1493 Cambridge St., Cambridge.
- T-Bus 69 (Harvard-Lechmere).
- T-Bus 83 (Rindge Ave.-Central) to Beacon & Cooney Sts.; 1-block walk.

Carney Hospital
2100 Dorchester Ave., Dorchester.
- Red Line to Ashmont; walk 1/2 mile S on Dorchester Ave.
- T-Bus 27 (Mattapan-Ashmont).
- T-Bus 217 (Wollaston Beach-Ashmont).
- T-Bus 240 (Avon Line-Ashmont).
- T-Bus 240A (Crawford Sq.-Ashmont).
The following T-Buses stop 2 blocks from the hospital:

- T-Bus 21 (Ashmont-Forest Hills).
- T-Bus 215 (Quincy Ctr.-Ashmont).

Central Hospital
26 Central St., Somerville.
- T-Bus 83 (Rindge Ave.-Central).
- T-Bus 87 (Arlington Ctr.-Lechmere).

Children's Hospital
300 Longwood Ave., Boston.
- Green Line-D to Longwood; 4-block walk.
- Green Line-E to Longwood/Hospitals; 4-block walk.
- T-Bus 8 (Harbor Pt.-Kenmore).
- T-Bus 47 (Central-Albany St.).
- T-Bus 60 (Chestnut Hill-Kenmore).
- T-Bus 65 (Brighton Ctr.-Kenmore).
- T-Bus 39 (Forest Hills-Back Bay Sta.) to Longwood/Hospitals; 4-block walk.
- Metrobus (Cambridge-Longwood Med. Area).

Dana-Farber Cancer Institute
44 Binney St., Boston.
Same directions as Children's Hospital.

Faulkner Hospital
1153 Centre St., Jamaica Plain.
- T-Bus 38 (Wren St.-Forest Hills).

Fernald State School
200 Trapelo Rd., Waltham.
- T-Bus 73 (Waverley-Harvard) to Waverley Sq.
- T-Bus 54 (Waverley-Newton Corner) to Waverley Sq.
Daily shuttle buses from Waverley Sq. (1 mile); call 894-3600 x2175.

Franciscan Children's Hospital
30 Warren St., Brighton.
- Green Line-B to Warren St.; 2-block walk.
- T-Bus 57 (Watertown-Kenmore) to Warren St.; 1/2 block walk.

Glover Memorial Hospital
148 Chestnut St., Needham.
- T-Bus 59 (Needham Jct.-Watertown).

Hahnemann Hospital
1515 Commonwealth Ave., Brighton.
- Green Line-B to Washington St.
- T-Bus 65 (Brighton Ctr.-Kenmore).

Hebrew Rehabilitation Center
1200 Centre St., Roslindale.
- T-Bus 38 (Wren St.-Forest Hills).

Jewish Memorial Hospital
59 Townsend St., Roxbury.
- T-Bus 42 (Forest Hills-Ruggles) to Townsend St.

Joslin Diabetes Center
1 Joslin Pl. (off 437 Brookline Ave.), Boston.
Same directions as Beth Israel Hospital.

Lahey Clinic Medical Center
41 Mall Rd., Burlington.
- T-Bus 350 (Burlington-Alewife).
- T-Bus 353 (Burlington Ind. Area-Haymarket).
- Hudson Airporter—from Logan Airport.

Lawrence Memorial Hospital
170 Governors Ave., Medford.
- Hudson Bus (Boston-Stoneham).
- T-Buses to Medford Sq.; 3/4 mile walk.

Malden Hospital
Hospital Rd., Malden.
- T-Bus 99 (Upper Highland-Wellington).

Massachusetts Eye and Ear Infirmary
243 Charles St., Boston.
- Red Line to Charles/MGH.

Massachusetts General Hospital
55 Fruit St., Boston.
- Red Line to Charles/MGH.

McLean Hospital
115 Mill St., Belmont.
- T-Bus 54 (Waverley-Newton Corner) to Waverley Sq.
- T-Bus 73 (Waverley-Harvard) to Waverley Sq.
Hospital is mile 1/4 walk up a steep hill from Waverley Sq. *Do not follow the signs "To McLean Hospital"*; this is the auto route which is considerably longer. Shuttle vans from Waverley Sq.; call 855-2121.

Melrose-Wakefield Hospital
585 Lebanon St., Melrose.
- T-Buses 136/137 (Reading-Malden Ctr.).
- T-Commuter Rail (Reading/Haverhill Line) to Melrose/Cedar Pk.; 1/2-mile.

Milton Hospital
92 Highland St., Milton.
- T-Bus 240 (Avon Line-Ashmont).
- T-Bus 240A (Crawford Sq.-Ashmont).

- T-Bus 245 (Quincy Ctr.-Mattapan); *trips "via Shadowlawn" do not serve the hospital.*

Mount Auburn Hospital
330 Mt. Auburn St., Cambridge.
- T-Bus 71 (Watertown-Harvard).
- T-Bus 73 (Waverley-Harvard).

New England Baptist Hospital
125 Parker Hill Ave., Roxbury.
- Green Line-E to Parker Hill Ave.
- T-Bus 39 (Forest Hills-Back Bay Sta.) to Parker Hill Ave.
- T-Bus 66 (Harvard-Dudley) to Parker Hill Ave.
- Mission Hill Link Bus—all routes.
Parker Hill Ave. has a very steep hill. You may wish to take Mission Hill Link (or a cab) from Brigham Circle.

New England Deaconess Hospital
185 Pilgrim Rd., Boston.
Same directions as Beth Israel Hospital.

New England Medical Center
See "Tufts-New England Medical Ctr."

New England Memorial Hospital
5 Woodland Rd., Stoneham.
- Hudson Bus (Boston-Stoneham).

New England Rehabilitation Hospital
Rehabilitation Way, Woburn.
- T-Bus 350 (Burlington-Alewife).

Newton-Wellesley Hospital
2014 Washington St., Newton Lower Falls.
- Green Line-D to Woodland.

Quincy City Hospital
114 Whitwell St., Quincy.
- T-Bus 245 (Quincy Ctr.-Mattapan).

St. Elizabeth's Hospital
736 Cambridge St., Brighton.
- T-Bus 57 (Watertown-Kenmore).
- T-Bus 65 (Brighton Ctr.-Kenmore).
- T-Bus 86 (Sullivan-Cleveland Cir.) to Brighton Ctr., 3-block walk.

St. Margaret's Hospital for Women
90 Cushing Ave., Dorchester.
- T-Bus 15 (Kane Sq.-Ruggles).
- T-Bus 17 (Fields Corner-Andrew).
Get off at Hancock and Powell Sts.

Salem Hospital
81 Highland Ave., Salem.
- T-Bus 450 (Salem-Haymarket).
- Michaud Bus (Salem Belt Line).

Sancta Maria Hospital
799 Concord Ave., Cambridge.
- T-Bus 74 (Belmont Ctr.-Harvard), *trips "via Concord Ave." only.*
- T-Bus 78 (Park Cir.-Harvard).

Lemuel Shattuck Hospital
170 Morton St., Jamaica Plain.
- Orange Line or T-Bus 39 to Forest Hills; 1/2 mile walk.
- T-Bus 21 (Ashmont-Forest Hills).
- T-Bus 31 (Mattapan-Forest Hills).

Shriners Burns Institute Shriners Hospital for Crippled Children
51 Blossom St., Boston.
- Red Line to Charles/MGH.

Somerville Hospital
230 Highland Ave., Somerville.
- T-Bus 88 (Clarendon Hill-Lechmere)
- T-Bus 90 (Davis-Wellington).

Spaulding Rehabilitation Hospital
125 Nashua St., Boston.
- Green Line (Lechmere) to Science Park.
- T-Commuter Rail to North Sta.

Symmes Hospital
39 Hospital Rd., Arlington.
- T-Bus 67 (Turkey Hill-Alewife) to Hospital Rd.
- T-Bus 77 (Arlington Hts.-Harvard) to Brattle St.; walk 1/2 mile up hill.

Tufts-New England Medical Center
750 Washington St., Boston.
- Orange Line to N. E. Medical Ctr.
- Green Line to Boylston; 4-block walk.
- T-Bus 11 (City Pt.-Downtown).
- T-Bus 43 (Ruggles-Park St.).
- T-Bus 49 (Dudley-Downtown).

The University Hospital
See "Boston University Medical Ctr."

Veterans Administration Clinic
251 Causeway St., Boston.
- Green Line, Orange Line, or T-Commuter Rail to North Sta.

Veterans Administration Hospital
200 Springs Rd., Bedford.
- T-Bus 62 (Bedford-Alewife), *before 7:00 pm only.*

Veterans Administration Hospital
150 S. Huntington Ave., Jamaica Plain.
- Green Line-E to Heath St.
- T-Bus 39 (Forest Hills-Back Bay Sta.).
- T-Bus 46 (Heath St.-Dudley).

Veterans Administration Hospital
1400 V.F.W. Parkway, West Roxbury.
- T-Bus 36A (V.A. Hospital-Forest Hills).
- T-Bus 52 (Dedham Mall-Watertown).

Waltham-Weston Hospital
Hope Ave., Waltham.
- T-Bus 53 (Roberts-Newton Corner).
- T-Bus 70 (Cedarwood-Central) to Main & South Sts.; walk 1/2 mile S on South St. to Hope Ave.
- T-Commuter Rail or any T-Bus to Central Sq./Waltham; 3/4 mile walk or take T-Bus 53 (Roberts).

Whidden Memorial Hospital
103 Garland St., Everett.
- T-Bus 110 (Wonderland-Wellington) to Woodlawn St.; 1/2 mile walk via Woodlawn St., left on Garland St.

Winthrop Hospital
40 Lincoln St., Winthrop.
- Paul Revere Bus (Orient Hts.-Winthrop Beach via Highlands).
- Paul Revere Bus (Orient Hts.-Winthrop Beach via Centre).
Get off at Main & Pleasant Sts.; walk 2 blocks S on Pleasant St. to Lincoln St.

Youville Hospital
1575 Cambridge St., Cambridge.
- T-Bus 69 (Harvard-Lechmere).

Chapter 16
Cities, Towns, and Neighborhoods

This chapter covers every city and town in Massachusetts directly served from Boston by public transportation, plus a number of towns in the Greater Boston area that are near transit, but are not directly served.

A number of towns outside the Greater Boston area that do not have direct service from Boston can be reached through an indicated (in **boldface**) connecting city or town listed in this chapter

Many cities and towns outside the metropolitan Boston area belong to regional transit authorities (RTAs), which provide local and regional bus service. For more information on services provided by the RTAs cited in this chapter (e.g., BAT, BRTA, CATA), see Chapter 20.

(P) indicates selected park-and-ride facilities near major highways. For more parking information, call 800-392-6100 or 722-3200.

Abington
- Carey's (Boston-Whitman), 2 rush hour trips serve Abington Ctr. and N. Abington.
- H. T. Drummond commuter vans.

Acton
- T-Commuter Rail (Fitchburg Line)—from North Sta. to S. Acton.
- Yankee Line (Boston-Littleton), rush hour only.
- (P) Off Main St. (Rt. 27), S of Rts. 2 and 111 (S. Acton).

Acushnet
- SRTA local bus from **New Bedford.**

Adams
See also North Adams.
- BRTA (Pittsfield-N. Adams).

Agawam
- PVTA local buses from **Springfield.**
- Peter Pan from Springfield, 4 trips daily.

Allston (Boston)
- Green Line-B (Boston College), serves Commonwealth Ave.
- T-Bus 57 (Watertown-Kenmore).
- T-Bus 64 (Oak Sq.-Central).
- T-Bus 66 (Harvard-Dudley, via Brookline).
- T-Bus 70 (Cedarwood-Central).
- T-Bus 86 (Sullivan-Cleveland Cir.).
Union Sq.: T-Buses 57, 64, 66.

Western Ave.: T-Buses 70, 86.

Amesbury
- The Coach Co. (Boston-Amesbury), rush hour only.
- MVRTA (Haverhill-Newburyport).

Amherst
- Peter Pan (Boston-Greenfield)—from Boston/Peter Pan and Riverside. Stops at Amherst Ctr. and U.Mass.; 3 trips/day also stop at Hampshire College.
- PVTA local buses.
- GMTA local bus to U.Mass. from Greenfield and Montague.

Andover
See also North Andover.
- T-Commuter Rail (Haverhill Line)—from North Sta. to Ballardvale and Andover.
- Trombly (Boston-N. Andover)—from Park Plaza and Essex St.
- Hudson Airporter—from Logan Airport.
- MVRTA local buses.

Arlington
- T-Bus 62 (Bedford-Alewife).
- T-Bus 67 (Turkey Hill-Alewife).
- T-Bus 77 (Arlington Hts.-Harvard).
- T-Bus 78 (Arlmont-Harvard).
- T-Bus 79 (Arlington Hts.-Alewife).
- T-Bus 80 (Arlington Ctr.-Lechmere, via Medford Hillside).
- T-Bus 84 (Alewife-Arlmont)
- T-Bus 87 (Arlington Ctr.-Lechmere, via Somerville Ave.).
- T-Bus 350 (Burlington-Alewife).

> ☞ Maps of selected cities, towns, and neighborhoods can be found elsewhere in this book:
>
> For the Boston area, including Brookline and Cambridge, see Chapter 5, "Downtown Boston and Cambridge." Also see the map on the inside front cover .
>
> For Falmouth, Framingham, Gloucester, Hyannis, Lowell, New Bedford, Rockport, Salem, Springfield, Worcester, and Providence, RI, see Chapter 9, "Day and Weekend Trips."

•Hudson Bus (Boston-Lexington)—from Park Plaza and Haymarket.
Primary service: T-Bus 77 from Harvard
Arlington Ctr.: T-Buses 67, 77, 79, 80, 87, 350; and Hudson Bus.
Arlington Hts.: T-Buses 62, 77, 79; and Hudson Bus.

Ashland
•Crystal Transport (Framingham-Milford), *connects w/T-Commuter Rail and Boston buses in Framingham.* Serves Rt.126.
•LIFT 5 (Framingham-Hopkinton), *connects w/T-Commuter Rail at Framingham.* Serves Rt.135.

Attleboro
•T-Commuter Rail (Attleboro Line)—from South Sta. and Back Bay Sta. to Attleboro and S. Attleboro.
•Mass Limousine—from Logan Airport to S. Attleboro.
•GATRA local buses.
ⓅMain St. (Rt. 152), S of Rt. 123 (downtown).

Auburn
•Peter Pan (Boston-Worcester, express), rush hour only.
•WRTA local bus from Worcester.

Auburndale (Newton)
•T-Commuter Rail (Framingham Line)-from South Sta. and Back Bay Sta.
•T-Express Bus 305 (Waltham-Downtown), rush hour only.
•T-Bus 58 (Auburndale-Newton Corner-Downtown), via Waltham.
•Green Line-D (Riverside) to Riverside; 1/2-mile walk.
•Hudson Airporter—from Logan Airport to Marriott Hotel.

Avon
•T-Bus 240 (Avon Line-Ashmont).
•BAT Bus 12 (Ashmont-Brockton)—from Ashmont (Red Line).

Ayer
See also Fort Devens.
•T-Commuter Rail (Fitchburg Line)—from North Sta.

Back Bay (Boston)
See Chapter 5 for subway, bus, and train service to Back Bay and map. See "Logan Airport" for service to the airport from Back Bay.

Barnstable
See also Hyannis.
•Plymouth & Brockton (Boston-Hyannis)—from Park Plaza, Boston/Peter Pan, and Logan Airport.
ⓅRoute 132 at Route 6, exit 6.

Bay Village (Boston)
•Green Line to Arlington.
•Orange Line to N. E. Medical Ctr.
•T-Bus 9 (City Pt.-Copley, via Broadway).
•T-Bus 43 (Ruggles-Park St.).

Beacon Hill (Boston)
•Red Line to Charles/MGH and Park St.
•Blue Line to Bowdoin.
•Green Line to Park St.
•T-Bus 43 (Ruggles-Park St.).
•T-Bus 55 (Queensberry St.-Park St.).

Bedford
•T-Bus 62 (Bedford-Alewife).
•T-Express Bus 353 (Burlington Ind. Area-Haymarket), rush hour "reverse commute" only.
•T-Bus 353A (Burlington Ind. Area-Dudley), rush hour "reverse commute" only.
•Hudson Airporter—from Logan Airport.
•M & L Transp.—from Logan Airport.

Belchertown
•PVTA local bus from **Amherst.**

Bellingham
*See **Franklin** for trains to Boston.*

Original Belmont R.R. Sta. with current station in background

Belmont
- T-Commuter Rail (Fitchburg Line)—from North Sta. to Belmont Ctr. and Waverley.
- T-Bus 54 (Waverley-Newton Corner-Downtown), via Waltham.
- T-Bus 73 (Waverley-Harvard).
- T-Bus 74 (Belmont Ctr.-Harvard).
- T-Bus 78 (Arlmont-Harvard).

Beverly
- T-Commuter Rail (Rockport Line)—from North Sta. to Beverly Depot, Montserrat, Prides Crossing (rush hour only), and Beverly Farms.
- T-Commuter Rail (Ipswich Line)—from North Sta. to Beverly Depot and N. Beverly.
- T-Bus 451 (N. Beverly-Salem).
- Beverly Shoppers' Shuttle.

Billerica
- T-Commuter Rail (Lowell Line)—from North Sta. to N. Billerica.
- LRTA local bus from Lowell.

Ⓟ Mt. Pleasant St. off Billerica Ave. (N. Billerica)

Boston
See Chapter 5 for service to downtown Boston and Back Bay.
See "Logan Airport" for service to the

airport from downtown and Back Bay. Transit service to Boston's neighborhoods is listed alphabetically under the following: Allston, Bay Village, Beacon Hill, Brighton, Charlestown, Chinatown, Dorchester, East Boston, Fenway, Fort Point Channel, Hyde Park, Jamaica Plain, Mattapan, Mission Hill, North End, Readville, Roslindale, Roxbury, South Boston, South End, West Roxbury.

Bourne
See also Buzzards Bay, Otis A.F.B.
- Bonanza (Boston-Woods Hole)—from Back Bay Sta. and Logan Airport.

Boxford
- The Coach Co. (Boston-Haverhill), rush hour only.

Boylston and W. Boylston
- WRTA local bus from **Worcester.**

Bradford
See Haverhill.

Braintree
- Red Line (Braintree) to Braintree.
- Carey's (Boston-Whitman), 2 rush hour trips serve E. Braintree.
- T-Bus 225 (Quincy Ctr.-Weymouth Landing), serves Quincy Ave.
- T-Bus 230 (Quincy Ctr.-Holbrook), serves Washington St.
- T-Bus 236 (Quincy Ctr.-South Shore Plaza), serves E. Braintree, Franklin St.
- T-Bus 238 (Quincy Ctr.-Crawford Sq.), serves Granite and Pond Sts.
- Green Harbor Transp.—from Logan Airport to Susse Chalet.
- Logan Express—from Logan Airport to Forbes Rd., off Granite St.

Brewster
- Plymouth & Brockton (Hyannis-Provincetown), *connects w/Boston buses at Hyannis.*

Bridgewater and W. Bridgewater
- Interstate (Boston-Middleborough), serves Bridgewater Ctr., West Bridgewater, Elm Sq., Hockomock, and Correctional Complex.

Brighton (Boston)
- Green Line-B (Boston College), serves Commonwealth Ave.
- Green Line-C (Cleveland Circle) to

Cleveland Circle.
- Green Line-D (Riverside) to Reservoir.
- T-Express Bus 301 (Brighton Ctr.-Downtown).
- T-Bus 57 (Watertown-Kenmore).
- T-Bus 64 (Oak Sq.-Central).
- T-Bus 65 (Brighton Ctr.-Kenmore).
- T-Bus 70 (Cedarwood-Central).
- T-Bus 86 (Sullivan-Cleveland Cir.).

Brighton Ctr.: T-Buses 57, 65, 86, 301.
Oak Sq.: T-Buses 57, 64, 301.
Western Ave.: T-Buses 70, 86.

Brockton
- BAT Buses 12 and 12X (Ashmont-Brockton)—from Ashmont *(Red Line).*
- Plymouth & Brockton (Boston-Brockton)—from Park Plaza and South Sta.
- BAT local buses.

Ⓟ Westgate Mall by Cinema 1 & 2, Route 27 at Route 24, exit 18A.

Brookfield and E. Brookfield
- WRTA local bus from **Worcester**.

Brookline
- Green Line-B (Boston College), serves Commonwealth Ave. in adjacent Allston and Brighton.
- Green Line-C (Cleveland Circle), serves Beacon St., Coolidge Corner.
- Green Line-D (Riverside) to Longwood, Brookline Village, Brookline Hills, Beaconsfield, and Reservoir.
- T-Bus 51 (Cleveland Cir.-Forest Hills).
- T-Bus 60 (Chestnut Hill-Kenmore), serves Boylston St. (Rt.9).
- T-Bus 65 (Brighton Ctr.-Kenmore), serves Washington St.
- T-Bus 66 (Harvard-Dudley), serves Harvard St.
- T-Bus 86 (Sullivan-Cleveland Cir.).
- Peter Pan (Boston-Worcester, Rt. 9 local), stops at Brookline Village and Chestnut Hill.

Burlington
- T-Bus 350 (Burlington-Alewife).
- T-Express Bus 352 (Burlington-Boston), rush hour only.
- T-Express Bus 353 (Burlington Ind. Area-Haymarket), rush hour "reverse commute" only.
- T-Bus 353A (Burlington Ind. Area-Dudley), rush hour "reverse commute" only.
- Hudson Airporter—from Logan Airport

to Lahey Clinic and hotels.
- M & L Transp.—from Logan Airport to hotels.
- Lexpress (Lexington-Burlington Mall).
- Burlington People Mover local buses.

Buzzards Bay
- Bonanza (Boston-Wareham)—from Back Bay Sta., 2 rush hour trips.

Byfield (Newbury)
- The Coach Co. (Boston-Amesbury), 1 rush hour trip.

Cambridge
See Chapter 5 for coverage of core transit lines in Cambridge.
E. Cambridge: Green Line (Lechmere) and T-Bus 69
Inman Sq.: T-Buses 69, 83, 91.
Mass. Ave.: Red Line (Central, Harvard, Porter); T-Bus 1 (Central, Harvard Sq.) and T-Buses 77, 77A (Harvard and Porter Sq.)
Mt. Auburn St.: T-Buses 71, 73
N. Cambridge: Red Line (Porter, Davis, and Alewife); Commuter Rail; and T-Buses 77, 77A, 83.

Ⓟ Route 2, junction Rt. 16 and U.S. 3 (Alewife).

Canton
- T-Commuter Rail (Stoughton Line)—from South Sta. and Back Bay Sta. to Canton Jct. and Canton Ctr.
- T-Commuter Rail (Attleboro Line)—from South Sta. and Back Bay Sta. to Canton Jct.
- Hudson Bus (Mattapan-Canton)—from Mattapan (Red Line).
- BAT local bus from Stoughton, serves Cobbs Corner.

Ⓟ Sherman St., between Chapman and Washington Sts. (Canton Junction)

Centerville
CCRTA from **Hyannis, Woods Hole**.

Charlemont
- Peter Pan (Boston-Bennington, VT)—from Boston/Peter Pan and Riverside

Charlestown (Boston)
- Orange Line to Community College and Sullivan.
- T-Commuter Boat—from Long Wharf.
- T-Bus 92 (Assembly Sq.-Downtown), serves Main St.
- T-Bus 93 (Sullivan-Downtown), serves

Bunker Hill St.
- T-Bus 111 (Woodlawn-Haymarket).
- Navy Yard Shuttle Bus.

Charlestown Navy Yard: T-Commuter
Boat; T-Bus 93; and shuttle bus
*See Orange Line map for other buses
to Sullivan.*

Chatham
- Plymouth & Brockton (Hyannis-
Chatham), *connects w/Boston buses
at Hyannis.*

Chelmsford
- LRTA local buses from **Lowell.**
- Hudson Airporter—from Logan Airport.
- M & L Transp.—from Logan Airport.

Chelsea
- T-Commuter Rail (Rockport/Ipswich
Line)—from North Sta.
- T-Bus 111 (Woodlawn-Haymarket).
- T-Bus 112 (Wellington-Maverick).
- T-Buses 116/117 (Wonderland-Maverick).

Cheshire
- BRTA from **Pittsfield** and **N. Adams.**

Chestnut Hill (Brookline/ Newton)
- Green Line-B (Boston College) to
Boston College.
- Green Line-D (Riverside) to Chestnut Hill.
- T-Bus 51 (Cleveland Cir.-Forest Hills).
- T-Bus 60 (Chestnut Hill-Kenmore).
- Peter Pan (Boston-Worcester, Rt. 9
local), stops at Chestnut Hill.

Chicopee
- Peter Pan (Boston-Springfield)—stops
at Quality Inn.
- PVTA local buses from Springfield and
Holyoke.

Chinatown (Boston)
- Orange Line to Chinatown and N. E.
Medical Ctr.
- Green Line to Boylston, cross Tremont
St., walk 1 block on Boylston St.
- T-Bus 3 (Chinatown-Marine Ind. Pk.).
- T-Bus 11 (City Pt.-Downtown, via
Bayview).
- T-Bus 49 (Dudley-Downtown).

Clinton
- WRTA local bus from **Worcester.**

Cohasset
- Plymouth & Brockton (Boston-

Scituate)—from Park Plaza, Boston/
Peter Pan and South Sta.
- H. T. Drummond commuter vans.

Concord
- T-Commuter Rail (Fitchburg Line)—
from North Sta. to Concord and W.
Concord.
- Vermont Transit (Boston-Rutland, VT).
Stops at W. Concord (Howard Johnson's).
- Yankee Line (Boston-Littleton), rush
hour only.
- Contran local buses.

Ⓟ Main St. (Rt. 62) and Commonwealth Ave. (W. Concord).

Cuttyhunk (Elizabeth Islands)
- Cuttyhunk Boat from **New Bedford.**

Dalton
- BRTA local bus from **Pittsfield.**

Danvers
- T-Bus 435 (Lynn-Danvers).
- T-Bus 458 (Salem-Danvers).
- T-Bus 458 (Haymarket-Danvers), rush
hour only.
- The Coach Co. (Boston-Haverhill),
rush hour only. Serves Danvers Plaza.

Dartmouth
- SRTA local buses from **New Bedford**
and **Fall River.**

Dedham
- T-Commuter Rail (Franklin Line)—
from South Sta. and Back Bay Sta. to
Endicott and Dedham Corp. Ctr.
- T-Commuter Rail (Attleboro/Stoughton
Lines)—from South Sta. and Back Bay
Sta. to Route 128 Sta.
- T-Bus 34E (Walpole Ctr.-Forest Hills),
serves Washington St. and Dedham Sq.
- T-Bus 35 (Dedham Mall-Forest Hills).
- T-Bus 52 (Dedham Mall-Watertown).
- Amtrak (Boston-New York, Shore
Line) stops at Route 128 Sta.
- Dedham Local Bus.
From Boston: Orange Line or Green
Line-E/T-Bus 39 to Forest Hills, then T-
Bus 34E; or Commuter Rail.

Ⓟ Allied Dr., off rotary at Route 128/I-
95, exit 14 (Dedham Corporate Center).

Deerfield
- Peter Pan (Boston- Benningon, VT)—
from Boston/Peter Pan and Riverside.
- FRTA local bus from **Greenfield.**
- PVTA from **Amherst** to S. Deerfield.

Dennis
- Plymouth & Brockton (Hyannis-Provincetown), *connects w/Boston buses at Hyannis.* Serves Dennis and E. Dennis.
- Plymouth & Brockton (Hyannis-Chatham), *connects w/Boston buses at Hyannis.* Serves Dennisport.

Dorchester (Boston)
- Red Line (Ashmont) to JFK/UMass, Savin Hill, Fields Corner, Shawmut, and Ashmont.
- Red Line (Mattapan) to Cedar Grove, Butler St., Milton, and Central Ave.
- T-Commuter Rail (Fairmount Line)—from South Sta. to Uphams Corner and Morton St.
- T-Bus 8 (Harbor Pt.-Kenmore).
- T-Bus 14 (Roslindale-Dudley).
- T-Bus 15 (Kane Sq.-Ruggles).
- T-Bus 16 (Forest Hills-JFK/UMass).
- T-Bus 17 (Fields Corner-JFK/UMass).
- T-Bus 18 (Ashmont-Broadway).
- T-Bus 19 (Fields Corner-Ruggles, via Grove Hall).
- T-Bus 20 (Fields Corner-Neponset & Adams).
- T-Bus 21 (Ashmont-Forest Hills).
- T-Bus 22 (Ashmont-Ruggles, via Jackson Sq.).
- T-Bus 23 (Ashmont-Ruggles, via Dudley Sq.).
- T-Bus 26 (Norfolk St.-Ashmont).
- T-Bus 27 (Mattapan-Ashmont).
- T-Bus 28 (Mattapan-Ruggles).
- T-Bus 29 (Mattapan-Jackson Sq.).
- T-Bus 44 (Jackson Sq.-Ruggles, via Humboldt Ave.).
- T-Bus 45 (Franklin Park-Ruggles, via Grove Hall).
- T-Bus 210F (Fields Corner-Quincy Ctr.).
- T-Bus 215 (Quincy Ctr.-Ashmont).
- T-Bus 217 (Wollaston Beach-Ashmont).
- T-Bus 240 (Avon Line-Ashmont).
- T-Bus 240A (Crawford Sq.-Ashmont.).

Codman Sq.: T-Buses 22, 23, 26; or walk from Shawmut, 3 blocks.
Edward Everett Sq.: T-Buses 8, 16, 17; or walk from JFK/U.Mass., 4 blocks.
Four Corners: T-Bus 23.
Grove Hall: T-Buses 14, 19, 23, 28, 45.
Lower Mills: Mattapan Line (Milton) and T-Buses 27, 217, 240, 240A.
Meeting House Hill: T-Buses 15, 17.
Neponset: T-Buses 20, 210F.
Uphams Corner: T-Buses 15, 16, 17; or walk from Commuter Rail, 3 blocks.

Douglas
- Local bus from **Worcester**; see WRTA listing.

Dover
- Brush Hill (Boston-Milford), rush hour only. Serves Rt.109.

*See **Needham** for train service to Boston.*

Dracut
- LRTA local bus from **Lowell.**

Duxbury
- Plymouth & Brockton (Boston-Plymouth Ctr.)—from Park Plaza, Boston/Peter Pan and South Sta. Serves Rt. 53.
- Plymouth & Brockton (Boston-S. Duxbury), rush hour only. Serves Millbrook, Snug Harbor, Hall's Corner, S. Duxbury.
- H. T. Drummond commuter vans.

East Boston
See also Logan Airport.
- Blue Line to Maverick, Airport, Wood Island, Orient Hts., and Suffolk Downs.
- T-Bus 112 (Wellington-Maverick).
- T-Buses 116/117 (Wonderland-Maverick).
- T-Bus 120 (Orient Hts.-Maverick).
- T-Bus 121 (Wood Island-Maverick).
- T-Bus 400 (Lynn-Haymarket).
- T-Bus 455 (Salem-Haymarket, via Loring Ave.).

Eastham
- Plymouth & Brockton (Hyannis-Provincetown), *connects w/Boston buses at Hyannis.*

Easthampton
- PVTA local bus from **Northampton.**

Easton
- Interstate (Boston-Middleborough), 1 trip Mon.-Fri.

*See **Stoughton** for train service to Boston.*

Egremont
- Bonanza from **Pittsfield** and **Lee** to S. Egremont, Fri. & Sun. only.

Everett
- T-Bus 97 (Malden Ctr.-Wellington, via Hancock St.).
- T-Bus 99 (Upper Highland-Wellington).

- T-Bus 104 (Malden Ctr.-Sullivan, via Ferry St.).
- T-Bus 105 (Malden Ctr.-Sullivan, via Faulkner).
- T-Bus 106 (Lebanon St.-Wellington).
- T-Bus 109 (Linden Sq.-Sullivan).
- T-Bus 110 (Wonderland-Wellington).
- T-Bus 111 (Woodlawn-Haymarket).
- T-Bus 112 (Wellington-Maverick).

Everett Sq.: T-Buses 97, 104, 109, 110, 112.
Glendale Sq.: T-Buses 104, 109.
Main St.: T-Buses 99, 105, 106.

Fairhaven
- SRTA local buses from New Bedford.
- American Eagle from Boston/Peter Pan.

Fall River
- Bonanza (Boston-Newport, RI)—from Back Bay Sta. and Logan Airport.
- SRTA local buses.

Falmouth
See also Woods Hole.
- Bonanza (Boston-Woods Hole)—from Back Bay Sta. and Logan Airport.
- Bonanza from New York, NY.
- Peter Pan from Springfield.
- CCRTA (from Hyannis-Woods Hole).
- Island Queen—ferry to Martha's Vineyard, May-Oct.

The Fenway (Boston)
- Green Line-D (Riverside) to Fenway and Longwood.
- Green Line-E (Heath St.) to Symphony, or stops along Huntington Ave.
- T-Bus 8 (Harbor Pt.-Kenmore).
- T-Bus 39 (Forest Hills-Back Bay Sta.).
- T-Bus 47 (Central-Albany St.).
- T-Bus 55 (Queensberry St.-Park St.).
- T-Bus 60 (Chestnut Hill-Kenmore).
- T-Bus 65 (Brighton Ctr.-Kenmore).
- Peter Pan (Boston-Worcester, Rt. 9 local), stops at Brigham Circle.

Fitchburg
- T-Commuter Rail (Fitchburg Line)—from North Sta.
- Vermont Transit (Boston-Rutland, VT)—from Boston/Greyhound, Logan Airport, and Riverside to "Fitchburg Jct.," 3-4 trips daily.
- MART local buses.

Ⓟ Main St. (Rt. 2A), E of Rt. 12 (downtown).

Fort Devens (Ayer)
- T-Commuter Rail (Fitchburg Line)—from North Sta. to Ayer and Shirley
- Vermont Transit (Boston-Rutland, VT)—from Boston/Greyhound,
- Logan Airport, and Riverside, 2-4 trips daily.
- MART local bus from Leominster.

Fort Point Channel (South Boston)
- Red Line to South Sta.
- T-Bus 3 (Chinatown-Marine Ind. Pk.).
- T-Bus 6 (Haymarket-Marine Ind. Pk.).
- T-Bus 7 (City Point-Franklin & Devonshire).

Foxborough
- Bonanza (Logan Airport-Providence, RI). *This bus does not stop in downtown Boston.*
- Mass Limousine—from Logan Airport. *See Chapter 10 for service to Patriots games; Chapter 12 for service to concerts at Foxboro Stadium.*
*See **Sharon** for train service to Boston.*

Framingham
- T-Commuter Rail (Framingham Line)—from South Sta. and Back Bay Sta.
- Peter Pan (Boston-Framingham, express)—from Boston/Peter Pan, Park Plaza, and Copley Sq.
- Peter Pan (Boston-Worcester, Rt. 9 local)—from Boston/Peter Pan, Park Plaza, Copley Sq., Brigham Cir. and Brookline Village.
- Logan Express—from Logan Airport.
- Amtrak—Trains to New York and Chicago stop at Framingham station.
- Crystal Transport (Framingham-Milford). Serves Rt.126. *Connects w/ Boston buses at Shoppers World; connects w/T-Commuter Rail at Framingham.*
- Gulbankian's (Framingham-Hudson), Sat. only.
- Natick Neighborhood Bus.
- LIFT local buses.

Downtown Framingham: T-Commuter Rail; Amtrak; Crystal Transport; and all LIFT routes.
Framingham Ctr.: Peter Pan (express and local); LIFT 2, 2X, and 3.
Shoppers World: Peter Pan (express and local); Logan Express; Crystal Transport; Gulbankian's; LIFT 1, 2, 3, and 4; and Natick Neighborhood Bus.
Waterview: Peter Pan (express and

local); LIFT 2X.

ⓅRt. 135, W of Rt. 126 (downtown). Rt. 9 (Shoppers World).

Franklin
- T-Commuter Rail (Franklin Line)— from South Sta. and Back Bay Sta. to Franklin and Forge Park/495.

ⓅRoute 140, 1/2 mile W of I-495, exit 17 (Forge Park/495).

Gardner
- T-Commuter Rail (Fitchburg Line)— from North Sta., 2-3 trips Mon.-Sat.
- Vermont Transit (Boston-Rutland, VT)—from Boston/Greyhound, Logan Airport, and Riverside, 3-4 trips daily.
- MART local buses.

Georgetown
- The Coach Co. (Boston-Haverhill), rush hour only.

Gloucester
- T-Commuter Rail (Rockport Line)— from North Sta. to W. Gloucester and Gloucester.
- AC Cruises—from Boston/Pier 1 to Rocky Neck, summer only.
- CATA local buses.

Granby
- PVTA local bus from **Holyoke.**

Great Barrington
- BRTA local bus from **Pittsfield** and **Lee.**
- Bonanza from Pittsfield and Lee, 3 trips daily.

Greenfield
- Peter Pan (Boston-Williamstown)— from Boston/Peter Pan.
- GMTA and FRTA local buses.

Groveland
- The Coach Co. (Boston-Haverhill), rush hour only. Serves So.Groveland.

Hadley
See also South Hadley.
- PVTA local bus from **Northampton** and **Amherst.**

Hamilton
- T-Commuter Rail (Ipswich Line)—from North Sta. to Hamilton/Wenham.

Hanover
- Plymouth & Brockton (Boston-Plymouth

Ctr.)—from Park Plaza, Boston/Peter Pan. Serves Rt. 53, Hanover Mall.
- Plymouth & Brockton (Braintree-Marshfield)—from Braintree (*Red Line)* to Hanover Mall, rush hour only.
- H. T. Drummond commuter vans.

ⓅRt. 53 at Rt. 3, exit 13 (Hanover Mall).

Harwich
- Plymouth & Brockton (Hyannis-Chatham), connects w/ Boston buses at Hyannis. Serves W. Harwich, Harwichport, S. Harwich.

Haverhill
- T-Commuter Rail (Haverhill Line)—from North Sta. to Bradford and Haverhill.
- The Coach Co. (Boston-Haverhill), rush hour only. Serves Bradford and Washington Sq.
- MVRTA local buses.

Hingham
- T-Commuter Boat—from Boston/ Rowes Wharf.
- Plymouth & Brockton (Boston-Scituate)—from Park Plaza, Boston/ Peter Pan and South Sta. Serves Rt. 228, East St.
- H. T. Drummond commuter vans.
- T-Bus 220 (Quincy Ctr.-Hingham).
- T-Bus 220A (Hingham Loop).
- People Care-iers (Hingham-Hull), connects w/T-Bus 220.
*See **Rockland** for service to Rt.3/228 interchange.*

Hinsdale
- BRTA local bus from **Pittsfield.**

Holbrook
- T-Bus 230 (Quincy Ctr.-Holbrook).

Holden
- WRTA local buses from **Worcester.**

Holliston
- Crystal Transport (Framingham-Milford), *connects w/Boston buses and trains in Framingham.*

Holyoke
- Peter Pan (Boston-Amherst)—from Boston/Peter Pan and Riverside, 13 trips daily.
- PVTA—frequent service from Springfield.
- PVTA local buses.

Hopkinton
- LIFT 5 (Framingham-Hopkinton), *connects w/ T-Commuter Rail at Framingham.*

Hudson
- Gulbankian's (Boston-Hudson)—from Park Plaza and Copley Sq.
- Gulbankian's (Framingham-Hudson)—from Shoppers World, Sat. only.

Hull
- People Care-iers (Hingham-Hull), *connects w/T-Bus 220 at Hingham.*
- Bay State Cruise Co. (Boston-Nantasket)—from Long Wharf, summer only.
- Bay State Cruise Co. (Boston-Pemberton)—from Long Wharf, year-round, rush hour only.

Hyannis
- Plymouth & Brockton (Boston-Hyannis)—from Park Plaza, Boston/Peter Pan, and Logan Airport.
- Plymouth & Brockton (Hyannis-Provincetown).
- Plymouth & Brockton (Hyannis-Chatham).
- CCRTA (Hyannis-Woods Hole).
- Amtrak from New York, NY, summer only.
- Bonanza from New York, NY.
- Peter Pan from Springfield.
- Steamship Authority—ferry to Nantucket, year-round.
- Hy-Line—ferries to Nantucket and Martha's Vineyard, May-Oct.

Hyde Park (Boston)
See also Readville.
- T-Commuter Rail (Attleboro/Stoughton/Franklin Lines)—from South Sta. and Back Bay Sta. to Hyde Park.
- T-Commuter Rail (Fairmount Line)—from South Sta. to Fairmount.
- T-Bus 24 (Wakefield Ave.-Mattapan).
- T-Bus 32 (Wolcott Sq.-Forest Hills).
- T-Bus 33 (Dedham Line-Mattapan).
- T-Bus 40 (Georgetowne-Forest Hills).
- T-Bus 50 (Cleary Sq.-Forest Hills, via Roslindale).
Cleary Sq.: T-Buses 32, 33, 50; and T-Commuter Rail (Hyde Park).
From Boston: Orange Line or Green Line-E/T-Bus 39 to Forest Hills, then T-Bus 32; or T-Commuter Rail.

Ipswich
- T-Commuter Rail (Ipswich Line)—from

North Sta.
- The Coach Co. (Boston-Newburyport), rush hour only. Serves Rt.1.
- Ⓟ Topsfield Rd., S of Market St., off Rt. 1A.

Jamaica Plain (Boston)
- Orange Line to Jackson Sq., Stony Brook, Green St., and Forest Hills.
- Green Line-E (Heath St.), serves S. Huntington Ave.
- Green Line-E/T-Bus 39 (Forest Hills-Back Bay Sta.), serves S. Huntington Ave., Centre St., South St.
- T-Commuter Rail (Needham Line)—from South Sta. and Back Bay Sta. to Forest Hills.
- T-Bus 38 (Wren St.-Forest Hills).
- T-Bus 41 (Centre & Eliot Sts.-Dudley).
- T-Bus 42 (Forest Hills-Ruggles).
- T-Bus 46 (Heath St.-Dudley).
- T-Bus 48 (Jamaica Plain Loop).
Centre St./The Monument: T-Buses 38, 39, 41, 48.
Washington St.: T-Bus 42; and Orange Line (Green St., Forest Hills).
See Orange Line map for other buses to Forest Hills.

Kingston
- Plymouth & Brockton (Boston-Plymouth Ctr.)—from Park Plaza, Boston/Peter Pan and South Sta.
- H. T. Drummond commuter vans.
- Green Harbor Transp.—from Logan Airport to Howard Johnson's.

Lanesboro
- BRTA local buses from **Pittsfield.**

Lawrence
- T-Commuter Rail (Haverhill Line)—from North Sta.
- Trombly (Boston-N. Andover)—from Park Plaza and Essex St.
- MVRTA local buses.

Lee
- Peter Pan (Boston-Albany, NY)—from Boston/Peter Pan and Riverside, 5 trips daily.
- Greyhound (Boston-Albany, NY)—from Boston/Greyhound and Riverside, 1 trip daily.
- BRTA local bus.

Leicester
- WRTA local buses from **Worcester.**

Lenox
- Peter Pan (Boston-Albany, NY)—from Boston/Peter Pan and Riverside, 5 trips daily.
- Greyhound (Boston-Albany, NY)—from Boston/Greyhound and Riverside, 1 trip daily.
- BRTA local bus.

Leominster
- T-Commuter Rail (Fitchburg Line)—from North Sta. to N. Leominster.
- Vermont Transit (Boston-Rutland, VT)—from Boston/Greyhound, Logan Airport, and Riverside to "Fitchburg Jct.," 3-4 trips daily.
- MART local buses.

Leverett
- GMTA local bus from **Greenfield** and **Amherst.**

Lexington
- Hudson Bus (Boston-Lexington)—from Park Plaza and Haymarket.
- T-Bus 62 (Bedford-Alewife).
- T-Bus 76 (Hanscom Field-Alewife).
- Lexpress local buses.
- Waltham-Lexington Express—from Alewife (*Red Line*) to participating employers.

Lincoln
- T-Commuter Rail (Fitchburg Line)—from North Sta.

Ⓟ Lincoln Rd., N of Route 117.

Littleton
- T-Commuter Rail (Fitchburg Line)—from North Sta. to Littleton/495.
- Yankee Line (Boston-Littleton), rush hour only.

Logan Airport
Service from downtown Boston and Back Bay:
- Blue Line to Airport
- Logan Link from South Station
- Airport Water Shuttle—from Rowes Wharf.
- Airways Transp.—from downtown and Back Bay hotels.
- City Transp.—from downtown and Back Bay hotels.
- Peter Pan—from Boston/Peter Pan.
Other Logan Airport service is listed by city or town in this chapter.

Longmeadow and E. Longmeadow
- PVTA local buses from **Springfield.**

Lowell
- T-Commuter Rail (Lowell Line)—from North Sta.
- Vermont Transit (Boston-White River Jct., VT)—from Boston/Greyhound and Logan Airport, 2-3 trips daily.
- Hudson Airporter—from Logan Airport.
- M & L Transp.—from Logan Airport.
- MVRTA local bus from **Lawrence.**
- LRTA local buses.

Ⓟ 145 Thorndike St. (Route 3A).

Ludlow
- PVTA local bus from **Springfield.**

Lynn
- T-Commuter Rail (Rockport/Ipswich Line)—from North Sta. to Lynn/Central Sq. and GE River Works.
- T-Bus 426 (Lynn-Haymarket, via Cliftondale).
- T-Bus 429 (Lynn-N. Saugus).
- T-Bus 433 (Lynn-Pine Hill).
- T-Bus 435 (Lynn-Danvers).
- T-Bus 436 (Lynn-Goodwin Cir.).
- T-Bus 436 (Haymarket-Goodwins Cir.), rush hour only.
- T-Bus 437 (Lynn-Lake Shore Park).
- T-Bus 439 (Lynn-Nahant).
- T-Buses 441/442 (Marblehead-Haymarket).
- T-Bus 450 (Salem-Haymarket, via Western Ave.)
- T-Bus 455 (Salem-Haymarke, via Loring Ave.)
- Lynn East/West Loop local buses.
Central Sq.: all of the above buses and trains except T-Bus 450.
West Lynn: T-Buses 426, 450 and West Lynn Loop.
From Boston: T-Bus 450 from Haymarket or T-Commuter Rail from North Sta.

Ⓟ Broad St. (Rt. 1A) and Market St. (downtown garage).

Lynnfield
- T-Bus 436 (Lynn-Goodwins Cir.).
- T-Bus 436 (Haymarket-Goodwins Cir.), rush hour only.

Malden
- Orange Line to Malden Ctr. and Oak Grove.

• T-Commuter Rail (Reading/Haverhill Line), stops at Malden Ctr.
• T-Bus 97 (Malden Ctr.-Wellington), serves Commercial St.
• T-Bus 99 (Upper Highland-Wellington).
• T-Bus 101 (Malden Ctr.-Sullivan, via Medford Sq.), serves Pleasant St.
• T-Bus 104 (Malden Ctr.-Sullivan, via Ferry St.).
• T-Bus 105 (Malden Ctr.-Sullivan, via Faulkner).
• T-Bus 106 (Lebanon St.-Wellington).
• T-Bus 108 (Linden Sq.-Wellington), serves Highland Ave.
• T-Bus 109 (Linden Sq.-Sullivan).
• T-Bus 119 (Northgate-Beachmont).
• T-Bus 130 (Lebanon St./Melrose-Malden Ctr.).
• T-Bus 130A (Wyoming Sq.-Malden Ctr.).
• T-Bus 131 (Melrose Highlands-Malden Ctr.).
• T-Buses 136/137 (Reading-Malden Ctr.).
• T-Bus 411 (Revere House-Malden Ctr.).
• T-Bus 426 (Lynn-Haymarket, via Cliftondale).
• T-Bus 426 (Granada Highlands-Haymarket), rush hour only.
• T-Bus 430 (Saugus-Malden Ctr.).
Granada Highlands: T-Bus 411; also T-Bus 426 in rush hour.
Linden Sq.: T-Buses 108, 109, 119, 411, 426.
Main St.: T-Buses 99, 106 (south of Malden Sq.); T-Buses 130, 131, 136, 137 (north of Malden Sq.).
Maplewood Sq./Salem St.: T-Buses 106, 108, 411, 430.
Ⓟ Entrance from Main St. at Malden/ Melrose line or from Winter St. E of Washington St. (Oak Grove).

Manchester-by-the-Sea
• T-Commuter Rail (Rockport Line)— from North Sta.

Mansfield
• T-Commuter Rail (Attleboro Line)— from South Sta. and Back Bay Sta.
• Mass Limousine—from Logan Airport.
See Chapter 12 for service to Great Woods.
Ⓟ Crocker St., off Main St., 1 block N of Route of Rt. 106 (downtown).

Marblehead
• T-Bus 441 (Marblehead-Haymarket, via Paradise Rd.).
• T-Bus 442 (Marblehead-Haymarket, via Humphrey St.).

*See **Swampscott** for train service to Boston.*

Marlborough
• Big W (Boston-Northborough), rush hour only. Serves Rt. 20.
• Gulbankian's (Boston-Hudson)—from Park Plaza and Copley Sq.
• Gulbankian's (Framingham-Hudson)— from Shoppers World, Sat. only.

Marshfield
• Plymouth & Brockton (Boston-S. Duxbury), rush hour only. Serves Furnace Brook School., Marshfield Ctr., Brant Rock, Green Harbor.
• Plymouth & Brockton (Braintree-Marshfield)—from Braintree *(Red Line)* to Furnace Brook Schl., rush hour only.
• H. T. Drummond commuter vans.
*See **Pembroke** for service to Rt.3/139 interchange.*

Marstons Mills
• CCRTA from **Hyannis, Woods Hole.**

Martha's Vineyard
Ferries to Vineyard Haven:
• Steamship Authority—from Woods Hole, year-round.
• Cape Island Express—from New Bedford, May-Oct.
Ferries to Oak Bluffs:
• Steamship Authority—from Woods Hole, May-Sept.
• Island Queen—from Falmouth, May-Oct.
• Hy-Line—from Hyannis, May-Oct.
• Hy-Line—from Nantucket, June-Sept.
Service on the island:
• Island Transport local buses, summer only.
• VTA local buses, summer only.
• Chappaquiddick Ferry—from Edgartown to Chappaquiddick, year-round, frequent service, daily.

Mashpee
• CCRTA from **Hyannis, Woods Hole.**

Mattapan (Boston)
• Red Line (Mattapan) to Mattapan.
• T-Commuter Rail (Fairmount Line)— from South Sta. to Morton St.
• T-Bus 21 (Ashmont-Forest Hills).
• T-Bus 24 (Wakefield Ave.-Mattapan).
• T-Bus 26 (Norfolk St.-Ashmont).
• T-Bus 27 (Mattapan-Ashmont).
• T-Bus 28 (Mattapan-Ruggles).
• T-Bus 29 (Mattapan-Jackson Sq.).

•T-Bus 30 (Mattapan-Roslindale).
•T-Bus 31 (Mattapan-Forest Hills).
•T-Bus 33 (Mattapan-Dedham Line).
Mattapan Sq.: Red Line; T-Buses 24, 27, 28, 29A, 30, 31, 33.
From Boston: Red Line; or: Orange Line to Forest Hills, then T-Bus 31; or: Orange Line to Ruggles, then T-Bus 28.

Mattapoisett
•SRTA local bus from **New Bedford.**

Maynard
*See **Acton** and **Concord** for train service to Boston.*

Medfield
•Brush Hill (Boston-Milford), rush hour only.

Medford
•Orange Line to Wellington.
•T-Commuter Rail (Lowell Line)—from North Sta. to W. Medford.
•T-Express Bus 325 (Elm St.-Haymarket), rush hour only.
•T-Express Bus 326 (W. Medford-Haymarket), rush hour only.
•T-Bus 80 (Arlington Ctr.-Lechmere, via Medford Hillside).
•T-Bus 90 (Davis-Wellington).
•T-Bus 94 (Medford Sq.-Davis).
•T-Bus 95 (W. Medford-Sullivan).
•T-Bus 96 (Medford Sq.-Harvard).
•T-Bus 99 (Upper Highland-Wellington).
•T-Bus 100 (Elm St.-Wellington).
•T-Bus 101 (Malden Ctr.-Sullivan, via Medford Sq.).
•T-Bus 108 (Linden Sq.-Wellington).
•T-Bus 134 (N. Woburn-Wellington).
•T-Bus 134M (Medford-Wellington).
•Hudson Bus (Boston-Lexington; Boston-Stoneham)—from Park Plaza and Haymarket.
•Hudson Bus (Meadow Glen Mall-Fulton St.).
Fellsway: T-Buses 100, 325.
*Medford Hillside:*T-Buses 80, 94, 96.
*Medford Sq.:*T-Buses 94, 95, 96, 101, 134, 134M, 326; and all Hudson Bus routes (hourly service from Boston).
*W. Medford:*T-Commuter Rail; T-Buses 80, 94, 95, 326; and Hudson Bus (Boston-Lexington).
Ⓟ Revere Beach Pkwy. (Route 16) E. of Route 28 (Wellington).

Medway
•Brush Hill (Boston-Milford), rush hour only. Serves W. Medway.

Melrose
•T-Commuter Rail (Reading/Haverhill Line)—from North Sta. to Wyoming, Melrose/Cedar Park, and Melrose Highlands.
•T-Bus 130 (Lebanon St./Melrose-Malden Ctr.).
•T-Bus 130A (Wyoming Sq.-Malden Ctr.).
•T-Bus 131 (Melrose Hlnds-Malden Ctr.).
•T-Buses 136/137 (Reading-Malden Ctr.).

Methuen
•MVRTA local buses from **Lawrence, Lowell,** and **Haverhill.**

Middleborough
•Interstate (Boston-Middleborough)—from Park Plaza and South Sta.
•Mass Limousine—from Logan Airport.

Milford
•Brush Hill (Boston-Milford), rush hour only.
•Crystal Transport (Framingham-Milford), *connects w/Boston buses and trains in Framingham.*

Millbury
•Peter Pan (Boston-Worcester, express)—from Boston/Peter Pan.
•WRTA local buses from Worcester.

Millers Falls
•GMTA local bus from **Greenfield.**

Millis
•Brush Hill (Boston-Milford), rush hour only.

Milton
•Red Line (Mattapan) to Milton, Central Ave., Valley Rd., and Capen St.
•Hudson Bus (Mattapan-Canton)—from Mattapan (Red Line).
•T-Bus 215 (Quincy Ctr.-Ashmont).
•T-Bus 217 (Wollaston Beach-Ashmont).
•T-Bus 240 (Avon line-Ashmont).
•T-Bus 240A (Crawford Sq.-Ashmont).
•T-Bus 245 (Quincy Ctr.-Mattapan).
•BAT local bus from Brockton.
Blue Hill Ave.: Hudson Bus.
E. Milton Sq.: T-Buses 215, 217, 245.
*Milton Village:*Red Line; T-Buses 217, 240, 240A; BAT.
*Town Ctr.:*T-Buses 240, 240A, 245.

Mission Hill (Boston)
•Green Line-E (Heath St.), serves Huntington Ave., S. Huntington Ave.
•Orange Line to Roxbury Crossing.

●T-Bus 39 (Forest Hills-Back Bay Sta.).
●T-Bus 66 (Harvard-Dudley, via Brookline).
●Peter Pan (Boston-Worcester, Rt. 9 local), stops at Brigham Cir.
●Mission Hill Link Bus.

Montague
See also Millers Falls and Turners Falls.
●GMTA local bus from **Greenfield** and **Amherst.**

Nahant
●T-Bus 439 (Lynn-Nahant). Through service from Haymarket on most trips. *See **Lynn** for train service to Boston.*

Nantasket
See Hull.

Nantucket
●Steamship Authority—ferry from Hyannis, year-round.
●Hy-Line—ferry from Hyannis, May-Oct.
●Hy-Line—ferry from Martha's Vineyard, June-Sept.
●Barrett's Tours local buses, June-Sept.

Natick
●T-Commuter Rail (Framingham Line)—from South Sta. and Back Bay Sta. to Natick and W. Natick.
●Peter Pan (Boston-Worcester, Rt. 9 local)—from Boston/Peter Pan, Park Plaza, Copley Sq., and Brigham Cir.
●Natick Neighborhood Bus.
●LIFT local buses from Framingham to Rt.9 malls.

Needham
●T-Commuter Rail (Needham Line)— from South Sta. and Back Bay Sta. to Hersey (Birds Hill), Needham Jct., Needham Ctr., and Needham Hts.
●T-Bus 59 (Needham Jct.-Watertown), via Newton Highlands.
●Hudson Airporter—from Logan Airport to Sheraton Needham.
Ⓟ Chestnut St., 1/2 mile S of Route 135 (Needham Jct.); Great Plain Ave. (Rt. 135, 3/4 mile W of Route 128/I-95, exit 18 (Hersey).

New Bedford
●American Eagle (Boston-New Bedford)—from Boston/Peter Pan.
●Cape Island Express—ferry to Martha's Vineyard, May-Oct.
●Cuttyhunk Boat—ferry to Cuttyhunk I.

●SRTA local buses.
Ⓟ Elm and Pleasant Sts. (downtown); U.S. 6 at Rt. 140 exit 1; Kings Hwy at Rt. 140 exit 4.

Newbury
Also see Byfield.
●The Coach Co. (Boston-Newburyport), rush hour only.

Newburyport
●C & J Trailways (Boston-Durham, NH)—from Boston/Peter Pan and Logan Airport, 13 trips daily.
●Greyhound (Boston-Portland, ME)— from Boston/Greyhound, 5 trips daily.
●The Coach Co. (Boston-Amesbury, Boston-Newburyport) rush hour only.
●MVRTA (Haverhill-Newburyport).
Downtown: The Coach Co. (Boston-Newburyport); and MVRTA.
Ⓟ Rt. 113, east of I-95, exit 57.

Newton
●Newton is served by Green Line-D, T-Commuter Rail (Framingham Line), T-Express Buses, Peter Pan (Boston-Worcester, Rt. 9 local), Hudson Airporter, and Peter Pan, Greyhound and Vermont Transit intercity buses. For more information, see the following neighbor-hoods: Auburndale; Chestnut Hill; Newton Centre; Newton Corner; Newton Highlands; Newton Upper Falls; Newtonville; Nonantum; Riverside; West Newton.

Newton Centre
●Green Line-D (Riverside) to Newton Centre.
●T-Bus 52 (Dedham Mall-Watertown).

Newton Corner
●T-Express Bus 301 (Brighton Ctr.-Downtown).
●T-Express Bus 302 (Watertown-Copley).
●T-Express Bus 304 (Watertown-Downtown).
●T-Express Bus 304A (Newton Corner-Downtown), through service to Roberts and Waverley.
●T-Bus 52 (Dedham Mall-Watertown).
●T-Bus 53 (Roberts-Newton Corner)
●T-Bus 54 (Waverley-Newton Corner), via Waltham.
●T-Bus 56 (Waltham Highlands-Newton Corner).
●T-Bus 57 (Watertown-Kenmore).
●T-Bus 58 (Auburndale-Newton

Corner), via Waltham.
●Hudson Airporter—from Logan Airport to Sheraton Tara.
From Boston: Green Line to Kenmore, then T-Bus 57; or any T-Express Bus.

Newton Highlands
●Green Line-D (Riverside) to Newton Highlands and Eliot.
●T-Bus 52 (Dedham Mall-Watertown).
●T-Bus 59 (Needham Jct.-Watertown).
●T-Bus 59A (Needham St.-Watertown).
●Peter Pan (Boston-Worcester, Rt. 9 local)—from Boston/Peter Pan, Park Plaza, Copley Sq., and Brigham Cir.

Newton Upper Falls
●T-Bus 59 (Needham Jct.-Watertown).
●Peter Pan (Boston-Worcester, Rt. 9 local)—from Boston/Peter Pan, Park Plaza, Copley Sq., and Brigham Cir.

Newtonville
●T-Commuter Rail (Framingham Line)— from South Sta. and Back Bay Sta.
●T-Bus 53 (Roberts-Newton Corner-Downtown).
●T-Bus 54 (Waverley-Newton Corner-Downtown).
●T-Bus 56 (Waltham Highlands-Newton Corner-Downtown).
●T-Bus 59 (Needham Jct.-Watertown).

Nonantum (Newton)
●T-Bus 56 (Waltham Highlands-Newton Corner-Downtown).
●T-Bus 58 (Auburndale-Newton Corner-Downtown).
●T-Bus 59 (Needham Jct - Watertown).

Norfolk
●T-Commuter Rail (Franklin Line)— from South Sta. and Back Bay Sta.

North Adams
●Peter Pan (Boston-Bennington, VT)— from Boston/Peter Pan and Riverside
●BRTA local buses.

Northampton
●Peter Pan (Boston-Amherst)—from Boston/Peter Pan and Riverside.
●PVTA local buses.

North Andover
●Trombly (Boston-N. Andover)—from Park Plaza and Essex St.
●MVRTA local buses from **Lawrence.**

Northborough
●Peter Pan (Boston-Worcester, Rt. 9 local)—from Boston/Peter Pan, Park Plaza, Copley Sq., and Brigham Cir.
●Big W (Boston-Northborough), rush hour only. Serves Rt.20.

Northbridge
●Local bus from **Worcester**; see WRTA listing.

North End (Boston)
●Green and Orange lines to Haymarket.
●T-Bus 6 (Marine Ind. Pk.-Haymarket).
See Green Line map in Ch.17 for other buses at Haymarket.

Norton
●GATRA local bus from Attleboro and Taunton, *connects w/T-Commuter Rail at Attleboro.*

Norwell
●Plymouth & Brockton (Boston-Plymouth Ctr.)—from Park Plaza, Boston/Peter Pan and South Sta., serves Rt. 53.

Norwood
●T-Commuter Rail (Franklin Line)— from South Sta. and Back Bay Sta. to Norwood Depot, Norwood Central, and Windsor Gardens.
●T-Bus 34E (Walpole Ctr.-Forest Hills).
●Hudson Airporter—from Logan Airport.

Orleans
●Plymouth & Brockton (Hyannis-Provincetown), *connects w/Boston buses at Hyannis.*

Osterville
●CCRTA from **Hyannis, Woods Hole.**

Otis A.F.B. (Bourne)
●Bonanza (Boston-Woods Hole)—from Back Bay Sta. and Logan Airport.

Palmer
●Peter Pan (Boston-Springfield)—from Boston/Peter Pan and Riverside, 4 trips daily.

Peabody
●T-Bus 435 (Lynn-Danvers).
●T-Bus 458 (Salem-Danvers).
●T-Bus 458 (Danvers-Haymarket), rush hour only.
●Michaud (Lake Shore-Northshore Shopping Ctr.).

•Michaud (Salem-Northshore Shop. Ctr.).

Pembroke
•Plymouth & Brockton (Boston-Plymouth Ctr.)—from Park Plaza, Boston/Peter Pan and South Sta. Serves Rt. 53.
•Plymouth & Brockton (Boston-Pembroke Ctr.), rush hour only.
•H. T. Drummond commuter vans.
•Green Harbor Transp.—from Logan Airport to Rts. 3/139.

Pittsfield
•Peter Pan (Boston-Albany, NY)—from Boston/Peter Pan and Riverside, 5 trips daily.
•Greyhound (Boston-Albany, NY)—from Park Plaza, Boston/Peter Pan and Riverside, 1 trip daily.
•Amtrak (Lake Shore Ltd.)—from South Sta., Back Bay Sta. and Framingham, 1 trip daily.
•BRTA local buses.

Plainville
•GATRA local bus from **Attleboro.**

Plymouth
•Plymouth & Brockton (Boston-Hyannis)—from Park Plaza, Boston/Peter Pan and Logan Airport.Express, stops at N. Plymouth (Industrial Park).
•Plymouth & Brockton (Boston-Plymouth Ctr.)—from Park Plaza, Boston/Peter Pan and South Sta. Local via Rt.53, Plymouth Ctr.
•H. T. Drummond commuter vans.
•Green Harbor Transp.—from Logan Airport.

Providence, RI
•T-Commuter Rail—from South Sta. and Back Bay Sta.
•Bonanza bus from Back Bay Sta.
•RIPTA buses
Ⓟ Gaspee St., opposite State House; parking off Canal St. (downtown); 1 Bonanza Way, off Cemetery St., off North Main St. (north).

Provincetown
•Bay State Cruise Co.—from Boston/Commonwealth Pier, summer only.
•Plymouth & Brockton (Hyannis-Provincetown), *connects w/Boston buses at Hyannis.*
•Lower Cape Bus—local bus in summer.

Quincy
•Red Line (Braintree) to N. Quincy, Wollaston, Quincy Ctr., and Quincy Adams.
•T-Bus 210 (Quincy Ctr.-N. Quincy)
•T-Bus 210F (Quincy Ctr.-Fields Corner), via N. Quincy, rush hour only.
•T-Bus 211 (Quincy Ctr.-Squantum).
•T-Bus 212 (Quincy Ctr.-N. Quincy, via Billings Rd.).
•T-Bus 214 (Quincy Ctr.-Germantown).
•T-Bus 215 (Quincy Ctr.-Ashmont).
•T-Bus 216 (Quincy Ctr.-Houghs Neck).
•T-Bus 217 (Wollaston Beach-Ashmont).
•T-Bus 220 (Quincy Ctr.-Hingham).
•T-Bus 221 (Quincy Ctr.-Fort Point).
•T-Bus 222 (Quincy Ctr.-E. Weymouth).
•T-Bus 225 (Quincy Ctr.-Weymouth Landing).
•T-Bus 230 (Quincy Ctr.-Holbrook).
•T-Bus 236 (Quincy Ctr.-South Shore Plaza, via E. Braintree).
•T-Bus 238 (Quincy Ctr.-Crawford Sq.).
•T-Bus 245 (Quincy Ctr.-Mattapan).

Randolph
•T-Bus 238 (Quincy Ctr.-Crawford Sq.).
•T-Bus 240 (Avon line-Ashmont).
•T-Bus 240A (Crawford Sq.-Ashmont).
•BAT local bus from Brockton.

Raynham
•Bloom (Boston-Taunton)—from Boston/Peter Pan.

Reading
•T-Commuter Rail (Reading/Haverhill Line)—from North Sta.
•T-Bus 136 (Reading-Malden Ctr., via Lakeside).
•T-Bus 137 (Reading-Malden Ctr., via North Ave.).

Readville (Hyde Park)
•T-Commuter Rail (Franklin Line)—from South Sta. and Back Bay Sta.
•T-Commuter Rail (Fairmount Line)—from South Sta.
•T-Bus 32 (Wolcott Sq.-Forest Hills).
•T-Bus 33 (Dedham Line-Mattapan).

Rehoboth
•GATRA local bus from **Taunton** and **Providence, RI.**

Revere
•Blue Line to Beachmont, Revere Beach, and Wonderland.

- T-Bus 110 (Wonderland-Wellington).
- T-Bus 116 (Wonderland-Maverick, via Revere St.).
- T-Bus 117 (Wonderland-Maverick, via Beach St.).
- T-Bus 119 (Northgate-Beachmont).
- T-Bus 400 (Lynn-Haymarket, via Lynn Common), serves American Legion Hwy.
- T-Bus 411 (Revere House-Malden Ctr.).
- T-Bus 426 (Lynn-Haymarket, via Cliftondale), serves Salem St.
- T-Buses 441/442 (Marblehead-Haymarket).
- T-Bus 450 (Salem-Haymarket, via Western Ave.), serves American Legion Hwy.
- T-Bus 455 (Salem-Haymarket, via Loring Ave.).

Revere Ctr.:T-Buses 110, 116, 117, 119, 411.

(P) Rt. 1A, N. of Bell Circle, Rt.60 (Wonderland).

Riverside (Newton)

- Green Line-D (Riverside) to Riverside.
- T-Express Bus 300 (Riverside-Downtown).
- T-Bus 353A (Burlington Ind. Area-Dudley), via Waltham.
- Hudson Airporter—from Logan Airport to Days Inn.

These buses stop at the Riverside Greyhound station:
- Greyhound to New York, NY, Islip, NY, and Albany, NY.
- Vermont Transit to Rutland, VT.

These buses stop at the Riverside Peter Pan station:
- Peter Pan to New York, NY, Albany, NY, Springfield, Amherst, and Worcester.

(P) Grove St. at Rt. 128/I-95 exit 22.

Rockland

- Carey's (Boston-Whitman), 1 rush hour trip.
- Plymouth & Brockton (several routes)—from Park Plaza, Boston/ Peter Pan and South Sta. to Rts. 3 & 228, frequent service Mon-Fri.
- H. T. Drummond commuter vans.
- Green Harbor Transp.—from Logan Airport to Rt.228 hotels.

(P) Rt. 228 at Rt. 3, exit 14, on Hingham/Norwell line.

Rockport

- T-Commuter Rail (Rockport Line)— from North Sta.
- CATA local buses.

Roslindale (Boston)

- T-Commuter Rail (Needham Line)— from South Sta. and Back Bay Sta.
- T-Bus 14 (Roslindale-Dudley).
- T-Bus 30 (Mattapan-Roslindale).
- T-Bus 32 (Wolcott Sq.-Forest Hills), serves Hyde Park Ave.
- T-Bus 34 (Dedham Line-Forest Hills).
- T-Bus 34E (Walpole Ctr.-Forest Hills).
- T-Bus 35 (Dedham Mall-Forest Hills, via Stimson).
- T-Bus 36 (Charles River-Forest Hills).
- T-Bus 36A (V.A. Hospital-Forest Hills).
- T-Bus 37 (Baker & Vermont-Forest Hills).
- T-Bus 38 (Wren St.-Forest Hills).
- T-Bus 40 (Georgetowne-Forest Hills).
- T-Bus 50 (Cleary Sq.-Forest Hills, via Roslindale).
- T-Bus 51 (Cleveland Cir.-Forest Hills).

*Roslindale Sq.:*T-Commuter Rail; and all of the above T-Buses *except* 32 and 38. *From Downtown Boston:* Orange Line or Green Line-E/T-Bus 39 to Forest Hills; then any of the T-Buses; or T-Commuter Rail.

Rowley

- The Coach Co. (Boston-Newburyport), rush hour only. Serves Rt.1.

See Ipswich for train service to Boston.

Roxbury (Boston)

See also Mission Hill and West Roxbury.
- Orange Line to Ruggles, Roxbury Crossing, and Jackson Sq.
- T-Bus 1 (Harvard-Dudley, via Mass. Ave.).
- T-Bus 8 (Harbor Pt.-Kenmore).
- T-Bus 14 (Roslindale-Dudley).
- T-Bus 15 (Kane Sq.-Ruggles).
- T-Bus 19 (Fields Corner-Ruggles, via Grove Hall).
- T-Bus 22 (Ashmont-Ruggles, via Jackson Sq.).
- T-Bus 23 (Ashmont-Ruggles, via Dudley Sq.).
- T-Bus 28 (Mattapan-Ruggles).
- T-Bus 29 (Mattapan- Jackson Sq.).
- T-Bus 41 (Centre & Eliot Sts.-Dudley).
- T-Bus 42 (Forest Hills-Ruggles).
- T-Bus 44 (Jackson Sq.-Ruggles, via Humboldt Ave.).
- T-Bus 45 (Franklin Park-Ruggles, via

Grove Hall), serves Blue Hill Ave.
- T-Bus 46 (Heath St.-Dudley).
- T-Bus 47 (Central-Albany St.).
- T-Bus 48 (Jamaica Plain Loop).
- T-Bus 49 (Dudley-Downtown).
- T-Bus 66 (Harvard-Dudley, via Brookline).
- T-Bus 353A (Burlington Ind. Area-Dudley), via Waltham.

Dudley Sq.: T-Buses 1, 8, 14, 15, 19, 23, 28, 41, 42, 44, 45, 46, 47, 49, 66, 353A.
From Boston: T-Bus 49 from Downtown; or: Orange Line to Mass. Ave., then T-Bus 1 (free transfer); or: Orange Line to Ruggles, then T-Bus 8, 15, 19, 23, 28, 42, 44, 45, or 47.
Egleston Sq.: T-Buses 22, 29, 42, 44.
Warren St.: T-Buses 19, 23, 28.

Sagamore
- Plymouth & Brockton (Boston-Hyannis)—from Park Plaza, Boston/Peter Pan and Logan Airport.

Ⓟ at rotary, Rt. 3, exit 1.

Salem
- T-Commuter Rail (Rockport/Ipswich Line)—from North Sta.
- T-Bus 450 (Salem-Haymarket, via Western Ave.).
- T-Bus 451 (N. Beverly-Salem).
- T-Bus 455 (Salem-Haymarket, via Loring Ave.).
- T-Bus 458 (Salem-Danvers).
- Michaud (Salem Belt Line).
- Michaud (Salem-Northshore Shop. Ctr.).

Ⓟ Bridge St. at North St. (Rts. 107 & 114)

Saugus
- T-Bus 426 (Lynn-Haymarket, via Cliftondale).
- T-Bus 426 (Oaklandvale-Haymarket), rush hour only.
- T-Bus 429 (Lynn-N. Saugus).
- T-Bus 430 (Saugus-Malden Ctr.).

Scituate
- Plymouth & Brockton (Boston-Scituate)—from Park Plaza, Boston/Peter Pan and South Sta. Serves Scituate, N. Scituate, Egypt, and Greenbush.
- H. T. Drummond commuter vans.

Seekonk
- GATRA local buses from **Attleboro, Taunton,** and **Providence, RI.**

Sharon
- T-Commuter Rail (Attleboro Line)—from South Sta. and Back Bay Sta.

Sheffield
- Bonanza from **Pittsfield** and **Lee,** 3 trips daily.

Shelburne Falls
- Peter Pan (Boston-Williamstown)—from Boston/Peter Pan.

Sherborn
*See **Framingham, Natick,** or **Wellesley** for train service to Boston.*

Shirley
- T-Commuter Rail (Fitchburg Line)—from North Sta.

Shrewsbury
- Peter Pan (Boston-Worcester, Rt. 9 local)—from Boston/Peter Pan, Park Plaza, Copley Sq., and Brigham Cir. Serves Fairlawn, South St., Levitz's.
- WRTA local buses from **Worcester.**

Somerset
- SRTA local buses from **Fall River.**

Somerville
- Red Line to Porter and Davis.
- Orange Line to Sullivan.
- T-Bus 80 (Arlington Ctr.-Lechmere, via Medford Hillside).
- T-Bus 83 (Rindge Ave.-Central).
- T-Bus 85 (Spring Hill-Kendall).
- T-Bus 86 (Sullivan-Cleveland Cir.).
- T-Bus 87 (Arlington Ctr.-Lechmere, via Somerville Ave.).
- T-Bus 88 (Clarendon Hill-Lechmere, via Highland Ave.).
- T-Bus 89 (Clarendon Hill-Sullivan).
- T-Bus 90 (Davis-Wellington), via Sullivan.
- T-Bus 91 (Sullivan-Central).
- T-Bus 92 (Assembly Sq.-Downtown).
- T-Bus 94 (Medford Sq.-Davis).
- T-Bus 95 (W. Medford-Sullivan).
- T-Bus 96 (Medford Sq.-Harvard).
- T-Bus 101 (Malden Ctr.-Sullivan, via Medford Sq.).

Ball Sq./Magoun Sq.: T-Buses 80, 89.
E. Somerville/Winter Hill: T-Buses 89, 101.
Highland Ave./City Hall: T-Buses 88, 90.
Powderhouse Sq.: T-Buses 80, 89, 94, 96; or walk from Davis, 1/2 mile.
Union Sq.: T-Buses 85, 86, 87, 91.

W. Somerville/Teele Sq.: T-Buses 87, 88, 89; or walk from Davis, 1/2 mile.

Southborough
- Peter Pan (Boston-Worcester, Rt. 9 local)—from Boston/Peter Pan, Park Plaza, Copley Sq., and Brigham Cir. Serves Fayville, White's Corner.
- Gulbankian's (Boston-Hudson)—from Park Plaza and Copley Sq. Serves Central St., Rt.30, Rt.85.
- Gulbankian's (Framingham-Hudson)— from Shoppers World, Sat. only.

See **Framingham** *for additional service.*

South Boston
- Red Line to Broadway and Andrew.
- T-Bus 3 (Chinatown-Marine Ind. Pk.).
- T-Bus 5 (City Pt.-McCormack Hsg.).
- T-Bus 6 (Marine Ind. Pk.-Haymarket).
- T-Bus 7 (City Pt.-Franklin & Devonshire)
- T-Bus 9 (City Pt.-Copley, via Broadway).
- T-Bus 10 (City Pt.-Copley, via Andrew).
- T-Bus 11 (City Pt.-Downtown).

Perkins Sq.: T-Buses 5, 9, 10.
See Red Line map for other buses to Andrew.

South End (Boston)
- Orange Line to Back Bay Sta. and Mass. Ave.
- Green Line (all trains) to Arlington and Copley, walk 3 blocks S.
- Green Line-E (Heath St.) to Prudential and Symphony, walk 2 blocks S.
- T-Bus 1 (Harvard-Dudley, via Mass. Ave.).
- T-Bus 8 (Harbor Pt.-Kenmore).
- T-Bus 9 (City Pt.-Copley, via Broadway).
- T-Bus 10 (City Pt.-Copley, via Andrew).
- T-Bus 43 (Ruggles-Park St.), serves Tremont St.
- T-Bus 47 (Central-Albany St.).
- T-Bus 49 (Dudley-Downtown), serves Washington St.

South Hadley
- Peter Pan (Boston-Amherst)—from Boston/Peter Pan and Riverside, 3 trips daily.
- PVTA local buses from **Holyoke** and **Amherst**.
- PVTA/Five Colleges buses to Mt. Holyoke College.

Spencer
- WRTA local bus from **Worcester**.

Springfield
See also West Springfield.

- Peter Pan (Boston-Springfield)—from Boston/Peter Pan and Riverside, 18 trips daily.
- Greyhound (Boston-Albany NY)—from Boston/Greyhound and Riverside, 2 trips daily.
- Amtrak (Inland Route and Lake Shore Ltd.)—from South Sta., Back Bay Sta., and Framingham, 3 trips daily.
- PVTA local buses.

Stockbridge
- BRTA local bus from **Pittsfield** and **Lee.**
- Bonanza from Pittsfield and Lee, 3 trips daily.

Stoneham
Hudson Bus (Boston-Stoneham)—from Park Plaza and Haymarket.

Stoughton
- T-Commuter Rail (Stoughton Line)— from South Sta. and Back Bay Sta.
- Interstate (Boston-Middleboro), 1 trip Mon.-Fri.
- Hudson Bus (Mattapan-Canton). Serves Cobbs Corner.
- BAT local bus.

Stow
See **Acton** *for train service to Boston.*

Sturbridge
- Peter Pan (Boston-Sturbridge)—from Boston/Peter Pan.

Sudbury
- Big W (Boston-Northborough), rush hour only. Serves Rt. 20.

See **Lincoln** *and* **Weston** *for train service to Boston.*

Sunderland
- PVTA local bus from Amherst.

Sutton
- Local bus from Worcester; see WRTA listing.

Swampscott
- T-Commuter Rail (Rockport/Ipswich Line)—from North Sta.
- T-Bus 441 (Marblehead-Haymarket, via Paradise Rd.).
- T-Bus 442 (Marblehead-Haymarket, via Humphrey St.).

Swansea
- SRTA local buses from **Fall River.**

Taunton
- American Eagle from Boston/Peter Pan to Silver City Galleria.
- Bloom (Boston-Taunton)—from Boston/Peter Pan.
- Mass Limousine—from Logan Airport.
- GATRA local buses.

Tewksbury
- Hudson Airporter—from Logan Airport.
- LRTA local bus from Lowell.

Topsfield
- The Coach Co. (Boston-Newburyport), rush hour only. Serves Rt.1.

Truro
- Plymouth & Brockton (Hyannis-Provincetown). *Connects w/Boston buses at Hyannis; connects w/Boston ferry at Provincetown.*

Turners Falls
- GMTA local bus from **Greenfield** and **Amherst.**

Tyngsboro
- LRTA local bus from **Lowell.**

Waban (Newton)
- Green Line-D (Riverside) to Waban.

Wakefield
- T-Commuter Rail (Reading/Haverhill Line)—from North Sta. to Greenwood and Wakefield.
- T-Bus 136 (Reading-Malden Ctr., via Lakeside).
- T-Bus 137 (Reading-Malden Ctr., via North Ave.).

Walpole
- T-Commuter Rail (Franklin Line)—from South Sta. and Back Bay Sta. to Plimptonville (rush hour only) and Walpole.
- T-Bus 34E (Walpole Ctr.-Forest Hills).
- Ⓟ West St., W of Route 1A (downtown).

Waltham
- T-Commuter Rail (Fitchburg Line)—from North Sta. to Waltham (Central Sq.) and Brandeis/Roberts.
- T-Express Bus 305 (Waltham-Downtown), rush hour only.
- T-Bus 53 (Roberts-Newton Corner-Downtown).
- T-Bus 54 (Waverley-Newton Corner-Downtown).
- T-Bus 56 (Waltham Highlands-Newton Corner-Downtown).
- T-Bus 58 (Auburndale-Newton Corner-Downtown).
- T-Bus 70 (Cedarwood-Central).
- T-Bus 70A (N. Waltham-Central).
- T-Bus 353A (Burlington Ind. Area-Dudley), via Riverside. Serves Waltham Ind. Area, rush hour only, "reverse commute."

Waltham-Lexington Express—from Alewife to participating employers.
Central Sq.: T-Commuter Rail; and T-Buses 53, 54, 56, 58, 70, 70A, 305.
From Boston: T-Commuter Rail; or T-Buses 53, 54, 56, 58, 305.
From Cambridge: T-Commuter Rail from Porter Sq.; or T-Bus 70 from Central Sq.
Or go to Watertown Sq. and transfer to T-Bus 70.

Wareham
- Bonanza (Boston-Wareham)—from Back Bay Sta.
- Ⓟ U.S. 6 at junction Rts. 28 and 25.

Watertown
- T-Express Bus 302 (Watertown-Copley).
- T-Express Bus 304 (Watertown-Downtown).
- T-Bus 52 (Dedham Mall-Watertown).
- T-Bus 54 (Waverley-Newton Corner-Downtown), via **Waltham**.
- T-Bus 57 (Watertown-Kenmore).
- T-Bus 58 (Auburndale-Newton Corner-Downtown).
- T-Bus 59 (Needham Jct.-Watertown).
- T-Bus 70 (Cedarwood-Central).
- T-Bus 70A (N. Waltham-Central).
- T-Bus 71 (Watertown-Harvard).
- T-Bus 73 (Waverley-Harvard).
Watertown Sq.: T-Buses 52, 57, 59, 70, 70A, 71, 302, 304.
From Boston: T-Buses 302, 304; or Green Line to Kenmore, then T-Bus 57.
From Cambridge: T-Bus 70 from Central Sq. or T-Bus 71 from Harvard Sq.

Wayland
- Big W (Boston-Northborough), rush hour only. Serves Rt. 20.
*See **Lincoln** and **Weston** for train service to Boston.*

Wellesley
- T-Commuter Rail (Framingham

Line)—from South Sta. and Back Bay Sta. to Wellesley Farms, Wellesley Hills, and Wellesley Sq.
- Peter Pan (Boston-Worcester, Rt. 9 local)—from Boston/Peter Pan, Park Plaza, Copley Sq., and Brigham Cir. Serves Wellesley Hills, Rt.9.

Ⓟ Washington St. at Jct. Routes 135 and 16, next to Post Office (Wellesley Sq.).

Wellfleet
- Plymouth & Brockton (Hyannis-Provincetown). *Connects w/ Boston buses at Hyannis; connects w/ Boston ferry at Provincetown.*

Wenham
- T-Commuter Rail (Ipswich Line)—from North Sta. to Hamilton/Wenham.

Westborough
- Peter Pan (Boston-Worcester, Rt. 9 local)—from Boston/Peter Pan, Park Plaza, Copley Sq., and Brigham Cir. Serves Rt. 9, Lyman St.
- Peter Pan (Boston-Westborough), rush hours only.
- Peter Pan (Logan Airport-Worcester), 4-6 trips daily.

West Bridgewater
See Bridgewater.

Westfield
- Peter Pan (Boston-Westfield), Fri and Sun only, no summer service.
- PVTA local buses from Springfield and Holyoke.

West Newton
- T-Commuter Rail (Framingham Line)—from South Sta. and Back Bay Sta.
- T-Express Bus 305 (Waltham-Downtown), rush hour only.
- T-Bus 53 (Roberts-Newton Corner-Downtown).
- T-Bus 54 (Waverley-Newton Corner-Downtown).

Weston
- T-Commuter Rail (Fitchburg Line)—from North Sta. to Kendal Green, Hastings, and Silver Hill. (Silver Hill: rush hour only.)
- Big W (Boston-Northborough), serves Rt.20, rush hour only.

Westport
- SRTA local bus from **New Bedford**

and **Fall River.**

West Roxbury (Boston)
- T-Commuter Rail (Needham Line)—from South Sta. and Back Bay Sta. to Bellevue, Highland, and West Roxbury.
- T-Bus 34 (Dedham Line-Forest Hills).
- T-Bus 34E (Walpole Ctr.-Forest Hills).
- T-Bus 35 (Dedham Mall-Forest Hills, via Stimson).
- T-Bus 36 (Charles River-Forest Hills).
- T-Bus 36A (V.A. Hospital-Forest Hills).
- T-Bus 37 (Baker & Vermont-Forest Hills).
- T-Bus 38 (Wren St.-Forest Hills).
- T-Bus 40 (Georgetowne-Forest Hills).
- T-Bus 51 (Cleveland Cir.-Forest Hills).
- T-Bus 52 (Dedham Mall-Watertown).
*Centre St.:*T-Commuter Rail; T-Buses 35, 36, 36A, 37.
Washington St.: T-Buses 34, 34E, 40.
From Downtown Boston: Orange Line or Green Line-E/T-Bus 39 to Forest Hills; then any of the above buses; or T-Commuter Rail.

West Springfield
- PVTA local buses from **Springfield** and **Holyoke.**

Westwood
- T-Commuter Rail (Attleboro/Stoughton Lines)—from South Sta. and Back Bay Sta. to Rt.128 Sta.
- T-Commuter Rail (Franklin Line)—from South Sta. and Back Bay Sta. to Islington.
- T-Bus 34E (Walpole Ctr.-Forest Hills), serves Washington St. (Rt.1A).
- Brush Hill (Boston-Milford), rush hour only. Serves Rt.109.
- Amtrak (Boston-New York, Shore Line) stops at Rt.128 Sta.

Ⓟ University Ave. (Rt 128 Sta.)

Weymouth
- Carey's (Boston-Whitman), rush hour only; 5 trips serve S. Weymouth, 2 trips serve Weymouth Landing.
- T-Bus 220 (Quincy Ctr.-Hingham).
- T-Bus 221 (Quincy Ctr.-Fort Point).
- T-Bus 222 (Quincy Ctr.-E. Weymouth).
- T-Bus 225 (Quincy Ctr.-Weymouth Landing).
- H. T. Drummond commuter vans.

Whitman
- Carey's (Boston-Whitman), rush hour only.
- H. T. Drummond commuter vans.

Wilbraham
●PVTA local bus from **Springfield.**

Williamsburg
●PVTA local bus from **Northampton.**

Williamstown
●Peter Pan (Boston-Bennington, VT)—
from Boston/Greyhound.
●BRTA local bus.

Wilmington
●T-Commuter Rail (Lowell Line)—from
North Sta. to Wilmington.
●T-Commuter Rail (Haverhill Line)—
from North Sta. to N. Wilmington.
Ⓟ Rt. 62, west of I-93, exit 40 (North
Wilmington).

Winchendon
●Vermont Transit (Boston-Rutland,
VT)—from Boston/Greyhound, Logan
Airport, and Riverside.

Winchester
●T-Commuter Rail (Lowell Line)—from
North Sta. to Wedgemere and
Winchester Ctr.
●T-Bus 134 (N. Woburn-Wellington),
serves Main St., Winchester Ctr.
●T-Bus 350 (Burlington-Alewife),

Winthrop
●Paul Revere bus local buses from Orient
Heights *(Blue Line).*Three routes:
●Paul Revere bus (Orient Hts.-
Winthrop Beach, via Highlands).
●Paul Revere bus (Orient Hts.-
Winthrop Beach, via Centre).
●Paul Revere bus (Winthrop Beach-
Point Shirley).

Woburn
●T-Commuter Rail (Lowell Line) to
Mishawum and Lechmere Sales
office.
●T-Express Bus 353 (Burlington Ind.
Area-Haymarket), rush hour "reverse

commute" only.
●T-Express Bus 354 (Woburn Sq.-
Haymarket), rush hour only.
●T-Bus 134 (N. Woburn-Wellington),
serves Main St., Woburn Sq.
●T-Bus 350 (Burlington-Alewife)
●Hudson Airporter—from Logan Airport
to Rt.128 hotels.
●M & L Transp.—from Logan Airport to
Rt.128 hotels.

Woods Hole
●Bonanza (Boston-Woods Hole)—from
Boston/Greyhound and Logan Airport.
●Bonanza from New York NY.
●Peter Pan from Springfield.
●CCRTA (Hyannis-Woods Hole).
●Steamship Authority—ferries to
Martha's Vineyard (year-round).

Worcester
●Peter Pan (Boston-Worcester,
express)—from Boston/Peter Pan and
Riverside, 20 trips daily.
●Peter Pan (Boston-Worcester, Rt. 9
local)—from Boston/Peter Pan, Park
Plaza, Copley Sq., and Brigham Cir., 9
trips Mon.-Fri.
●Greyhound (Boston-New York NY,
Boston-Albany, NY)—from Boston/
Greyhound and Riverside, 7 trips daily.
●Amtrak (Inland Route, Lake Shore
Ltd.)—from South Sta., Back Bay Sta.,
and Framingham, 3 trips daily.
●Peter Pan from Logan Airport, 9-15
trips daily.
●WRTA local buses.

Wrentham
See **Franklin** *or* **Norfolk** *for train service
from Boston.*

Yarmouth
●Plymouth & Brockton (Hyannis-
Provincetown), *connects w/Boston
buses at Hyannis.*
●Plymouth & Brockton (Hyannis-
Chatham), *connects w/Boston buses
at Hyannis.* Serves S. Yarmouth.

Commuter train at South Station, Boston.

FIRST & LAST RAPID TRANSIT TRAINS

Except Red Line trains to Braintree, the last trains on all lines wait at Park Street, Government Center, and Downtown Crossing for the last trains on connecting lines, so riders can transfer between lines.

The last trains to all Green Line and Red Line destinations (except Braintree) leave Park Street at 12:45 am. Last trains on the Blue and Orange lines depart Government Center and Downtown Crossing after the arrival of the last trains from Park Street.

Buses scheduled to leave subway stations after 12:45 am wait for the last train before departing.

	First Train Mon.-Sat.	Sun.	Last Train Every Day
Blue Line			
Wonderland-Government Ctr.	5:25	5:58	11:56[1]
Orient Heights-Government Ctr.	5:13	6:04	12:26
Government Ctr. - Wonderland	5:27	6:18	12:48[2]
Green Line			
B–Boston College-Government Ctr	5:01	5:40	12:10
B–Government Ctr.-Boston College	5:28	6:07	12:40
C–Cleveland Circle-North Station	5:01	5:40	12:10
C–North Station-Cleveland Circle	5:34[3]	6:10	12:40
D–Riverside-Government Ctr.	5:01	5:40	12:10[4]
D–Government Ctr.-Riverside	5:34	6:16	12:45
E–Heath St.-Lechmere	5:30	6:15	12:14[5]
E–Lechmere-Heath St.	5:01	5:40	12:20[6]
E–Forest Hills-Back Bay Sta. (bus)	5:01	5:45	11:58[7]
E–Back Bay Sta.-Forest Hills (bus)	5:29[3]	6:13	1:00
Orange Line			
Oak Grove-Forest Hills	5:16	6:00	12:26
Forest Hills-Oak Grove	5:16	6:00	12:22
Red Line			
Alewife-Ashmont & Mattapan	5:16	6:00	12:22
Alewife-Braintree	5:24	6:08	12:14[8]
Ashmont-Alewife	5:16	6:00	12:30
Braintree-Alewife	5:16	6:00	12:18
Mattapan-Ashmont & Alewife	5:05	5:51	12:19[9]

1 On Sat. & Sun., last train leaves Wonderland at 12:20.
2 Connecting buses from Orient Heights to Wonderland on Mon.-Fri.; last through train to Wonderland leaves Government Ctr. at 11:32 pm.
3 Saturday service begins 1-2 minutes earlier.
4 On Sat. & Sun., last train leaves Riverside at 12:05.
5 Last train connecting to other lines leaves Heath St. at 12:14; other trains operate until 12:55.
6 On Sat. & Sun., last train connecting to other lines leaves Lechmere at 12:15; another train leaves at 12:30.
7 Last bus connecting to trains at Heath St. leaves Forest Hills at 11:58; other buses operate until 12:30. (Bus to train connections are not guaranteed.)
8 For later service to N. Quincy, Wollaston, and Quincy Ctr., take the last Ashmont train to Fields Corner and then a connecting bus.
9 Last train connecting to trains at Ashmont leaves Mattapan at 12:19 Mon.-Fri., 12:15 Sat.-Sun.; other trains operate until 12:50.

Chapter 17

MBTA Rapid Transit and Buses

The charts on the following pages show the approximate frequency (time between trains or buses), in minutes, of all MBTA bus and rapid transit routes as of Spring 1992. Trip time is approximately how long it takes to go from one end of the route to the other.

Rush hour figures show service *to* Boston (inbound) in the morning and *away from* Boston in the evening; service in the other direction may be less frequent.

A dash (—) means there is no service at the time indicated.

Listings for bus routes also show the major streets which the route serves; some minor streets have been omitted. A slash (/) between two street names means that inbound buses operate via one street and outbound buses use the other.

For precise schedules and route information, **call the MBTA at 722-3200 or 800-392-6100;** or see the printed schedules issued for all MBTA routes. Schedules are available from some bus drivers and T employees; at Park Street station; and at other locations listed in Chapter 1.

MBTA Rapid Transit	Trip Time	Mon.-Fri. frequency (min.)			Sat. Freq.	Sun. Freq.
		Rush	Midday	Night		

Blue Line
Wonderland—Bowdoin   18   4   8   11   9   11
Stations: Wonderland, Revere Beach, Beachmont, Suffolk Downs, Orient Hts., Wood Island, Airport, Maverick, Aquarium, State, Government Ctr., Bowdoin.
Nights & weekends: Wonderland—Government Ctr. only, **Bowdoin closed.**
Trip times from Gov't Ctr.: Airport 7 min., Orient Hts. 11 min., Wonderland 17 min.

Orange Line
Oak Grove—Forest Hills   33   5   8   13   10   14
Stations: Oak Grove, Malden Ctr., Wellington, Sullivan, Community College, North Sta., Haymarket, State, Downtown Crossing (Washington), Chinatown, New England Medical Ctr., Back Bay Sta., Massachusetts Ave., Ruggles, Roxbury Crossing, Jackson Sq., Stony Brook, Green, Forest Hills.
Trip times from Downtown Crossing: Sullivan 8 min., Oak Grove 16 min.; Back Bay Sta. 5 min., Ruggles 8 min., Forest Hills 17 min.

Red Line
Alewife—Ashmont   37   8   12   12   13   15
Stations: Alewife, Davis, Porter, Harvard, Central, Kendall, Charles/MGH, Park St., Downtown Crossing (Washington), South Sta., Broadway, Andrew, JFK/UMass, Savin Hill, Fields Corner, Shawmut, Ashmont.
Trip times from Park St.: Kendall 5 min., Harvard 10 min., Alewife 18 min.; Andrew 7 min., Fields Corner 14 min., Ashmont 19 min.
Alewife—Braintree   44   8   12   12   13   15
Stations: Alewife, Davis, Porter, Harvard, Central, Kendall, Charles/MGH, Park St., Downtown Crossing , South Sta., Broadway, Andrew, JFK/UMass, N. Quincy, Wollaston, Quincy Ctr., Quincy Adams, Braintree.
Trip times from Park St.: N. Quincy 14 min., Quincy Ctr. 19 min., Braintree 26 min.
Ashmont—Mattapan   9-10   4   8   11   8   11
Stations: Ashmont, Cedar Grove, Butler St., Milton, Central Ave., Valley Rd., Capen St., Mattapan. *Connects w/Alewife-Ashmont trains at Ashmont.*

MBTA Rapid Transit

	Trip Time	Rush	Midday	Night	Sat. Freq.	Sun. Freq.
			Mon.–Fri. frequency (min.)			

Green Line

B
Boston College—Gov't Ctr.   27-39   5   5   10   7   5-10
Brighton, Allston: Commonwealth Ave.
Stations: Kenmore, Hynes Convention Ctr./ICA, Copley, Arlington, Boylston, Park St.,
Government Ctr.
Trip times from Park St.: Copley 5 min., Kenmore 10 min.,
Harvard Ave. 18-33 min., Boston College 26-37 min.

C
Cleveland Circle–North Sta.   25-40   7   5   10   5-8   7-10
Brookline: Beacon St.
Stations: Kenmore, Hynes Convention Ctr./ICA, Copley, Arlington, Boylston, Park St.,
Government Ctr., Haymarket, North Sta.
Trip times from Park St.: Coolidge Cor. 13-21 min., Cleveland Cir. 20-33 min.

D
Riverside–Government Ctr.   35-45   8   10   10   6   7-10
Stations: Riverside, Woodland, Waban, Eliot, Newton Highlands, Newton Centre, Chestnut
Hill, Reservoir, Beaconsfield, Brookline Hills, Brookline Village, Longwood, Fenway, Kenmore,
Hynes Convention Ctr./ICA, Copley, Arlington, Boylston, Park St., Government Ctr.
Trip times from Park St.: Reservoir 18-25 min., Riverside 33-43 min.

E
Heath St.–Lechmere   25-31   8   9   10   7-10   7-10
Jamaica Plain: S. Huntington Ave; *Mission Hill, Fenway:* Huntington Ave.
Stations: Symphony, Prudential, Copley, Arlington, Boylston, Park St., Government Ctr.,
Haymarket, North Sta., Science Park, Lechmere.
Trip times from Park St.: North Sta. 6 min., Lechmere 9 min.;
Brigham Cir. 13-16 min., Heath St. 16-22 min.

Arborway—Park St.   Service temporarily suspended.

Blue Line

RAPID TRANSIT STATIONS	STREET ADDRESS & CONNECTING SERVICES

Wonderland ○

1300 North Shore Rd. (Rt. 1A), opposite dog track/Revere

110-Wellington	441-Marblehead-Haymarket,
116-Maverick, via Revere St.	via Paradise Rd.
117-Maverick, via Beach St.	442-Marblehead-Haymarket,
411-Revere House-Malden Ctr.	via Humphrey St. (Mon.-Sat.)

Revere Beach ○

220 Shirley Ave. and 300 Ocean Ave./Revere

110-Wonderland-Wellington	411-Revere House-Malden
117-Wonderland-Maverick,	Ctr.
via Beach St.	

Beachmont ○

630 Winthrop Ave. at 1 Bennington St./Revere

119-Northgate	119-Beachmont Loop

Suffolk Downs ○

1230 Bennington St. and Walley St./East Boston
Does not open until 9:30 am on Sat.; 10:45 am on Sun.

Orient Heights ○

1000 Bennington St., north of 990 Saratoga St./East Boston

Paul Revere buses:	Highlands
—Winthrop Beach via Centre	120-Maverick
—Winthrop Beach via	120-Orient Hts. Loop

Wood Island ○

450 Bennington St., north of Rt. 1A/East Boston

120-Orient Hts.-Maverick	121-Maverick (AM rush)

Airport ○

Airport access road and Porter St./East Boston
Airport shuttle buses to airline terminals

Maverick ○

220 Sumner St. at Chelsea and Meridian Sts./East Boston

112-Wellington	120-Orient Hts.
116-Wonderland, via Revere St.	120-Jeffries Point Loop
117-Wonderland, via Beach St.	121-Wood Island, via Eagle Sq.

Aquarium ○

200 Atlantic Ave. at 300 State St./Boston

Commuter Boats	Long Wharf ferries*
6-Marine Ind. Park-Haymarket	Rowes Wharf ferries*

State ○

200 Washington St. at 1 State St./Boston
Wheelchair access only for outbound platform (to Wonderland).
Wheelchair users coming inbound should go to Government Ctr.,
then cross platform and come back to State.

Orange Line	93-Sullivan, via Bunker Hill St.
92-Assembly Sq., via Main St.	

Government Center ○
Scollay Sq.

1 Cambridge St. at Court and Tremont Sts./Boston
Green Line

Bowdoin ○

Cambridge St. at New Chardon and Bowdoin Sts./Boston
Open Mon.-Fri. 5:15 am-6:30 pm. Closed Sat. & Sun.

***See "Boston Terminals"
map for complete list of
carriers.**

Orange Line

Oak Grove–State

RAPID TRANSIT STATIONS   **STREET ADDRESS & CONNECTING SERVICES**

Oak Grove

Washington St. at Winter St./Malden

130A-Wyoming Sq.-Malden Ctr. 136-Reading-Malden Ctr.,
131-Melrose Highlands-   via Lakeside
Malden Ctr.   137-Reading-Malden Ctr.,
                                via North Ave.

Malden Center

230 Pleasant St. at Summer and Commercial St./Malden
Commuter Rail—Reading/   108-Linden Sq.-Wellington,
Haverhill Line   via Highland Ave.
97-Wellington, via Hancock St. 130-Lebanon St., Melrose
99-Upper Highland-Wellington,   130A-Wyoming Sq.
via Main St.   131-Melrose Highlands
101-Sullivan, via Medford Sq.   136-Reading, via Lakeside
104-Sullivan, via Ferry St.   137-Reading, via North Ave.
105-Sullivan, via Faulkner   411-Revere House
106-Lebanon. St.-Wellington,   (Wonderland)
via Main St.   430-Saugus

Wellington

Revere Beach Pkwy. (Rt. 16), east of Rt. 28/Medford
90-Davis, via Sullivan   108-Linden Sq., via
97-Malden Ctr., via Hancock St.   Highland Ave. & Malden
99-Upper Highland, via Main St.   Ctr.
& Malden Ctr.   110-Wonderland
100-Elm St., Medford   112-Maverick
106-Lebanon St., via Main St. & 134-N. Woburn
Malden Ctr.   134M-Medford

Sullivan

1 Broadway and 1 Cambridge St./Charlestown
86-Cleveland Cir., via Harvard 95-W. Medford
89-Clarendon Hill-Lechmere   101-Malden Ctr., via
90-Davis-Wellington   Medford Sq.
91-Central   104-Malden Ctr., via Ferry St.
92-Assembly Sq.-Downtown, via   105-Malden Ctr., via Faulkner
Main St.   109-Linden Sq.
93-Downtown, via Bunker Hill St.

Community College

Austin St., west of Rutherford Ave./Charlestown

North Station

135 Causeway St. at Canal St./Boston
Commuter Rail   Green Line

Haymarket

Congress St. at New Sudbury St./Boston
Green Line   426-Lynn, via Cliftondale
Commuter buses*   441-Marblehead, via
6-Marine Ind. Park, via South Sta. Paradise Rd.
92-Assembly Sq.-Downtown,   442-Marblehead, via
via Main St.   Humphrey St.
93-Sullivan-Downtown, via   450-Salem, via Highland Ave.
Bunker Hill St.   455-Salem, via Loring Ave.
111-Woodlawn (Chelsea)   Special rush hour service:
325-Elm St., Medford (express) 426-Granada Highlands or
326-W. Medford (express)   Oaklandvale
352-Burlington (express)   436-Happy Valley
353-Burlington Ind. Area   439-Nahant
354-Woburn (express)   458/468-Danvers

State

200 Washington St. at 1 State St./Boston
Blue Line   93-Sullivan, via Bunker Hill
92-Assembly Sq., via Main St.   St.

To Forest Hills via Downtown Crossing

*See "Boston Terminals"
map for complete list of
carriers.

Orange Line

RAPID TRANSIT STATIONS

STREET ADDRESS & CONNECTING SERVICES

To Oak Grove via State

Downtown Crossing
Washington

450 Washington St. at 1 Summer St./Boston
Red Line
Green Line via walkway to Park St.
7-City Pt., via Summer St.
11-City Pt., via Bayview
49-Dudley
53-Roberts, via Waltham & Newton Corner
54-Waverley, via Waltham & Newton Corner
92-Assembly Sq., via Main St.

93-Sullivan, via Bunker Hill St.
300-Riverside (express)
301-Brighton Ctr. (express)
304-Watertown (express)
304A-Newton Corner (express)
305-Waltham (express)
Special rush hour service:
56-Waltham Highlands or Cedarwood
58-Auburndale

Chinatown
Essex

640 Washington St. at 1 Boylston St./Boston
11-City Pt., via Bayview   49-Dudley

New England Medical Ctr.
South Cove

750 Washington St., south of Stuart St./Boston
3-Marine Ind. Pk.   43-Ruggles
11-City Pt., via Bayview   49-Dudley

Back Bay Station
South End

145 Dartmouth St., south of Stuart St./Boston
Commuter Rail
Amtrak
Bonanza

Greyhound Terminal*, 3 blocks
10-City Pt., via Andrew
39-Forest Hills (free transfer)

Massachusetts Ave.

380 Massachusetts Ave., south of St. Botolph St./Boston
1-Harvard-Dudley (free transfer to/from Dudley)

Ruggles

800 Columbus Ave. at Melnea Cass Blvd./Roxbury
Commuter Rail—Attleboro/ Stoughton, Franklin, Needham Lines
8-Harbor Pt.-Kenmore
15-Kane Sq.
19-Fields Corner, via Grove Hall
22-Ashmont, via Jackson Sq.

23-Ashmont, via Dudley Sq.
28-Mattapan, via Dudley Sq.
42-Forest Hills
43-Park St.
44-Jackson Sq., via Humboldt Ave.
45-Franklin Park Zoo
47-Central-Albany St.

Roxbury Crossing

1400 Tremont St., west of 1200 Columbus Ave./Roxbury
66-Harvard-Dudley, via Brookline

Mission Hill Link Bus, Blue Route

Jackson Sq.

1500 Columbus Ave. at 240 Centre St./Jamaica Plain
22-Ashmont-Ruggles
29-Mattapan-Jackson Sq.
41-Centre & Eliot Sts.-Dudley

44-Ruggles, via Humboldt Ave.
46-Heath St.-Dudley
48-Jamaica Plain Loop

Stony Brook

100 Boylston St. at 180 Lamartine St./Jamaica Plain
48-Jamaica Plain Loop

Green

150 Green St. at 380 Amory St./Jamaica Plain
48-Jamaica Plain Loop

Forest Hills

3700 Washington St., south of Morton St./Jamaica Plain
Commuter Rail—Needham Line
Green Line-E [T-Bus 39]
Franklin Park Zoo bus (weekends)
16-JFK/UMass
21-Ashmont
31-Mattapan
32-Wolcott Sq., via Hyde Park Ave.
34-Dedham Line (Washington St.)

34E-Walpole Ctr.
35-Dedham Mall, via Stimson
36-Charles River
36A-V.A. Hospital
37-Baker & Vermont Sts.
38-Wren St.
39-Back Bay Sta.
40-Georgetowne
42-Ruggles
50-Cleary Sq., via Roslindale
51-Cleveland Circle

RAPID TRANSIT STATIONS	STREET ADDRESS & CONNECTING SERVICES

Alewife ⬤

Alewife Brook Pkwy. at Rindge Ave. and Rt. 2/Cambridge

Waltham-Lexington Express	79-Arlington Hts.
62-Bedford	83-Central
67-Turkey Hill	84-Arlmont Village
76-Hanscom Field	350-Burlington

Davis ⬤
Tufts U.

1 College Ave. and 1 Holland St./Somerville

87-Arlington Ctr.-Lechmere, via Somerville Ave.	90-Wellington, via Sullivan
88-Clarendon Hill-Lechmere, via Highland Ave.	94-Medford Sq., via W. Medford
	96-Medford Sq.-Harvard, via George St.

Porter ⬤

1900 Massachusetts Ave. at 830 Somerville Ave./Cambridge

Commuter Rail—Fitchburg Line	83-Rindge Ave.-Central
77-Arlington Hts.-Harvard	96-Medford Sq.-Harvard
77A-N. Cambridge-Harvard	

Harvard ⬤

1400 Massachusetts Ave. at 1 Brattle St./Cambridge

1-Dudley, via Mass. Ave.	74-Belmont Ctr.
66-Dudley, via Brookline	77-Arlington Hts.
69-Lechmere	77A-N. Cambridge
71-Watertown	78-Arlmont
72-Huron Ave.	86-Sullivan-Cleveland Circle
73-Waverley	96-Medford Sq.

Central ⬤

650 Massachusetts Ave. at 1 Prospect St./Cambridge

Metrobus to Longwood Ave.	70-Cedarwood (Waltham)
1-Harvard-Dudley	70A-N. Waltham
47-Albany St.	83-Rindge Ave.
64-Oak Sq.	91-Sullivan
64-Kendall (rush hours)	

Kendall ⬤
MIT

330 Main St. at Carleton St. and 3 Cambridge Ctr./Cambridge

64-Oak Sq. (rush hours)	85-Spring Hill

Charles/MGH ⬤

Charles Circle, 350 Cambridge St. at 160 Charles St./Boston

Park St. ⬤

120 Tremont St. at 1 Park St./Boston

Green Line	43-Ruggles
Orange Line via walkway to Downtown	55-Queensberry St. (Mon.-Fri.)

Downtown Crossing ⬤
Washington

450 Washington St. at 1 Summer St./Boston

Orange Line	93-Sullivan, via Bunker Hill St.
Green Line via walkway to Park St.	300-Riverside (express)
7-City Pt., via Summer St.	301-Brighton Ctr. (express)
11-City Pt., via Bayview	304-Watertown (express)
49-Dudley	304A-Newton Corner (express)
53-Roberts, via Waltham & Newton Corner	305-Waltham (express)
54-Waverley, via Waltham & Newton Corner	Special rush hour service:
92-Assembly Sq., via Main St.	56-Waltham Highlands or Cedarwood
	58-Auburndale

South Station ⬤

Dewey Sq., 200 Summer St. at 600 Atlantic Ave./Boston

Commuter Rail	Logan Link
Amtrak	6-Marine Ind. Pk.-Haymarket
Peter Pan Terminal*	7-City Pt., via Summer St.
South Sta. commuter buses*	

Broadway ⬤

100 Dorchester Ave. at 1 W. Broadway/South Boston

3-Chinatown-Marine Ind. Pk.	11-City Pt.-Downtown, via Bayview
9-City Pt.-Copley	18-Broadway

To Ashmont or Braintree

See "Boston Terminals" map for complete list of carriers.

RAPID TRANSIT STATIONS

STREET ADDRESS & CONNECTING SERVICES

To Alewife via Park St.

Andrew

580 Dorchester Ave. at 500 Southampton St./South Boston
5-City Pt.-McCormack Hsg.   16-Forest Hills-JFK/UMass
10-City Pt.-Copley

JFK/UMass
Columbia

900 Columbia Rd. at 1 Morrissey Blvd./Dorchester
Red Line to Braintree   16-Forest Hills
UMass buses   16-U Mass (rush hours)
Kennedy Library bus   17-Fields Corner
8-Harbor Pt.-Kenmore

Savin Hill

100 Savin Hill Ave. at Sidney St./Dorchester
18-Ashmont-Broadway

Fields Corner

1470 Dorchester Ave. at Charles St./Dorchester
15-Ruggles, via Kane Sq.   18-Ashmont-Broadway
  (nights & Sun.)   19-Ruggles, via Grove Hall
17-JFK/UMass, via Uphams   20-Neponset & Adams Sts.
  Corner   210F-Quincy Ctr.

Shawmut

Dayton St. at Clementine Pk., north of Centre St./Dorchester

Ashmont

1900 Dorchester Ave. at 200 Ashmont St./Dorchester
BAT Buses 12 & 12X to   24-Wakefield Ave. (nights)
  Brockton   26-Norfolk St.
18-Broadway   27-Mattapan, via River St.
21-Forest Hills   215-Quincy Ctr, via E. Milton
22-Ruggles, via Talbot Ave. & 217-Wollaston Beach
  Jackson Sq.   240-Avon Line
23-Ruggles, via Washington 240A-Crawford Sq.
  St. & Dudley Sq.   240/238-Quincy Ctr., via
    South Shore Plaza

Ashmont

[Free transfer from Ashmont train to Mattapan trolley]

Cedar Grove

Hillsdale St., off 950 Adams St./Dorchester

Butler St.

Butler St., off 1120 Adams St./Dorchester

Milton

1 Adams St. at 1 Eliot St./Milton
217-Wollaston Beach-Ashmont 240A-Crawford Sq.-Ashmont
240-Avon Line-Ashmont   240/238-Quincy Ctr., via
    South Shore Plaza

Central Ave.

Central Ave. at Eliot St./Milton

Valley Rd.

Valley Rd. at 320 Eliot St./Milton

Capen St.

Capen St., off Eliot St./Milton

Mattapan

500 River St. at 1670 Blue Hill Ave./Mattapan
Hudson Bus to Canton   30-Roslindale
24-Wakefield Ave.   31-Forest Hills
27-Ashmont, via River St. 33-Dedham Line (River &
28-Ruggles, via Dudley Sq.   Milton Sts.)
29A-Franklin Field Hsg.   245-Quincy Ctr., via E. Milton

⬭ Rapid Transit
⬤ Surface Streetcar

Red Line

RAPID TRANSIT STATIONS	STREET ADDRESS & CONNECTING SERVICES

To Alewife via Park St.

Andrew

580 Dorchester Ave. at 500 Southampton St./South Boston
5-City Pt.-McCormack Hsg.　　16-Forest Hills-JFK/UMass
10-City Pt.-Copley

JFK/UMass
Columbia

900 Columbia Rd. at 1 Morrissey Blvd./Dorchester
Red Line to Braintree　　　16-Forest Hills
UMass buses　　　　　　16-UMass (rush hours)
Kennedy Library bus　　　17-Fields Corner
8-Harbor Pt.-Kenmore

North Quincy

Newport Ave. at 70 W. Squantum St./Quincy
210-Quincy Ctr., via Hancock St.　211-Quincy Ctr.-Squantum
210F-Quincy Ctr.-Fields Corner　212-Quincy Ctr., via Billings Rd.

Wollaston

300 Newport Ave. at 90 Beale St./Quincy
211-Quincy Ctr.-Squantum　　217-Wollaston Beach-
　　　　　　　　　　　　　　Ashmont

◄— FARE ZONE beyond this point:
Inbound—pay 2 tokens when boarding.
Combo pass required.
Outbound—no fare.

Quincy Center

1300 Hancock St. at Washington St./Quincy
210-N. Quincy., via Hancock St.　221-Fort Point
210F-Fields Corner　　　　　222-E. Weymouth
211-Squantum　　　　　　　225-Weymouth Landing
212-N. Quincy, via Billings Rd.　230-Brockton Line
214-Germantown　　　　　　236-South Shore Plaza, via
215-Ashmont, via E. Milton　　　E. Braintree
216-Hough's Neck　　　　　238-Crawford Sq.
220-Hingham　　　　　　　238/240-Ashmont, via
220A-Hingham Loop　　　　　Randolph
　　　　　　　　　　　　245-Mattapan, via E. Milton

◄— FARE ZONE beyond this point:
Inbound—pay 2 tokens when boarding.
Combo Plus pass required.
Outbound—pay 1 additional token when exiting.

Quincy Adams

Burgin Pkwy. and 200 Independence Ave./Quincy
238-Quincy Ctr.-Crawford Sq.　238/240-Ashmont, via
(Mon.-Sat.)　　　　　　　　Randolph (Mon.-Sat.)

Braintree

Union St. at Ivory St., west of Rt. 3/Braintree
230-Quincy Ctr.-Brockton Line　Plymouth & Brockton to
236-South Shore Plaza-Quincy　Marshfield, via Hanover
Ctr.　　　　　　　　　　　Mall

Lechmere – Kenmore

Green Line

RAPID TRANSIT STATIONS	STREET ADDRESS & CONNECTING SERVICES

Lechmere ○

1 Cambridge St. at O'Brien Hwy./Cambridge
Exact change required after
  8:50 pm daily.
69-Harvard
80-Arlington Ctr., via Medford
  Hillside

87-Arlington Ctr., via
  Somerville Ave.
88-Clarendon Hill, via
  Highland Ave.
Shuttle bus to
  CambridgeSide Galleria

Science Park ○

Leverett Circle, Charles St. at Nashua St./Boston
Exact change required at all times.

North Station ○

135 Causeway St. at Canal St./Boston
Commuter Rail   Orange Line

Haymarket ○

Congress St. at New Sudbury St./Boston
Orange Line
Commuter buses*
6-Marine Ind. Pk., via South
  Sta.
92-Assembly Sq.-Downtown,
  via Main St.
93-Sullivan-Downtown, via
  Bunker Hill St.
111-Woodlawn (Chelsea)
325-Elm St., Medford (express)
326-W. Medford (express)
352-Burlington (express)
353-Burlington Ind. Area
354-Woburn (express)

426-Lynn, via Cliftondale
441-Marblehead, via Paradise
  Rd.
442-Marblehead, via
  Humphrey St.
450-Salem, via Highland Ave.
455-Salem, via Loring Ave.
Special rush hour service:
426-Granada Highlands or
  Oaklandvale
436-Happy Valley
439-Nahant
458/468-Salem-Danvers

Government Center ○
Scollay Sq.

1 Cambridge St. at Court and Tremont Sts./Boston
Blue Line

Park St. ○

120 Tremont St. at 1 Park St./Boston
Red Line
Orange Line via walkway to
  Downtown Crossing

43-Ruggles
55-Queensberry St. (Mon.-
  Fri.)

Boylston ○
Theatre District

186 Tremont St. at 80 Boylston St./Boston
Park Plaza commuter buses*   43-Ruggles

Arlington ○
Park Plaza

300 Boylston St. at 20 Arlington St./Boston
Greyhound Terminal*
Park Plaza commuter buses*

9-City Pt.-Copley, via
  Broadway

Copley ○

640 Boylston St. at 230 Dartmouth St./Boston
[No free transfer between inbound and outbound at Copley;
  use Arlington instead.]
Commuter buses*
Back Bay Sta., 2 blocks
  (Commuter Rail and Amtrak)
9-City Pt., via Broadway
10-City Pt., via Andrew
39-Forest Hills (free transfer)

55-Queensberry St.-Park St.
300-Riverside (nights)
302-Watertown (express)
304-Watertown (express)
  (middays & Sat.)
352-Burlington (express)
  (some trips)

To E-Brigham Circle or Arborway

Hynes Convention Ctr./ ○
ICA

100 Massachusetts Ave. at 360 Newbury St./Boston
1-Harvard-Dudley   55-Queensberry St.-Park St.

Kenmore ○

500 Commonwealth Ave. at 1 Brookline Ave./Boston
8-Harbor Pt.
57-Watertown
60-Chestnut Hill

65-Brighton Ctr., via Brookline
  Village

To B-Boston College, C-Cleveland
Circle, D-Riverside

*See "Boston Terminals" map
for complete list of carriers.

125

RAPID TRANSIT STATIONS **STREET ADDRESS & CONNECTING SERVICES**

To North Station via Park St.

Kenmore

500 Commonwealth Ave. at 1 Brookline Ave./Boston
Green Line-B (Boston College)   60-Chestnut Hill
Green Line-D (Riverside)   65-Brighton Ctr., via
8-Harbor Pt.   Brookline Village
57-Watertown

◀— FARE ZONE beyond this point:
Inbound—pay 85¢, exact change, when boarding.
Local Bus or Subway pass accepted.
Outbound—no fare.

St. Mary's St.   47-Central-Albany St., 1 block

Hawes St.

Kent St./Powell St.

St. Paul St.

Coolidge Corner
Harvard St.   66-Harvard-Dudley

Summit Ave.

Brandon Hall

Fairbanks St.

Washington Sq.
Washington St.   65-Brighton Ctr.-Kenmore, via Brookline Village

Tappan St./Williston Rd.

Dean Rd./Corey Rd.

Englewood Ave.   Beacon St.

Cleveland Circle
Green Line-B (Boston College)   51-Forest Hills, 1 block
at Chestnut Hill Ave., 2   86-Sullivan, via Harvard
blocks N.   Boston College bus
Green Line-D (Riverside) at   Newbury College bus
Reservoir, 1 block S.

◐ Rapid Transit
● Surface Streetcar

Green Line-B

Kenmore – Boston College

RAPID TRANSIT STATIONS

STREET ADDRESS & CONNECTING SERVICES

To Government Center via Park St.

Kenmore ○ — **500 Commonwealth Ave. at 1 Brookline Ave./Boston**
Green Line-C (Cleveland Circle) 60-Chestnut Hill
Green Line-D (Riverside) 65-Brighton Ctr., via
8-Harbor Pt. Brookline Village
57-Watertown

← FARE ZONE beyond this point:
Inbound—pay 85¢, exact change, when boarding.
Local Bus or Subway pass accepted.
Outbound—no fare.

Blandford St. ●

Boston Univ. East ●
Cummington St.

Boston Univ. Central ● 47-Central-Albany St.
St. Mary's St./B.U. Bridge

Boston Univ. West ●
Amory St.

St. Paul St. ●

Pleasant St. ●

Babcock St. ●

Packard's Corner ● 57-Watertown-Kenmore
Brighton Ave.

Fordham Rd. ●

Harvard Ave. ● 66-Harvard-Dudley

Long Ave. ●

Allston St. ●

Warren St./Kelton St. ●

Summit Ave. ●

Washington St. ● 65-Brighton Ctr.-Kenmore, via Brookline Village

Mt. Hood Rd. ●

Colborne Rd./ ●
Sutherland Rd.

Chiswick Rd. ●

Chestnut Hill Ave. ● Green Line-C at Cleveland 51-Forest Hills, 2 blocks
Circle, 2 blocks 86-Sullivan, via Harvard
Green Line-D (Riverside) at Boston College bus
Reservoir, 2 blocks

South St. ●

Greycliff Rd. ●

Boston College ●
Lake St.

Commonwealth Ave.

○ Rapid Transit
● Surface Streetcar

Green Line-D

Kenmore – Riverside

RAPID TRANSIT STATIONS   **STREET ADDRESS & CONNECTING SERVICES**

To Government Center via Park St.

Kenmore
500 Commonwealth Ave. at 1 Brookline Ave./Boston
Green Line-B (Boston College)   60-Chestnut Hill
Green Line-C (Cleveland Circle) 65-Brighton Ctr., via
8-Harbor Pt.   Brookline Village
57-Watertown

◄— FARE ZONE beyond this point:
Inbound—pay $1.00, exact change, when boarding.
Local Bus or Subway pass accepted.

Fenway
400 Park Dr., west of Riverway/Boston
47-Central-Albany St.

Longwood
Chapel St., north of 200 Longwood Ave./Brookline

Brookline Village
Station St. and Pearl St./Brookline
Green Line-E (Heath St.) at S.   65-Brighton Ctr.-Kenmore
Huntington Ave., 3 blocks   66-Harvard-Dudley
39-Forest Hills-Back Bay Sta.,   Peter Pan to Worcester,
3 blocks   Rt. 9 local
60-Chestnut Hill-Kenmore

Brookline Hills
Tappan St., west of 100 Cypress St./Brookline

Beaconsfield
100 Beaconsfield Rd. at 30 Dean Rd./Brookline

Reservoir
400 Chestnut Hill Ave., south of 1960 Beacon St./Brookline
Green Line-B (Boston College)   86-Sullivan, via Harvard
at Chestnut Hill Ave., 2 blocks Boston College bus
Green Line-C (Cleveland Circle) Newbury College bus
51-Forest Hills

◄— FARE ZONE beyond this point:
Inbound—pay $2.00, exact change, when boarding.
Combo pass required.
Outbound—no fare.

Chestnut Hill
500 Hammond St., north of Rt. 9/Newton

Newton Centre
Union St., off 750 Beacon St. and Langley Rd./Newton
52-Dedham Mall-Watertown

Newton Highlands
1160 Walnut St. at Lincoln St./Newton
59-Needham Jct.-Watertown

Eliot
250 Lincoln St. and Meredith Ave./Newton

Waban
Wyman St., off 1620 Beacon St./Newton

Woodland
1960 Washington St. at Longfellow Rd./Newton

Riverside
390 Grove St., east of Rt. 128/Newton
Greyhound   Regis College bus
Peter Pan   300-Downtown (express)
Vermont Transit   353A-Burlington &
Hudson Airporter   Waltham Ind. Areas
Mass. Bay Comm. College bus

Rapid Transit
Surface Streetcar

RAPID TRANSIT STATIONS

STREET ADDRESS & CONNECTING SERVICES

To Lechmere via Park St.

Copley	[No free transfer between inbound and outbound at Copley; use Arlington instead.]
Prudential	*150 Huntington Ave. at W. Newton St./Boston*
Symphony	*240 Huntington Ave. at 300 Massachusetts Ave./Boston* 1-Harvard-Dudley

◄— FARE ZONE beyond this point:
Inbound—pay 85¢, exact change, when boarding.
Local Bus or Subway pass accepted.
Outbound—no fare.

Station	Address & Connecting Services
Northeastern	39-Forest Hills-Back Bay Sta.
Museum	8-Harbor Pt.-Kenmore 47-Central-Albany St..
Longwood Ave.	
Brigham Circle Tremont St./Francis St.	Mission Hill Link Bus 39-Forest Hills-Back Bay Sta. Peter Pan to Worcester, Rt. 9 66-Harvard-Dudley, via local Brookline
Fenwood Rd.	
Parker Hill Ave.	66-Harvard-Dudley, via Brookline
Huntington Ave./ **S. Huntington Ave.**	Green Line-D (Riverside) at 66-Harvard-Dudley, via Brookline Village, 3 blocks W. Brookline
Back of the Hill	
Heath St.	39-Forest Hills-Back Bay Sta. 46-Dudley
V.A. Hospital	◄— [Service south of Heath St. is temporarily provided by T-bus 39 (Forest Hills-Back Bay Sta.)]
Goddard House	
Bynner St.	
Perkins St.	
Boylston/Centre Sts.	41-Centre & Eliot Sts.-Dudley 48-Jamaica Plain Loop
Robinwood Ave.	
Lakeville Rd.	
Pond St.	
Burroughs St.	
The Monument Eliot St.	38-Wren St.-Forest Hills 48-Jamaica Plain Loop 41-Dudley
Custer St.	
McBride St.	
St. Rose St.	
St. Mark St.	
Forest Hills Arborway	

(vertical labels: Huntington Ave., S. Huntington Ave., Centre St., South St.)

○ Rapid Transit
● Surface Streetcar

Commuter Rail—Needham Line   35-Dedham Mall, via Stimson
Orange Line   36-Charles River
Franklin Park Zoo bus (weekends)   36A-V.A. Hospital
16-JFK/U. Mass.   37-Baker & Vermont Sts.
21-Ashmont   38-Wren St.
31-Mattapan   40-Georgetowne
32-Wolcott Sq., via Hyde Park Ave. 42-Ruggles
34-Dedham Line (Washington St.)   50-Cleary Sq., via Roslindale
34E-Walpole Ctr.   51-Cleveland Circle

MBTA Buses

	Trip Time	Mon.–Fri. frequency (min.)			Sat. Freq.	Sun. Freq.
		Rush	Midday	Night		

1 **Harvard—Dudley** 26-38 8/7 12 16 12 18-20
via Mass. Ave.—Cambridge: Mass. Ave., Central Sq., MIT; Harvard Bridge; *Back Bay:* Mass. Ave., Symphony Hall; South End: Boston City Hosp.; *Roxbury:* Melnea Cass Blvd., Washington St.
➤Red Line @ Harvard, Central; Green Line-(B,C,D) @ Hynes Convention Ctr./ICA; Green Line-E @ Symphony; Orange Line @ Mass. Ave. **Free transfer** (with 85¢ fare) between Dudley Sq. and Orange Line at Mass. Ave. station.

3 **Chinatown—Marine Ind. Pk.** 17-19 20/23 — — — —
*Boston:*Washington St., Kneeland St., Harrison Ave., Broadway; S. Boston: A St., Congress St., Fargo St., Northern Ave., Black Falcon Ave., Summer St.
➤Orange Line @ N. E. Med. Ctr., Red Line @ Broadway.

5 **City Point—McCormack Housing** 19-20 — 60 — 60 —
S. Boston: E. 4th St./E. Broadway, Perkins Sq., Dorchester St., Andrew Sq., Preble St., Old Colony Ave.
➤Red Line @ Andrew.

6 **Marine Ind. Pk.—Haymarket** 23-26 30 — — — —
S. Boston: Black Falcon Ave., Summer St., Congress St.; *Boston*: South Sta., Atlantic Ave., Commercial St., Hanover St. **Add'l service Marine Ind. Pk.—South Sta. every 15 min.**
➤Red Line @ South Sta.; Blue Line @ Aquarium; Green & Orange lines @ Haymarket.

7 **City Point—Franklin/D'shire Sts.** 17-26 12/14 25 40 25 —
S. Boston: E. 4th St./E. Broadway, L St., Summer St., Congress St.; *Boston*: South Sta., Federal St., Franklin St., Otis St., Summer St. **Nights: City Pt.—South Sta. only.**
➤Red Line @ South Sta.;

8 **Harbor Pt.—Kenmore** 29-45 20 45 45 45 45
Dorchester: UMass/Boston, Mt. Vernon St., Columbia Rd., Mass. Ave.; *South End:* Boston City Hosp., Harrison Ave.; *Roxbury:* Washington St., Dudley Sq., Melnea Cass Blvd.; *Fenway*: Ruggles St., Ave. Louis Pasteur, Longwood Ave., Longwood Med. Area, Brookline Ave.
Bus 8A—*Rush hours:* add'l service Dudley-Kenmore every 13/20 min.
➤Red Line @ JFK/UMass; Orange Line @ Ruggles; Green Line-E @ Ruggles St.; Green Line-(B,C,D) @ Kenmore

9 **City Point—Copley** 16-31 8/9 15 30 15-20 30
via Broadway—S. Boston: E. 4th St./E. Broadway, Perkins Sq., W. Broadway; *South End:* Herald St., Berkeley/Arlington Sts.; *Back Bay:* St. James Ave./Boylston St.
➤Red Line @ Broadway; Green Line @ Copley, Arlington.

10 **City Point—Copley** 26-44 25 35 60 40 —
via Andrew—S. Boston: E. 4th St./E. Broadway, Perkins Sq., Dorchester St., Andrew Sq., Southampton St.; *South End:* Newmarket Sq., Mass. Ave., Albany St., Boston City Hosp., E. Newton St., W. Dedham St.; *Back Bay:* Dartmouth St.
➤Red Line @ Andrew; Orange Line @ Back Bay Sta.; Green Line @ Copley.

11 **City Pt.—Downtown** 19-28 6/8 15 30 15 20
via Bayview—S. Boston: E. 8th St., W. 7th St., Dorchester Ave.; *Boston:* Herald St., Washington St., Chauncy St., Bedford St. **Nights: City Pt.—Kneeland & Washington Sts. only.**
➤Red Line @ Broadway; Orange Line @ N. E. Med. Ctr.; Orange Line @ Chinatown (except nights); Red & Orange lines @ Downtown (except nights).

14 **Roslindale—Dudley** 25-28 60 60 — — —
Roslindale: Cummins Hwy., Hyde Park Ave., Bradlees, American Legion Hwy.; *Dorchester:* Blue Hill Ave., Franklin Park, Grove Hall; *Roxbury:* Warren St.

15 **Kane Sq.—Ruggles** 21-35 7/9 13 30 16 60
Dorchester: Hancock St., Uphams Corner, Dudley St.; *Roxbury:* Dudley Sq., New Dudley St. **Nights & Sun.: Fields Corner—Ruggles—***Dorchester:* Geneva Ave., Bowdoin St., Kane Sq., then regular route.
➤Orange Line @ Ruggles; Red Line @ Fields Corner (nights & Sun. only).

Crosstown Bus Routes

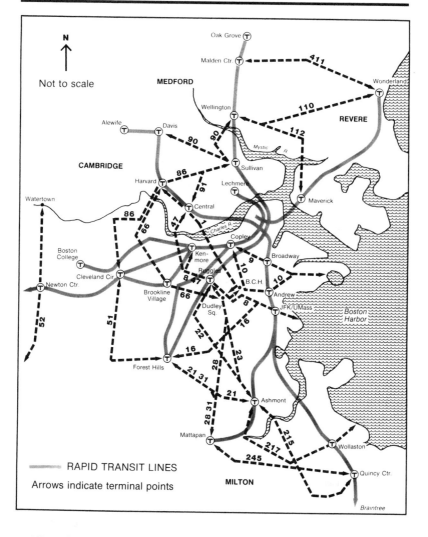

RAPID TRANSIT LINES

Arrows indicate terminal points

1-Harvard-Dudley
8-Harbor Pt.-Kenmore
9-City Pt.-Copley
10-City Pt.-Copley
16-Forest Hills-JFK/U.Mass.
21-Ashmont-Forest Hills
22-Ashmont-Ruggles
23-Ashmont-Ruggles

28-Mattapan-Ruggles
31-Mattapan-Forest Hills
47-Central-Albany St.
51-Cleveland Cir.-Forest Hills
52-Dedham Mall-Watertown
66-Harvard-Dudley
86-Sullivan-Cleveland Cir.
90-Davis-Wellington

91-Sullivan-Central
110-Wonderland-Wellington
112-Wellington-Maverick
215-Quincy Ctr.-Ashmont
217-Wollaston Beach-Ashmont
245-Quincy Ctr.-Mattapan
411-Revere House-Malden Ctr.

MBTA Buses	Trip Time	Mon.–Fri. frequency (min.)			Sat. Freq.	Sun. Freq.
		Rush	Midday	Night		

16 **Forest Hills—JFK/UMass**   17-23   15/18   25   40   25   40
Jamaica Plain: Morton St., J.W.V. Dr., Franklin Park; *Dorchester:* Columbia Rd., Uphams
Corner, Boston St., Andrew Sq., Preble St., Old Colony Ave.; **Rush hours: Forest Hills—
UMass.**—regular route, then Morrissey Blvd., University Rd.
➤Orange Line, Green Line [Bus 39] @ Forest Hills; Red Line @ JFK/UMass, Andrew.

17 **Fields Corner—JFK/UMass**   13-12   12   20   —   20   —
Dorchester: Geneva Ave., Bowdoin St., Kane Sq., Hancock St., Uphams Corner,
Columbia Rd. *Nights & Sun.:* Buses operate **Fields Corner-Ruggles** (see Bus 15).
➤Red Line @ Fields Corner, JFK/UMass.

18 **Ashmont—Broadway**   23-27   35   70   —   70   —
Dorchester: Dorchester Ave., Fields Corner; *S. Boston:* Andrew Sq.
➤Red Line @ Ashmont, Fields Corner, Savin Hill, Andrew, Broadway

19 **Fields Corner—Ruggles**   19-28   13/20   —   —   —   —
via Grove Hall—*Dorchester:* Geneva Ave., Grove Hall; *Roxbury:* Warren St., Dudley Sq.,
New Dudley St.
➤Red Line @ Fields Corner; Orange Line @ Ruggles.

20 **Fields Cor.—Neponset & Adams**   8-10   12/15   15   30   15   30-60
Dorchester: Adams St., Gallivan Blvd., Neponset Cir., Neponset Ave. (loop). **Middays &
weekends: also serves Hilltop St., Hallet Sq.**
➤Red Line @ Fields Corner.

21 **Ashmont—Forest Hills**   12-19   11   20   40   45   —
Dorchester: Gallivan Blvd.; *Mattapan, Jamaica Plain:* Morton St.
➤Red Line @ Ashmont; Orange Line, Green Line [Bus 39] @ Forest Hills.

22 **Ashmont—Ruggles**   20-31   6/7   13   20   11-16   15-25
via Jackson Sq.—*Dorchester:* Talbot Ave., Codman Sq., Blue Hill Ave., Franklin Park,
Seaver St.; *Roxbury:* Columbus Ave., Egleston Sq., Jackson Sq.
➤Red Line @ Ashmont; Orange Line @ Jackson Sq., Ruggles.

23 **Ashmont—Ruggles**   20-30   5/6   13   20   13-16   20-30
via Dudley Sq.—*Dorchester:* Talbot Ave., Codman Sq., Washington St., Grove Hall;
Roxbury: Warren St., Dudley Sq., New Dudley St.
➤Red Line @ Ashmont; Orange Line @ Ruggles.

24 **Wakefield Ave.—Mattapan**   11-22   20/25   50   60   50   60
Hyde Park: Metropolitan Ave., Highland St., Washington St., Truman Pkwy. (loop), Fairmount
Ave.*; *Mattapan:* River St. * *Nights: Through service Wakefield Ave.—Ashmont.*
➤Red Line @ Mattapan; Red Line @ Ashmont (nights only).

26 **Norfolk St.—Ashmont**   10-13   15   30   30   30   60
Dorchester: Washington St., Gallivan Blvd., Norfolk St. (loop); Codman Sq., Talbot Ave.
➤Red Line @ Ashmont.

27 **Mattapan—Ashmont**   11-12   30   30   30   30   60
Mattapan: River St., Mattapan Hosp.; *Dorchester:* Lower Mills, Dorchester Ave. **Nights:**
Through service on some trips **Wakefield Ave.—Ashmont** via Bus 24.
➤Red Line @ Mattapan, Ashmont.

28 **Mattapan—Ruggles**   23-41   8/12   13   20   11   17-30
via Dudley Sq.—*Mattapan:* Blue Hill Ave.; *Dorchester:* Franklin Park, Grove Hall;
Roxbury: Warren St., Dudley Sq., New Dudley St.
➤Red Line @ Mattapan; Orange Line @ Ruggles.

29 **Mattapan—Jackson Sq.**   17-29   8   —   —   —   —
via Jackson Sq.—*Dorchester:* Blue Hill Ave., Franklin Park, Seaver St.; *Roxbury:*
Columbus Ave. *Some midday trips serve Franklin Field Housing Project.*
➤Orange Line @ Jackson Sq.; Red Line @ Mattapan.

MBTA Buses

		Trip Time	Mon.–Fri. frequency (min.)			Sat. Freq.	Sun. Freq.
			Rush	Midday	Night		

30   **Mattapan—Roslindale**   9-15   20   30   60   40   60
Mattapan, Roslindale: Cummins Hwy.
➤Red Line @ Mattapan.

31   **Mattapan—Forest Hills**   10-19   8   12   20   10-15   20
Mattapan: Blue Hill Ave.; *Jamaica Plain*: Morton St.
➤Red Line @ Mattapan; Orange Line, Green Line [Bus 39] @ Forest Hills

32   **Wolcott Sq.—Forest Hills**   14-22   12/8   15   30   12   30
Readville: Hyde Park Ave.; *Hyde Park*: Cleary Sq.; *Roslindale, Jamaica Plain*: Hyde Park Ave. **AM rush: add'l service Cleary Sq.—Forest Hills every 6 min.**
➤Orange Line, Green Line [Bus 39] @ Forest Hills.

33   **Dedham Line—Mattapan**   21-27   60   60   —   60   —
Readville: River St.; *Hyde Park*: Turtle Pond Pkwy., Alwin St., River St., Cleary Sq.; *Mattapan*: River St.
➤Red Line @ Mattapan.

34   **Dedham Line—Forest Hills**   13-24   9/8   15   30   15   30
W. Roxbury: Washington St.; *Roslindale*: Roslindale Sq.
➤Orange Line, Green Line [Bus 39] @ Forest Hills.

34E   **Walpole Ctr.—Forest Hills**   44-59   20   45   60   45   60
Walpole: East St., High Plain Ave., E. Walpole; *Norwood, Westwood*: Washington St.; *Dedham*: Dedham Sq., Dedham Mall; *W. Roxbury*: Washington St.; *Roslindale*: Roslindale Sq. **Nights & Sun.: E. Walpole—Forest Hills only.** Zone fares, 60¢-$1.00.
➤Orange Line, Green Line [Bus 39] @ Forest Hills.

35   **Dedham Mall—Forest Hills**   20-31   20/12   30   2 trips   30   60
via Stimson St.—*Dedham*: Washington St.; *W. Roxbury*: Stimson St., Centre St.; *Roslindale*: Belgrade Ave., Roslindale Sq., Washington St. **AM rush: Stimson St.—Forest Hills only.**
➤Orange Line, Green Line [Bus 39] @ Forest Hills.

36   **Charles River—Forest Hills**   16-21   11/12   30   30   30   30
W. Roxbury: Spring St., Centre St.; *Roslindale*: Belgrade Ave., Roslindale Sq., Washington St.
➤Orange Line, Green Line [Bus 39] @ Forest Hills.

36A   **V.A. Hospital—Forest Hills**   18-25   22/30   30   —   30   60
W. Roxbury: Spring St., Centre St.; *Roslindale*: Belgrade Ave., Roslindale Sq., Washington St.
➤Orange Line, Green Line [Bus 39] @ Forest Hills.

37   **Baker & Vermont—Forest Hills**   15-23   20/13   30   —   30   60
W. Roxbury: Vermont St., Baker St., Lasell St., LaGrange St., Centre St.; *Roslindale*: Belgrade Ave., Roslindale Sq., Washington St.
➤Orange Line, Green Line [Bus 39] @ Forest Hills.

38   **Wren St.—Forest Hills**   12-19   22   40   2 trips   40   40
W. Roxbury: Park St., Anawan Ave.; *Roslindale*: Centre St.; *Jamaica Plain*: Faulkner Hosp., Arnold Arboretum, The Monument, South St.
➤Green Line [Bus 39] @ The Monument; Orange Line, Green Line [Bus 39] @ Forest Hills.

39   **Forest Hills—Back Bay Sta.**   24-38   3/4   7   6   7   7
Substitutes for Green Line-E (Arborway) streetcar.
Jamaica Plain: South St., The Monument, Centre St., V. A. Hospital, S. Huntington Ave., *Mission Hill, Fenway*: Huntington Ave.; *Back Bay*: Boylston St./St. James Ave.
➤Orange Line @ Forest Hills; Green Line-E @ Forest Hills @ Heath St., Brigham Cir., Northeastern; Green Line @ Copley; Orange Line @ Back Bay Sta. **Free transfer** (with 85¢ fare) at Copley and Back Bay Sta.

40   **Georgetowne—Forest Hills**   18-25   30   50   —   60   —
Hyde Park: Alwin St., Georgetowne Dr., W. Boundary Rd.; *W. Roxbury*: Washington St.; *Roslindale*: Roslindale Sq.

MBTA Buses

		Trip Time	**Mon.–Fri. frequency (min.)**			Sat. Freq.	Sun. Freq.
			Rush	Midday	Night		

41 **Centre & Eliot Sts.—Dudley**   10-17   18/20   34   30   35   —
Jamaica Plain: Centre St., Hyde Sq.; *Roxbury:* Jackson Sq., Centre St.
➤Green Line [Bus 39] @ Forest Hills; Orange Line @ Jackson Sq.

42 **Forest Hills—Ruggles**   18-24   20   20   50   18   50
Jamaica Plain: Washington St.; *Roxbury:* Egleston Sq., Dudley Sq., New Dudley St.
AM Rush: add'l service Forest Hills—Dudley every 10 min.
➤Orange Line, Green Line [Bus 39] @ Forest Hills; Orange Line @ Ruggles.

43 **Ruggles—Park St.**   13-21   8/10   15   20   15   20
South End: Tremont St.; *Boston:* Park Plaza, circles Boston Common.
➤Orange Line @ Ruggles, N. E. Med. Ctr.; Green Line @ Boylston; Red & Green lines @ Park St.

44 **Jackson Sq.—Ruggles**   17-27   8/9   16   30   16   45
via Humboldt Ave.—*Roxbury:* Columbus Ave., Egleston Sq.; *Dorchester:* Seaver St., Humboldt Ave.; *Roxbury:* Walnut St., Warren St., Dudley Sq., New Dudley St.
➤Orange Line @ Jackson Sq., Ruggles.

45 **Franklin Park Zoo—Ruggles**   15-25   7/8   16   30   16   45
via Grove Hall—*Dorchester:* Blue Hill Ave., Grove Hall; *Roxbury:* Dudley St., Dudley Sq., New Dudley St.
➤Orange Line @ Ruggles.

46 **Heath St.—Dudley**   10-13   30   30   —   30   —
Jamaica Plain: Heath St.; *Roxbury:* Jackson Sq., Centre St.
➤Green Line-E @ Heath St.; Orange Line @ Jackson Sq.

47 **Central—Albany St.**   24-40   20   20   30   20   35
Cambridge: Pearl/Brookline Sts.; *Fenway:* Park Dr., Brookline Ave., Longwood Med. Area, Longwood Ave., Ave. Louis Pasteur, Ruggles St.; *Roxbury:* Melnea Cass Blvd., Dudley Sq., Washington St.; *South End:* Boston City Hospital, University Hospital.
➤Red Line @ Central; Green Line-B @ B.U. Central; Green Line-C @ Mary's St. (1 block walk); Green Line-D @ Fenway; Green Line-E @ Museum; Orange Line @ Ruggles.

48 **Jamaica Plain Loop**   19   —   30   —   30   —
Jamaica Plain: Centre St., Paul Gore St., Chestnut Ave.; *Roxbury:* Jackson Sq., Egleston Sq.; *Jamaica Plain:* Washington St., Amory St., Lamartine St., Green
➤Green Line-E @ The Monument, Centre St.; Orange Line @ Jackson Sq., Stony Brook, Green.

49 **Dudley—Downtown**   15-25   6/8   11   13   9-12   11-15
Roxbury, South End: Washington St.; *Boston:* Chauncy St., Bedford St.
➤Orange Line @ N. E. Med. Ctr., Chinatown; Red & Orange Lines @ Downtown Crossing. Free inbound with transfer from Orange Line at N. E. Med. Ctr. and outbound at Surface Artery.

50 **Cleary Sq.—Forest Hills**   15-19   20   60   —   60   —
via Roslindale—*Hyde Park:* Gordon Ave., West St.; *Roslindale:* Metropolitan Ave., Roslindale Sq., Washington St.
➤Orange Line, Green Line [Bus 39] @ Forest Hills.

51 **Cleveland Cir.—Forest Hills**   25-33   20   60   60   60   —
Brookline: Chestnut Hill Ave., Lee St., Newton St., Grove St., Putterham Sq., Hancock Village; *W. Roxbury:* V.F.W. Pkwy., Weld St.; *Roslindale:* Walter St., Roslindale Sq., Washington St.
➤Green Line-C @ Cleveland Circle; Green Line-D @ Reservoir; Orange Line, Green Line [Bus 39] @ Forest Hills.

52 **Dedham Mall—Watertown**   37   30   45   —   45   —
Dedham: V.F.W. Pkwy.; *W. Roxbury:* Charles River Loop, Spring St., Baker St.; *Newton:* Oak Hill, Wiswall Rd., Dedham St., Parker St.*, Newton Centre, Centre St., Newton Corner; *Watertown:* Galen St. *Alternate trips *Newton:* Jewish Community Ctr., Winchester St., Centre St. *instead of* Parker St. **AM rush: Charles River Loop—Watertown only.**
➤Green Line-D @ Newton Centre

MBTA Buses

		Trip Time	Mon.–Fri. frequency (min.)			Sat. Freq.	Sun. Freq.
			Rush	Midday	Night		

53 **Roberts—Newton Corner**   28-31   30/60   60   —   60   —
Waltham: South St., Brandeis U., Waltham Hosp., Main St., Central Sq., Moody St.; *Newton:* River St., W. Newton, Washington St., Newtonville. *Through service* **Roberts—Downtown** via Bus 304.

54 **Waverley—Newton Corner**   35-36   30/60   60   —   60   —
Belmont: Lexington St.; *Watertown:* Belmont St.; *Waltham:* Beaver St., Bentley College, Lyman St., Central Sq., Moody St.; *Newton:* River St., W. Newton, Washington St., Newtonville. *Through service* **Waverley—Downtown** via Bus 304.

55 **Queensberry St.—Park St.**   14-27   17/30   60   30   30   30
Fenway: Ipswich St.; *Back Bay:* Boylston St., Copley Sq.; *Boston:* circles Boston Common. (Outbound trips: Stuart St., St. James Ave., Copley Sq., Newbury St.) Nights & weekends: **Queensberry St.—Copley only.**
➤Green Line @ Hynes Convention Ctr./ICA, Copley; Red & Green lines @ Park St.

56 **Waltham Hlnds.—Newton Corner** 27   30   60   —   60   —
Waltham: Bacon St., Dale St., Hammond St., Main St., Central Sq., Moody St., High St.; *Newton:* Crafts St., Nonantum, Walnut St., Newtonville, Washington St. **Rush hours:** alternate trips **Cedarwood—Newton Corner**—*Waltham:* Stow St., Main St., Central Sq., then regular route. **Rush hours:** through service **Waltham Highlands—Downtown** or **Cedarwood—Downtown** via Bus 304.

57 **Watertown—Kenmore**   21-32   6/8   9   15   9   15-30
Watertown: Galen St.; *Newton:* Newton Corner, Tremont St.; *Brighton:* Oak Sq., Washington St., Brighton Ctr., Cambridge St.; *Allston:* Union Sq., Brighton Ave., Commonwealth Ave.
➤Green Line-B @ Packard's Corner; Green Line-(B,C,D) @ Kenmore.

58 **Auburndale—Newton Corner**   27-28   30   —   —   —   —
Newton: Commonwealth Ave., Lexington St., Rumford Ave.; *Waltham:* Woerd Ave., Crescent St., Central Sq., River St.; *Watertown:* Pleasant St., Bemis; *Newton:* Chapel St., Nonantum, Adams St., Washington St. *Through service* on some trips **Auburndale—Downtown** via Bus 304.

59 **Needham Jct.—Watertown**   35-40   30   45   —   45   —
Needham: Chestnut St., Needham Ctr., Highland Ave., Needham Hts., Hillside Ave., Webster St., Central Ave.; *Newton:* Newton Upper Falls, Chestnut St., Oak St., Elliott St.*, Lincoln St.*, Newton Highlands, Walnut St., Newtonville, Nonantum, Watertown St. * **Mon.-Fri.:** some trips **via Needham St.—** *Newton:* Needham St. *instead of* Elliott & Lincoln Sts.
➤Green Line-D @ Newton Highlands.

60 **Chestnut Hill—Kenmore**   19-33   17/18   30   30-60   30-32   60
Brookline: Boylston St. (Rt.9), Cypress St., High St., Brookline Village; *Fenway:* Brookline Ave., Longwood Med. Area.
➤Green Line-D @ Brookline Village; Green Line-(B,C,D) @ Kenmore.

62 **Bedford—Alewife**   38-42   30   60   1 trip   60   —
Bedford: V.A. Hosp., Springs Rd., Bedford Ctr., South Rd., Loomis St., Great Rd.; *Lexington:* Bedford St., Lexington Ctr., Mass. Ave.; *Arlington:* Arlington Hts., Park Ave., Rt. 2. **Nights:** Bedford Ctr.-Alewife only. Zone fares, 60¢-$2.00.
➤Red Line @ Alewife.

64 **Oak Sq.—Central**   19-29   18   30   60   60   60
Brighton: Faneuil St., Hobart St., Brooks St., Birmingham Pkwy., N. Beacon St.; *Allston:* Union Sq., Cambridge St.; *Cambridge:* Magazine St./Western Ave. **Rush hours:** Oak Sq.—Kendall—regular route, then Cambridge: Central Sq., Main St.
➤Red Line @ Central; Red Line @ Kendall (rush hours only).

65 **Brighton Ctr.—Kenmore**   21-33   20/25   30   2 trips   32   —
via Brookline—*Brighton:* Washington St.; *Brookline:* Washington St., Brookline Village; *Fenway:* Brookline Ave., Longwood Med. Area.
➤Green Line-B @ Washington St.; Green Line-C @ Washington Sq.; Green Line-D @ Brookline Village; Green Line-(B,C,D) @ Kenmore.

MBTA Buses

		Trip Time	Mon.–Fri. frequency (min.)			Sat. Freq.	Sun. Freq.
			Rush	Midday	Night		

66   **Harvard—Dudley**   26-43   8/9   14   40   15   40
via Brookline—*Cambridge:* Kennedy St.; *Allston:* N. Harvard St., Cambridge St., Union Sq., Brighton Ave.; *Brookline:* Harvard St., Coolidge Corner, Brookline Village; *Mission Hill:* Huntington Ave., Brigham Cir., Tremont St.; *Roxbury:* Roxbury Crossing, New Dudley St.
➤Red Line @ Harvard; Green Line-B @ Harvard Ave.; Green Line-C @ Coolidge Corner; Green Line-D @ Brookline Village; Green Line-E @ S. Huntington Ave., Brigham Cir.; Orange Line @ Roxbury Crossing.

67   **Turkey Hill—Alewife**   15-20   25   45   —   —   —
Arlington: Washington St., Forest St., Summer St., Symmes Hosp., Mill St., Arlington Ctr., Pleasant St., Rt. 2.
➤Red Line @ Alewife.

69   **Harvard—Lechmere**   11-18   14/17   23   30   20   30
Cambridge: Cambridge St., Inman Sq., E. Cambridge.
➤Red Line @ Harvard; Green Line @ Lechmere.

70   **Cedarwood—Central**   32-53   14/15   30   60   40-60   30
Waltham: Stow St., Main St., Central Sq.; *Watertown:* Watertown Sq., Arsenal St.; *Brighton, Allston:* Western Ave.; *Cambridge:* River St./Western Ave. **Sat.:** *Add'l service* **Watertown Sq.—Central** every 10 min. (afternoon & early evenings only)
➤Red Line @ Central.

70A   **North Waltham—Central**   31-38   60   120   —   40-60   —
Waltham: Trapelo Rd., Smith St., Lincoln St., Lake St., Lexington St., Central Sq., Main St., then same route as Bus 70. *Rush hours:* some trips *Waltham:* Totten Pond Rd.
➤Red Line @ Central.

71   **Watertown—Harvard**   13-16   7/91230   12-15 50-60
Watertown, Cambridge: Mt. Auburn St., E. Watertown, Mt. Auburn Hosp.
➤Red Line @ Harvard.

72   **Huron Ave.—Harvard**   9-10   15   30   30   30   30
Cambridge: Aberdeen Ave., Huron Ave., Concord Ave.
➤Red Line @ Harvard.

73   **Waverley—Harvard**   14-22   5   1230 12-15 50-60
Belmont: Trapelo Rd., Cushing Sq.; *Watertown:* Belmont St.; *Cambridge:* Mt. Auburn St., Mt. Auburn Hosp.
➤Red Line @ Harvard.

74   **Belmont Ctr.—Harvard**   13-22   14/15   30   40   30   40
via Concord Ave.—*Belmont:* Leonard St., Concord Ave., Bright Rd.; *Cambridge:* Blanchard Rd.*, Sancta Maria Hosp.*, Concord Ave.*, Fresh Pond*. ***Mon.-Fri.: some trips via Huron Towers**—*Belmont:* Leonard St., Concord Ave., Bright Rd.; *Cambridge:* Grove St., Huron Ave., Fresh Pond Pkwy., Concord Ave.
➤Red Line @ Harvard.

76   **Hanscom Field—Alewife**   36-41   30   60   60   60   —
Lexington: Wood St., Mass. Ave., Marrett Rd., Five Forks, Waltham St., Worthen Rd., Lexington Ctr., Mass. Ave., Pleasant St.; *Arlington:* Rt. 2. **Nights:** Five Forks—Alewife only. **Zone fares**, 60¢-$1.00.
➤Red Line @ Alewife.

77   **Arlington Hts.—Harvard**   22-35   8   11   10-12   8   15-20
Arlington: Mass. Ave., Arlington Ctr.; *Cambridge:* Mass. Ave., N. Cambridge, Porter Sq. *Rush hours:* no local stops N. Cambridge—Harvard; see Bus 77A.
➤Red Line @ Porter, Harvard.

77A   **North Cambridge—Harvard**   8-13   7/9   12   —   —   —
Cambridge: Mass. Ave., Porter Sq. **Nights & weekends:** see Bus 77.
➤Red Line @ Porter @ Harvard.

MBTA Buses

| | | Trip Time | **Mon.–Fri. fre**. Rush | Midda. | | | | |

78 Arlmont—Harvard 15-30 14/15 30
Arlington: Appleton St., Wachusett Ave., Park Cir., Rt. 2; *Belmont:* Brig
Cambridge: Blanchard Rd., Sancta Maria Hosp., Concord Ave., Fresh Pt
➤Red Line @ Harvard.

79 Arlington Hts.—Alewife 16-24 8/9 25 45, — —
Arlington: Mass. Ave., Arlington Ctr.; *Cambridge:* Alewife Brook Pkwy.
➤Red Line @ Alewife.

80 Arlington Ctr.—Lechmere 19-34 15 35 60 35 60
via Medford Hillside—*Arlington:* Medford St.; *Medford:* High St., W. Medford, Boston
Ave., Medford Hillside, Tufts U.; *Somerville:* College Ave., Powderhouse Sq., Broadway,
Ball Sq., Magoun Sq., Medford St., McGrath Hwy.
➤Green Line @ Lechmere.

83 Rindge Ave.—Central 16-27 10/15 30 60 25 40-60
Cambridge: Rindge Ave., Mass Ave., Porter Sq.; *Somerville:* Somerville Ave., Park St.,
Beacon St.; *Cambridge:* Inman Sq., Prospect St.
➤Red Line @ Alewife, Porter, Central.

84 Arlington—Alewife 20 30 — — — —
Arlington: Appleton St., Wachusett Ave., Park Ave., Rt. 2 [New Service].
➤Red Line @ Alewife.

85 Spring Hill—Kendall 10-14 30/40 40 — — —
Somerville: Summer St., Union Sq., Webster Ave.; *Cambridge:* Windsor/Columbia Sts.,
Hampshire St., Tech Sq.
➤Red Line @ Kendall.

86 Sullivan—Cleveland Cir. 24-37 20/18 35 35-60 40 70
Somerville: Washington St., Union Sq.; *Cambridge:* Kirkland St., Harvard Sq., Kennedy St.;
Allston: N. Harvard St., Western Ave.; *Brighton:* Market St., Brighton Ctr., Chestnut Hill Ave.
➤Orange Line @ Sullivan; Red Line @ Harvard; Green Line-B @ Chestnut Hill Ave.;
Green Line-C @ Cleveland Cir.; Green Line-D @ Reservoir.

87 Arlington Ctr.—Lechmere 22-28 16/15 25 30 24 30
via Somerville Ave.—*Arlington:* Broadway; *Somerville:* Clarendon Hill, Broadway, Teele
Sq., Holland St., Davis Sq., Elm St., Somerville Ave., Union Sq., McGrath Hwy. **Nights &
weekends: Clarendon Hill—Lechmere only.**
➤Red Line @ Davis, Porter (1 block walk); Green Line @ Lechmere.

88 Clarendon Hill—Lechmere 17-22 8/12 25 30 24 30
via Highland Ave.—*Somerville:* Broadway, Teele Sq., Holland St., Davis Sq., Highland
Ave., Somerville Hosp., City Hall, McGrath Hwy.
➤Red Line @ Davis; Green Line @ Lechmere.

89 Clarendon Hill—Sullivan 14-24 9 30 60 30 60
Somerville: Broadway, Teele Sq., Powderhouse Sq., Ball Sq., Magoun Sq., Winter Hill, E.
Somerville.
➤Orange Line @ Sullivan.

90 Davis—Wellington 26-28 30/35 70 60 60 —
Somerville: Highland Ave., Somerville Hosp., City Hall, Cross St., Broadway;
Charlestown: Sullivan Sq.; *Somerville:* Middlesex Ave., Assembly Sq.; *Medford:* Fellsway.
➤Red Line @ Davis; Orange Line @ Sullivan, Wellington.

91 Sullivan—Central 12-20 25 25 60 20 40
Somerville: Washington St., Union Sq., Newton St., Springfield St.; *Cambridge:* Inman
Sq., Prospect St.
➤Orange Line @ Sullivan; Red Line @ Central.

A Buses

		Trip Time	Mon.–Fri. frequency (min.)			Sat. Freq.	Sun. Freq.
			Rush	Midday	Night		

92 **Assembly Sq.-Downtown** — Trip Time 18-24 — Rush 10/13 — Midday 30 — Night 60 — Sat. 30 — Sun. —
via Main St.—*Somerville:* Middlesex Ave.; Charlestown: Sullivan Sq., Main St., Thompson Sq., City Sq.; *Boston:* N. Washington St., Haymarket, Congress St., Franklin St., Washington St. **Rush hours: Sullivan—Downtown only. Nights: Sullivan—Haymarket only.**
➤Orange Line @ Sullivan; Green & Orange lines @ Haymarket; Blue & Orange lines @ State (except nights); Red & Orange lines @ Downtown (except nights).

93 **Sullivan—Downtown** — 14-24 — 6/7 — 20 — 30-60 — 20 — 40
via Bunker Hill St.—*Charlestown:* Bunker Hill St., Charlestown Navy Yard, Chelsea St., City Sq.; *Boston:* N. Washington St., Haymarket, Congress St., Franklin St., Washington St. Nights: **Sullivan—Haymarket** only.
➤Orange Line @ Sullivan; Green & Orange lines @ Haymarket; Blue & Orange lines @ State (except nights); Red & Orange lines @ Downtown (except nights).

94 **Medford Sq.—Davis** — 13-22 — 22/20 — 40 — 40 — 22 — 40
via W. Medford—*Medford:* High St., W. Medford, Boston Ave., Medford Hillside, Tufts U.; *Somerville:* College Ave., Powderhouse Sq.
➤Red Line @ Davis.

95 **West Medford—Sullivan** — 18-30 — 15 — 30 — 60 — 30 — 60
Medford: Playstead Rd., High St., Medford Sq., Mystic Ave.; *Somerville:* Assembly Sq.
➤Orange Line @ Sullivan.

96 **Medford Sq.—Harvard** — 17-30 — 20 — 40 — 20-60 — 30 — 60
Medford: Main St., George St., Winthrop St., Medford Hillside, Boston Ave., Tufts U.; *Somerville:* College Ave., Powderhouse Sq., Davis Sq., Elm St.; *Cambridge:* Beech St., Porter Sq., Mass. Ave.
➤Red Line @ Davis, Porter, Harvard.

97 **Malden Ctr.—Wellington** — 16-18 — 30 — 60 — — — 50 — —
via Hancock St.—*Malden:* Commercial St., Medford St., Main St.; *Everett:* Belmont St., Hancock St., Everett Sq., Broadway.
➤Orange Line @ Malden Ctr., Wellington.

99 **Upper Highland—Wellington** — 22-28 — 20 — 30 — 60 — 30 — 60
Medford: Highland Ave.; *Malden:* Malden Hosp., Clifton St., Summer St., Malden Ctr., Malden Sq.; *Everett:* Main St. **AM rush: add'l service Upper Highland—Malden Ctr.**
➤Orange Line @ Malden Ctr., Wellington.

100 **Elm St.—Wellington** — 10-21 — 20 — 20 — 60 — 30 — 60
Medford: Fellsway West, Fellsway.
➤Orange Line @ Wellington.

101 **Malden Ctr.—Sullivan** — 21-38 — 12 — 30 — 60 — 30 — 60
via Medford Sq.—*Malden:* Malden Sq., Pleasant St.; *Medford:* Salem St., Medford Sq., Main St.; *Somerville:* Broadway, Winter Hill, E. Somerville. **AM rush: add'l service Medford Sq.-Sullivan every 6 min.**
➤Orange Line @ Malden Ctr., Sullivan.

104 **Malden Ctr.—Sullivan** — 17-30 — 12/15 — 30 — 60 — 30 — 60
via Ferry St.—*Malden:* Malden Sq., Ferry St.; *Everett:* Glendale Sq., Broadway, Everett Sq.
➤Orange Line @ Malden Ctr., Sullivan.

105 **Malden Ctr.—Sullivan** — 25-31 — 30 — 60 — — — 65 — 60
via Faulkner—*Malden:* Malden Sq., Eastern Ave., Bowdoin St., Newland St., Bryant St., Cross St.; *Everett:* Main St., Broadway.
➤Orange Line @ Malden Ctr., Sullivan.

106 **Lebanon St.—Wellington** — 21-30 — 20 — 30 — 60 — 30 — 60
Malden: Lebanon St., Maplewood Sq., Salem St., Malden Sq., Malden Ctr.; *Everett:* Main St. **AM rush: add'l service Lebanon St.—Malden Ctr.**
➤Orange Line @ Malden Ctr., Wellington.

MBTA Buses

		Trip Time	Mon.–Fri. frequency (min.)			Sat. Freq.	Sun. Freq.
			Rush	Midday	Night		

108 **Linden Sq.—Wellington** 23-30 25/20 30 60 30 60
Malden: Lynn St., Beach St., Salem St., Maplewood Sq., Malden Sq., Malden Ctr., Pleasant St., Highland Ave.; *Medford:* Middlesex Ave. **AM rush: add'l service Linden Sq.—Malden Ctr.**
➤Orange Line @ Malden Ctr., Wellington.

109 **Linden Sq.—Sullivan** 16-27 12/15 30 60 30 60
Malden: Eastern Ave.; *Everett:* Broadway, Glendale Sq., Everett Sq.
➤Orange Line @ Sullivan.

110 **Wonderland—Wellington** 21-30 20 30 60 306 0
Revere: Beach St., Revere Ctr., Park Ave.; *Everett:* Woodlawn, Elm St., Ferry St., Chelsea St., Everett Sq., Broadway. **Rush hours: add'l service Revere Ctr.—Wellington** every 10 min. **Nights: Woodlawn—Wellington** *only.*
➤Blue Line @ Wonderland (except nights), Revere Beach (except nights); Orange Line @ Wellington.

111 **Woodlawn—Haymarket** 19-31 5/6 15 15-20 15-20 25
Chelsea: Washington Ave., Prattville, Bellingham Sq., Chelsea Sq.; Tobin Bridge; *Charlestown:* City Sq.; *Boston:* N. Washington St.
➤Green & Orange lines @ Haymarket.

112 **Wellington—Maverick** 33-42 30 30 — 35-50 50
Everett: Broadway, Everett Sq., Chelsea St.; *Chelsea:* Everett Ave., Mystic Mall, Spruce St., Admiral's Hill, Bellingham Sq., Chelsea Sq.; *E. Boston:* Meridian St.
➤Orange Line @ Wellington; Blue Line @ Maverick.

116 **Wonderland—Maverick** 24-28 15 30 60 30 60
via Revere St.—*Revere:* Revere St., Broadway, Revere Ctr.; *Chelsea:* Bellingham Sq., Chelsea Sq.; *E. Boston:* Meridian St.
➤Blue Line @ Wonderland, Maverick.

117 **Wonderland—Maverick** 22-26 15 30 60 30 60
via Beach St.—*Revere:* Beach St., Revere Ctr., Broadway; *Chelsea:* Bellingham Sq., Chelsea Sq.; *E. Boston:* Meridian St.
➤Blue Line @ Wonderland, Revere Beach, Maverick.

119 **Northgate—Beachmont** 20-27 30 60 40 60 60
Revere: Squire Rd.; *Malden:* Linden Sq.; *Revere:* Malden St., Cooledge St., Broadway, Revere Ctr., Winthrop Ave., Crescent Ave., Endicott Ave. **Nights: Revere Ctr.— Beachmont only.**
➤Blue Line @ Beachmont.

120 **Orient Hts.—Maverick** 29-31 14/15 20 60 30 50
E. Boston: Boardman St., Waldemar Ave., Orient Ave., Orient Hts., Bennington St., Meridian St., Maverick Sq., Sumner St., Jeffries Pt., Maverick St.
➤Blue Line @ Orient Hts., Wood Island, Maverick.

121 **Wood Island—Maverick** 11-12 30/25 — — — —
E. Boston: Chelsea St., Eagle Sq., Lexington St., Meridian St. **PM rush: Eagle Sq.— Maverick only.**
➤Blue Line @ Wood Island (AM Rush only), Maverick.

130 **Lebanon St./Melrose—Malden Ctr.** 14 30 60 — 60 —
Melrose: Linwood Ave., Lebanon St., Forestdale; *Malden:* Sylvan St., Forest St., Main St., Malden Sq.
➤Orange Line @ Malden Ctr.

130A **Wyoming Sq.—Malden Ctr.** 13 30 60 — 60 —
Melrose: Lynde Ave., Wyoming Ave., Pleasant St., Washington St.; *Malden:* Summer St.
➤Orange Line @ Oak Grove, Malden Ctr.

MBTA Buses

		Trip Time	Mon.–Fri. frequency (min.)			Sat. Freq.	Sun. Freq.
			Rush	Midday	Night		

131   **Melrose Highlands—Malden Ctr.** 27-28   30   60   —   —   —
Melrose: Franklin St., East Side, Porter St., Waverly Ave., Grove St., Main St.; *Malden:*
Main St., Malden Sq.
➤Orange Line @ Oak Grove, Malden Ctr.

134   **North Woburn—Wellington**   42-48   60   60   —   60   —
Woburn: Main St., Elm St., Main St., Woburn Sq.; *Winchester:* Main St., Winchester Ctr.;
Medford: Winthrop St., High St., Medford Sq., Riverside Ave. *M-Sat*: add'l service:
Playstead Rd. & Winthrop St.-Wellington. Zone fares, 60¢-$1.00.
➤Orange Line @ Wellington.

134A   **Medford—Wellington**   15-22   20   30   40   30   60
Medford: Winthrop St., High St., Medford Sq., Riverside Ave. ***Nights & Sun.:* Medford
Sq.—Wellington only**.
➤Orange Line @ Wellington.

136   **Reading—Malden Ctr.**   32-40   30   60   —   60   —
via Lakeside—*Reading:* Reading Depot, Reading Sq., Salem St.; *Wakefield:* Main St.,
Wakefield Sq.; *Melrose:* Main St., Melrose Ctr.; *Malden:* Main St., Malden Sq. **Zone fares**,
60¢-$1.00
➤Orange Line @ Oak Grove, Malden Ctr.

137   **Reading—Malden Ctr.**   30-38   30   60   70   60   —
via North Ave.—*Reading:* Reading Depot, Reading Sq., John St.; *Wakefield:* North Ave.,
Main St., Wakefield Sq.; *Melrose:* Main St., Melrose Ctr.; *Malden:* Main St., Malden Sq.
Zone fares, 60¢-$1.00.
➤Orange Line @ Oak Grove, Malden Ctr.

210   **Quincy Ctr.—N. Quincy**   12   30   30   —   30   —
via Hancock St.—*Quincy:* Hancock St.
➤Red Line @ Quincy Ctr., N. Quincy.

210F   **Quincy Ctr.—Fields Corner**   22-25   30   —   —   —   —
Quincy: Hancock St., N. Quincy, Newport Ave.; *Dorchester:* Neponset Cir., Neponset Ave.
➤Red Line @ Quincy Ctr., N. Quincy, Fields Corner.

211   **Quincy Ctr.—Squantum**   18-24   30   60   —   60   —
Quincy: Newport Ave., Beale St., Highland Ave., Montclair, W. Squantum St., N. Quincy,
E. Squantum St.
➤Red Line @ Quincy Ctr., Wollaston, N. Quincy.

212   **Quincy Ctr.—N. Quincy**   12-14   30/60   —   —   60   —
via Billings Rd.—*Quincy:* Hancock St., Elm Ave., Billings Rd.
➤Red Line @ Quincy Ctr., N. Quincy.

214   **Quincy Ctr.—Germantown**   12   11/20   30   —   20   —
Quincy: Coddington St., Sea St., Palmer St., Oceanview. ***Nights & Sun.:* see Bus 216.**
➤Red Line @ Quincy Ctr.

215   **Quincy Ctr.—Ashmont**   24-32   20   30   60   30   60
via Granite Ave.—*Quincy:* Hancock St., Franklin St., Water St., Copeland St., W. Quincy,
Willard St., Robertson St.; *Milton:* Adams St., E. Milton Sq., Granite Ave.; *Dorchester:*
Gallivan Blvd. **Sun.: alt. trips** *Quincy:* Whitwell St.; *Milton:* Adams St., then regular route.
➤Red Line @ Quincy Ctr., Ashmont.

216   **Quincy Ctr.—Hough's Neck**   11-17   9/20   30   60   20   40
Quincy: Coddington St., Sea St. ***Nights & Sun.:* also serves** *Quincy:* Germantown,
Palmer St., Oceanview.
➤Red Line @ Quincy Ctr.

217   **Wollaston Beach—Ashmont**   23-28   30   60   —   60   —
Quincy: Beach St., Wollaston, Beale St.; *Milton:* Adams St., E. Milton Sq.; *Dorchester:*
Lower Mills, Dorchester Ave.
➤Red Line @ Wollaston, Milton, Ashmont.

MBTA Buses

		Trip Time	Mon.–Fri. frequency (min.) Rush	Midday	Night	Sat. Freq.	Sun. Freq.

220   **Quincy Ctr.—Hingham**   22-24   10/15   30   60   30   60
Quincy: Washington St.; *Weymouth:* Bridge St., N. Weymouth; *Hingham:* Lincoln St., Broad Cove Rd., Otis St., Station St.
➤Red Line @ Quincy Ctr.

220A   **Quincy Ctr.—Hingham Loop**   22-31   10/15   60   —   60   —
Same route as Bus 220, then *Hingham:* Main St., Central St., Hingham Ctr.
➤Red Line @ Quincy Ctr.

221   **Quincy Ctr.—Fort Point**   16-18   3/1 trips   1 trip   —   —   —
Quincy: Washington St.; *Weymouth:* Bridge St., N. Weymouth, Neck St., River St.
➤Red Line @ Quincy Ctr.

222   **Quincy Ctr.—E. Weymouth**   21-23   10/15   30   60   30   60
Quincy: Washington St.; *Weymouth:* Bridge St., N. Weymouth, Sea St., North St., Commercial St., Middle St., Broad St.
➤Red Line @ Quincy Ctr.

225   **Quincy Ctr.—Weymouth Landing**   15-28   10   30   60   30   60
via Des Moines Rd.—*Quincy:* Hancock St., Quincy Ave., Scammell St., South St., Des Moines Rd., Fore River Shipyard; *Braintree:* Quincy Ave.; *Weymouth:* Front Rd., Summer St., Federal St., Washington St.
Bus 225A: *Mon.-Sat.:* **alternate trips via Quincy Ave.**—*Quincy:* Hancock St., Quincy Ave.; *Braintree:* W. Howard St., Shaw St., Hayward St., Quincy Ave., then regular route.
➤Red Line @ Quincy Ctr.

230   **Quincy Ctr.—Brockton Line**   33-43   15/20   60   60   60   60
Quincy: Hancock St., Franklin St., Independence Ave.; *Braintree:* Washington St., Braintree Sta., S. Braintree Sq., Washington St.; *Holbrook:* Franklin St., Holbrook Sq., Brookville Sq. to Brockton line. **Zone fares**, 60¢-$1.00.
➤Red Line @ Quincy Ctr., Braintree.

236   **Quincy Ctr.-South Shore Plaza**   28-32   30   60   —   60   —
via E. Braintree—*Quincy:* Hancock St., Franklin St.; *Braintree:* Commercial St., Elm St., Middle St., Union St., Braintree Sta., S. Braintree Sq., Franklin St., Five Corners, Granite St. **AM rush: Quincy Ctr.-Braintree** *only.*
➤Red Line @ Quincy Ctr., Braintree.

238   **Quincy Ctr.—Crawford Sq.**   31-39   30   60   60   60   60
Quincy: Hancock St., Franklin St., Water St., Liberty St., Centre St., West St., Willard St.; *Braintree:* Granite St., South Shore Plaza, Five Corners, Pond St.; *Randolph:* North St. **Through service (except nights) Quincy Ctr.—Ashmont via Bus 240A.** *Sat.:* **add'l service South Shore Plaza—N. Randolph via Bus 240A, every 30 min. Zone fares**, 60¢-75¢ to Crawford Sq.; 60¢-$1.50 on Ashmont through buses.
➤Red Line @ Quincy Ctr., Quincy Adams (Mon.-Sat. only).

240   **Avon Line—Ashmont**   27-31   20   60   60   60   60
Randolph: Main St., Crawford Sq.; *Milton:* Randolph Ave., Reedsdale Rd., Milton Hosp., Central Ave.; *Dorchester:* Lower Mills, Dorchester Ave. **Zone fares**, 60¢-$1.00.
➤Red Line @ Milton, Ashmont.

240A   **Crawford Sq.—Ashmont**   23-25   10   30   60   30   60
Same route as Bus 240 except originates at Crawford Sq. **Through service** (except nights) **Quincy Ctr.—Ashmont via Bus 238. Zone fares**, 60¢-75¢ to Crawford Sq.; 60¢-$1.50 on Quincy Ctr. through buses.
➤Red Line @ Milton, Ashmont.

225   **Quincy Ctr.—Mattapan**   12-14   30   60   —   60   —
Quincy: Whitwell St., Adams St.; *Milton:* E. Milton Sq., Edge Hill Rd.*, Pleasant St.*, Reedsdale Rd.*, Milton Hosp.*, Brook Rd. * -**Rush hour:** alternate trips via Shadowlawn—*Quincy:* Whitwell St., Adams St.; *Milton:* E. Milton Sq., Brook Rd. **Sun.: see Bus 215.**
➤Red Line @ Quincy Ctr., Mattapan.

MBTA Buses

	Trip Time	Mon.–Fri. frequency (min.)			Sat. Freq.	Sun. Freq.
		Rush	Midday	Night		

300 **Riverside—Downtown**   22   5/6   —   4 trips   —   —
express—*Newton:* Riverside; Mass. Pike; *Boston:* Federal St., Franklin St., Otis St. **Nights: via Copley Sq. and Newton Corner. Fare** $2.25.
➤Green Line-D @ Riverside; Red & Orange lines @ Downtown Crossing.

301 **Brighton Ctr.—Downtown**   25   5   —   —   —   —
express—*Brighton:* Washington St., Oak Sq., Tremont St.; Mass. Pike; *Boston:* Federal St., Franklin St., Otis St. **Fare** $1.50.
➤Red & Orange lines @ Downtown Crossing.

302 **Watertown—Copley**   18   10/12   —   —   —   —
express—*Watertown:* Galen St.; *Newton:* Newton Corner; Mass. Pike; *Boston:* Prudential Ctr., Boylston St. **Midday & Sat.: see Bus 304. Nights: see Bus 300. Fare** $1.50.
➤Green Line @ Copley.

304 **Watertown—Downtown**   18-33   8/10   30   —   35   —
express—*Watertown:* Galen St.; *Newton:* Newton Corner; Mass. Pike; *Boston:* Federal St., Franklin St., Otis St. **Midday & Sat.:** *Boston:* Copley Sq. **Fare** $1.50.
➤Red & Orange lines @ Downtown Crossing; Green Line @ Copley (middays & Sat. only).

304A **Newton Cor.—Downtown**   15-22   4/5   15   —   30   —
express—*Newton:* Newton Corner; Mass. Pike; *Boston:* Federal St., Franklin St., Otis St. *Through service* on most trips to Waverley, Roberts, and other Waltham points via Buses 53, 54, 56, 58. **Nights: see Bus 300. Fare** $1.50.
➤Red & Orange lines @ Downtown Crossing.

305 **Waltham—Downtown**   30   10   —   —   —   —
express—*Waltham:* Central Sq., Moody St.; *Newton:* Lexington St., Auburndale, Commonwealth Ave., Washington St., W. Newton; Mass. Pike; *Boston:* Federal St., Franklin St., Otis St. **Non-rush hours: see Buses 53, 54. Fare** $2.25.
➤Red & Orange lines @ Downtown Crossing.

325 **Elm St./Medford—Haymarket**   13-20   10/12   —   —   —   —
express—*Medford:* Fellsway West, Salem St.; I-93. **Fare** $1.50.
➤Green & Orange lines @ Haymarket.

326 **West Medford—Haymarket**   16-23   10/15   —   —   —   —
express—*Medford:* Playstead Rd., High St., Medford Sq.; I-93. **Fare** $1.50.
➤Green & Orange lines @ Haymarket.

350 **Burlington—Alewife**   34-54   14/20   60   60   60   50-60
Burlington: Chestnut Ave., Cambridge St., Mall Rd., Burlington Mall; *Woburn:* Cambridge Rd.; *Winchester:* Cambridge St.; *Arlington:* Mystic St., Arlington Ctr., Mass. Ave.; Alewife Brook Pkwy. **Zone fares**, 60¢-$1.00.
➤Red Line @ Alewife.

352 **Burlington—Boston**   43   10   —   —   —   —
express—*Burlington:* Chestnut Ave., Cambridge St.; Rt. 128, I-93; *Boston:* Haymarket Sq. **AM:** to Copley Sq. via Govt. Ctr., Park Plaza. **PM:** from Haymarket, except 1 trip from Park Plaza, Copley Sq. **Fare** 60¢ local, $2.25 to Boston.
➤Green & Orange lines @ Haymarket; Green Line @ Copley.

353 **Burlington Ind. Area—Haymarket**   41-46   30   —   —   —   —
express—*Bedford:* Crosby Dr.; *Burlington:* Middlesex Tpk., 2nd Ave., Mall Rd., Cambridge St.; *Woburn:* Cambridge Rd., Lexington St., Woburn Sq., Montvale Ave., Bow St., Salem St., Washington St., Cummings Ind. Pk.; I-93. **AM: from Boston only; PM: to Boston only. Zone fares**: 60¢ local; $2.25 to Haymarket.
➤Green & Orange lines @ Haymarket.

353A **Burlington Ind. Area—Dudley**   45-60   2/1 trips   —   —   —   —
express—*Bedford:* Crosby Dr.; *Burlington:* Middlesex Tpk., 2nd Ave.; Rt. 128; *Waltham:* 2nd Ave., Bear Hill Rd.; Riverside; Mass. Pike. **AM: from Dudley only; PM: to Dudley only. Fare** $2.25.
➤Green Line-D @ Riverside.

MBTA Buses

		Trip Time	Mon.–Fri. frequency (min.) Rush	Midday	Night	Sat. Freq.	Sun. Freq.

354   **Woburn—Haymarket**   28-31   10   —   —   —   —
express—*Woburn:* Cambridge Rd., Lexington St., Woburn Sq., Montvale Ave., Bow St., Salem St., Pine St.; I-93. **Fare** 60¢ local; $2.25 to Haymarket.
➤Green & Orange lines @ Haymarket.

400   **Lynn—Haymarket**
This bus is now combined with bus 455 (Salem-Haymarket). Some buses may still be signed "400."

411   **Revere House—Malden Ctr.**   36-47   35/50   60   —   60   —
Revere: Ocean Ave., Wonderland, Revere/Beach Sts., Malden St., Northgate Mall; *Malden:* Linden Sq., Lynn St., Granada Hlds., Kennedy Dr., Broadway, Salem St., Maplewood Sq., Malden Sq. **AM rush: Granada Hlds.—Malden Ctr. only.**
➤Blue Line @ Wonderland, Revere Beach; Orange Line @ Malden Ctr.

426   **Lynn—Haymarket**   47-60   10   60   80   60   60
via Cliftondale—*Lynn:* Lynn Common, W. Lynn, Summer St.; *Saugus:* E. Saugus, Lincoln Ave., Cliftondale; *Revere:* Salem St.; *Malden:* Lynn St., Linden Sq.; **express via Tobin Bridge.** *Rush hours:* 3/2 trips **Oaklandvale—Haymarket**—*Saugus:* Main St., Saugus Ctr., Winter St., E. Saugus, then regular route. *Rush hours:* 2 trips **Granada Hlds.—Haymarket**—*Malden:* Kennedy Dr., Lynn St., then regular route. **Zone fares**, 60¢-$2.00.
➤Green & Orange lines @ Haymarket.

429   **Lynn—North Saugus**   21-24   30   60   —   60   —
Lynn: Franklin St., Lynn Hosp., Boston St., Myrtle St., Holyoke St., O'Callaghan Way, King's Lynne, Garfield/Fairmount Aves.; *Saugus:* Walnut St.

430   **Saugus—Malden Ctr.**   30-51   35/45   60   —   60   —
Saugus: Appleton St., Summer St., Main St., Saugus Ctr., Central St., Cliftondale, Essex St., New England Shopping Ctr.; *Malden:* Broadway, Salem St., Maplewood Sq., Malden Sq.
➤Orange Line @ Malden Ctr.

433   **Lynn/Central Sq.—Pine Hill**   14   40   1 trip   —   —   —
Lynn: Lynn Common, Lynn Hosp., Mall/Park Sts., Lovers Leap Ave., Linwood St., Thistle St.

435   **Lynn—Danvers**   38-53   —/1 trip   60   1 trip   30-60   —
Lynn: Franklin St., Lynn Hosp., Western Ave., Chestnut St., Wyoma Sq., Broadway; *Peabody:* Lynn St., Peabody Ctr., Andover St., N. Shore Shopping Ctr.; *Danvers:* Liberty Tree Mall, Sylvan St., Park St., Danvers Sq. **Rush Hours: 1 trip. Sun: Lynn-Liberty Tree Mall only. Zone fares**, 60¢-$1.00.

436   **Lynn—Goodwins Cir.**   19   30   60   —   60   90
Lynn: Union St., Chestnut St., Wyoma Sq., Lynnfield St., AtlantiCare Hosp.; *Lynnfield:* Goodwins Cir. **Rush hours: 1 trip Happy Valley—Haymarket**—*Lynnfield:* Goodwins Cir.; *Lynn:* Lynnfield St., Wyoma Sq., Chestnut St., Western Ave., *through service* via Bus 450. **Fare** 60¢ local, $2.00 to Haymarket.

437   **Lynn/Central Sq.—Lake Shore Park** 15-22   30   60   —   60   90
Lynn: Union St., Timson St., Eastern Ave.,Euclid Ave., Jenness St., Saunders Rd., Broadway.

439   **Lynn—Nahant**   15-17   30   1 trip   —   —   —
Lynn: Nahant St.; *Nahant:* Nahant Rd., Castle Rd., Spring Rd., Willow Rd., Wharf St. **Rush hours: through service Nahant—Haymarket via Bus 455. Fare** 60¢ local, $2.00 to Haymarket.

440   **Lynn—Haymarket**   25-36   10   30   60   30   60*
This bus is now combined with buses 441 and 442. Some buses may still be signed "440."

441   **Marblehead—Haymarket**   48-63   30/10   60   —   60   —
via Paradise Rd.—*Marblehead:* Washington St., Pleasant St., Humphrey St.; *Swampscott:* Salem St., Vinnin Sq., Paradise Rd.; *Lynn:* Lewis St., Broad St., Central Sq.; Lynnway; Gen. Edwards Bridge; *Revere:* N. Shore Rd., Wonderland, Bell Cir.; **express** via Rt. 1A. **Mon.-Sat.:** *through service* on most trips **Marblehead—Haymarket** via 442. *-**Sun.: Lynn—Wonderland** only. **Zone fares**, 60¢-$2.25. **Nights & Sun.:** see Bus 442.
➤Blue Line @ Wonderland; Green & Orange lines @ Haymarket.

MBTA Buses

	Trip Time	Mon.–Fri. frequency (min.) Rush	Midday	Night	Sat. Freq.	Sun. Freq.

442   **Marblehead—Haymarket**   47-62   15   60   60   60   60
via Humphrey St.—*Marblehead:* Washington St., Pleasant St., Humphrey St.;
Swampscott: Swampscott Ctr.; *Lynn:* Lewis St., Broad St., Central Sq., Lynnway; Gen.
Edwards Bridge; *Revere:* N. Shore Rd., Wonderland, Bell Cir.; **express** via Rt. 1A.
Mon.—Sat.: through service on most trips Marblehead—Haymarket via 441. *-**Sun.:**
Lynn—Wonderland *only.,* or Bus 455 (Sun.). Zone fares, 60¢-$2.25.
➤Blue Line @ Wonderland (Mon.-Sat.); Green & Orange lines @ Haymarket.

450   **Salem—Haymarket**   35-50   20   60   2 trips   60   60
via Highland Ave.—*Salem:* Essex St., Highland Ave.; *Lynn:* Western Ave., W. Lynn;
Saugus: Marsh Rd., (Salem Tpk.); *Revere:* American Legion Hwy., Bell Cir.; **express** via
Rt. 1A. **Rush hours:** *through service* on some trips **Danvers—Haymarket** via Bus 458.
Rush hours: add'l service Essex St.—Haymarket—*Lynn:* Eastern Ave., Western Ave.,
then regular route, every 10 min. **Zone fares,** 60¢-$2.25.
➤Green & Orange lines @ Haymarket.

451   **North Beverly—Salem**   22-27   60   60   —   —   —
Beverly: Sohier Rd., Cabot St., Beverly Ctr.; *Salem:* Bridge St. **Sat.: see** Beverly
Shoppers Shuttle in Chapter 13

455   **Salem—Haymarket**   60   30/15   30   60   30   60
via Loring Ave.—*Salem:* Lafayette St., Loring Ave.; *Swampscott:* Vinnin Sq., Essex St.;
Lynn: Union St., Central Sq., Lynn Common, Western Ave., W. Lynn; *Saugus:* Marsh Rd.
(Salem Tpk.); *Revere:* American Legion Hwy., Bell Cir.; **express** via Rt. 1A. *Through
service* on most trips **Salem—Haymarket via Bus 455, daily, or Marblehead—
Haymarket via Bus 442, Sun. Zone fares,** 60¢-$2.25.
➤Green & Orange lines @ Haymarket.

458/   **Salem—Danvers**   25-31   30/60   60   —   —   —
468   *Salem:* North St.; *Peabody:* Margin St.; *Danvers:* Water St., Endicott Plaza, Liberty Tree
Mall, Purchase St., Danvers Sq. Some trips serve Danvers State Hospital, Essex
Agricultural School (see schedule). **Rush hours: through service** Danvers—Haymarket
via Bus 450. **Zone fares,** 60¢ local; $2.50 to Haymarket.

Chapter 18

MBTA Commuter Rail and Boats

The charts for commuter rail and commuter boat service show the number of trains or
boats on weekdays and Saturdays and Sundays, as well as the trip time from one end of the
route to the other.

The rush-hour column shows the number of trains or boats going to Boston in the morning
and away from Boston in the evening (e.g., "4/4").

Numbers in parentheses—(1A), (2), etc.—indicate fare zones. A dash (—) means there
is no service at the time indicated. An asterisk (*) indicates limited service (check schedule).

**Seven-day-a-week service began during the summer of 1992 for the Attleboro,
Framingham, Franklin, and Needham lines. THIS SERVICE IS EXPERIMENTAL.
FOR THE LATEST INFORMATION, CALL 800-392-6099.**

MBTA Commuter Rail

	Trip Time	**Weekday Trips** Rush	**Weekday Trips** Day	**Weekday Trips** Nite	Sat. Trips	Sun. Trips

Rockport/Ipswich Line

North Sta.—Beverly Depot	:35	8/8	8	4	12	7

Stations: Chelsea (1B), G.E. River Works* (2), Lynn (2), Swampscott (3), Salem (3), Beverly Depot (4).
➤Green & Orange lines @ North Sta.

North Sta.—Rockport	1:10	4/4	6	5	6	6

Stations: Beverly Depot (4), Montserrat (4), Prides Crossing* (5), Beverly Farms (5), Manchester-by-the-Sea (6), W. Gloucester (7), Gloucester (7), Rockport (8).
➤Green & Orange lines @ North Sta.

North Sta.—Ipswich	:55	4/4	4	2	5	—

Stations: Beverly Depot (4), N. Beverly (5), Hamilton/Wenham (5), Ipswich (6).
➤Green & Orange lines @ North Sta.

Reading/Haverhill Line

North Sta.—Reading	:30	7/7	6	5	6	6

Stations: Malden Ctr. (1B), Wyoming Hill (1), Melrose/Cedar Park (1), Melrose Hlds. (1), Greenwood (2), Wakefield (2), Reading (2).
➤Green & Orange lines North Sta.; Orange Line Malden Ctr.

North Sta.—Haverhill	1:05	6/3	2	6	6	5

Stations: Reading (2), N. Wilmington (3), Ballardvale (4), Andover (5), Lawrence (6), Bradford (7), Haverhill (7).
➤Green & Orange lines @ North Sta.; Orange Line @ Malden Ctr.

Lowell Line

North Sta.—Lowell	:45	6/6	7	5	8	8

Stations: W. Medford* (1B), Wedgemere (1), Winchester Ctr. (1), Lechmere Sales office* (2), Mishawum (2), Wilmington (3), N. Billerica (5), Lowell (6).
➤Green & Orange lines @ North Sta.

Fitchburg Line

North Sta.—S. Acton	:50	5/5	5	4	8	7

Stations: Porter (1B), Belmont Ctr.* (1), Waverley* (1), Waltham (2), Brandeis/Roberts (2), Kendal Green (3), Hastings* (3), Silver Hill* (3), Lincoln (4), Concord (5), W. Concord (5), S. Acton (6).
➤Green & Orange lines @ North Sta.; Red Line @ Porter.

North Sta.—Fitchburg	1:30	4/4	4	2	5	4

Stations: S. Acton (6), Littleton/495 (7), Ayer (8), Shirley (8), N. Leominster (9), Fitchburg (9).
➤Green & Orange lines @ North Sta.; Red Line @ Porter.

Fitchburg—Gardner	:30	2/2	1	—	3	—

Nonstop bus to Gardner (11). *Connects w/ Boston trains at Fitchburg.*

Framingham Line

South Sta.—Framingham	:45	5/5	4	3	—	—

Stations: Back Bay Sta. (1A), Newtonville* (1), W. Newton* (2), Auburndale* (2), Wellesley Farms (3), Wellesley Hills (3), Wellesley Sq. (3), Natick (4), W. Natick (4), Framingham (5).
➤Red Line @ South Sta.; Orange Line @ Back Bay Sta.

Needham Line

South Sta.—Needham Jct.	:30	5	4	4	6	—

Stations: Back Bay Sta. (1A), Ruggles* (1A), Forest Hills* (1B), Roslindale (1), Bellevue (1), Highland (1), W. Roxbury (1), Hersey (Bird's Hill) (2), Needham Jct. (2). *Connects w/ T-Bus 59 to Needham Ctr. and Needham Hts.*

MBTA Commuter Rail

	Trip	Weekday Trips			Sat.	Sun.
	Time	Rush	Day	Nite	Trips	Trips

➤Red Line @ South Sta.; Orange Line @ Back Bay Sta., Ruggles, Forest Hills.

South Sta.—Needham Hts.   :40   3/5   —   4   2   —
Stations: Needham Jct. (2), Needham Ctr. (2), Needham Hts. (2).
➤Red Line @ South Sta.; Orange Line @ Back Bay Sta., Ruggles, Forest Hills.

Franklin Line

South Sta.—Forge Park/495   1:00   6/4   4   4   3   —
Stations: Back Bay Sta. (1A), Ruggles* (1A), Readville (2), Endicott (2), Dedham Corp. Ctr. (2), Islington (3), Norwood Depot (3), Norwood Central (3), Windsor Gardens (4), Plimptonville* (4), Walpole (4), Norfolk (5), Franklin (6), Forge Park/495 (7).
➤Red Line @ South Sta.; Orange Line @ Back Bay Sta., Ruggles.

Attleboro/Stoughton Line

South Sta.—Attleboro   :50   6/5   4   3   6   —
Stations: Back Bay Sta. (1A), Ruggles* (1A), Hyde Park (1), Rt. 128 Sta. (2), Canton Jct. (3), Sharon (4), Mansfield (6), Attleboro (7).
➤Red Line @ South Sta.; Orange Line @ Back Bay Sta., Ruggles.

South Sta.—Providence, RI   1:05   4/4   —   —   —   —
Stations: Attleboro (7), S. Attleboro (7), Providence, RI (9).
➤Red Line @ South Sta.; Orange Line @ Back Bay Sta., Ruggles.

South Sta.—Stoughton   :40   4/4   4   3   2   —
Stations: Back Bay Sta. (1A), Ruggles* (1A), Hyde Park (1), Rt. 128 Sta. (2), Canton Jct. (3), Canton Ctr. (3), Stoughton (4).
➤Red Line @ South Sta.; Orange Line @ Back Bay Sta., Ruggles.

Fairmount Line

South Sta.—Readville   :19   7/6   7   3   —   —
Stations: Uphams Corner (1A), Morton St. (1B), Fairmount (1), Readville (2).
➤Red Line @ South Sta.

MBTA Commuter Boats

	Trip	Weekday Trips			Sat.	Sun.
	Time	Rush	Day	Nite	Trips	Trips

Long Wharf—Charlestown   :10   10/12   15   1   17   17
Navy Yard Water Shuttle to Pier 4, Charlestown Navy Yard. *Operated for the MBTA by Boston Harbor Cruises.* **Fare** $1.00. Rush hour service operates every 15 min.; off-peak and weekends, every 30 min. Free connecting shuttle bus service to points within the Navy Yard.
➤Blue Line @ Aquarium.

Rowes Wharf—Hingham   35   8/9   3   1   —   —
Operated by Boston Harbor Commuter Service and by Massachusetts Bay Lines. **Fare** $4.00.
➤Blue Line @ Aquarium; Red Line @ South Sta.

Airport Water Shuttle—see Chapter 6 ("Logan Airport")
For other non-MBTA ferry services, see Chapter 19.

Chapter 19
Other Trains, Ferries, Buses

The Americans With Disabilities Act (ADA), which requires all public carriers to provide services for persons with disabilities, became effective in July 1992. During the initial period of compliance, call the individual train, bus, or ferry line for the latest information on these services.

Phone numbers are listed on pages 167 and 168. The Boston Terminals map is found on page 18.

Trains

Amtrak
Boston terminals:
South Station; Back Bay Station
Suburban terminals:
Route 128 Sta. (Dedham/Westwood);
Framingham (downtown)
Northeast Corridor (Shore Line)
Boston-New York, NY
Via Rt. 128 Sta., Providence RI; New London, New Haven, CT; through trains to Philadelphia, PA, and Washington, DC.
    Daily: 9-10 trips
    Trip time: 4 3/4–5 hours
Inland Route
Boston-New York, NY
Via Framingham, Worcester, Springfield; Hartford, New Haven, CT; through trains to Philadelphia, PA, and Washington, DC.
    Daily: 2 trips from Boston;

plus 7 trips Springfield-New York
    Trip time: 6 1/4 hours
Lake Shore Limited
Boston-Chicago
Via Framingham, Worcester, Springfield, Pittsfield; Albany, Buffalo, NY; Cleveland, OH; connecting train to Michigan points.
    Daily: 1 trip
    Trip time: Boston-Albany, 5 1/2 hours;
    Boston-Chicago, 21 1/2 hours
Cape Codder
New York, NY-Hyannis, MA
Via New Haven, New London, CT; Providence, RI; Taunton, Wareham, Buzzards Bay, Sandwich, W. Barnstable. *Does not stop in Boston.*
    Late June-Labor Day only:
    Fri, Sat, & Sun, 1 trip
    Trip time: 6 1/4–7 hours

Ferries

A.C. Cruise Line
Boston terminal: Pier One
Boston-Gloucester (Rocky Neck)
    Late June-Labor Day: 1 trip daily
    Mem'l Day-mid June : weekends only
    Trip time: 2 1/2 hours

Airport Water Shuttle
Boston terminal: Rowes Wharf
Downtown Boston-Logan Airport
Connecting shuttle bus to all airline terminals.
    M-F: every 15 min., 6:00 am-8:00 pm
    Sat-Sun-Hol: every 30 min., 12:00 n-8:00 pm
    Trip time: 7 min.

Bay State Cruise Co.
Boston terminals:
Long Wharf; Commonwealth Pier
Unless noted otherwise, all Bay State boats operate daily, mid June-Labor Day; and weekends only, early May-early June & mid Sept.-late Oct.
Boston-Georges Island
From Long Wharf.
    M-F: 3 trips
    Sat-Sun-Hol: 4 trips
    Trip time: 45 min.
Boston-Nantasket
From Long Wharf.
    M-F: 2 trips
    Sat-Sun-Hol: 3 trips
    Trip time: 1 hour

Boston-Peddocks Island
From Long Wharf.
　Daily: 1 trip
　Trip time: 45 min.
Boston-Pemberton (Hull)
From Long Wharf.
　M-F rush hours: 1 trip (year-round)
　Trip time: 50 min.
Boston-Provincetown
_From Commonwealth Pier; shuttle
boat available from Long Wharf._
　_Mid June-Labor Day:_1 trip daily
　_Memorial Day-mid June &
　Labor Day-mid Sept._: weekends only
　Trip time: 3 hours
Nantasket (Hull)-Georges Island
　M-F only: 1 trip
　Trip time: 45 min.

Boston Harbor Commuter Service
Boston terminal: Rowes Wharf
Boston-Hingham
See _"MBTA Commuter Boat" in
Chapter 18._

Boston Harbor Cruises
Boston terminal: Long Wharf
Navy Yard Water Shuttle
Boston-Charlestown Navy Yard
_See "MBTA Commuter Boat" in
Chapter 18._
Boston-JFK Library
　M-F: 5 trips
　Trip Time: 45 min.

Cape Island Express Lines
**New Bedford-Martha's Vineyard
(Vineyard Haven)**
　Mid June-Labor Day: 3 trips daily
　_Mid May-early June & Labor Day-
　Columbus Day:_ 1-3 trips daily
　Trip time: 1 hours

Cuttyhunk Boat Lines
New Bedford-Cuttyhunk Island
_Connects w/American Eagle buses at
New Bedford on Mon-Fri only._
　Mid June-mid Sept.:1-2 trips daily
　_Memorial Day-early June & late Sept.-
　Columbus Day:_ Tue, Fri, Sat, Sun,
　& Hol, 1 trip
　Rest of year: Tues & Fri only
　Trip time: 1 3/4 hours

Harbor Islands Water Taxi
Operated by the Boston Harbor Islands
State Park.
All Harbor Islands boats operate daily

in summer; weekends in May, Sept., Oct.
Georges I.-Bumpkin I. & Peddocks I.
　Daily: 2 trips
Georges I.-Gallops I. & Lovells I.
　M-F: 3 trips
　Sat-Sun-Hol: 5 trips
Georges I.-Grape I.
　Daily: 3 trips

Hy-Line
**Hyannis-Martha's Vineyard
(Oak Bluffs)**
_Connects w/Plymouth & Brockton buses
from Boston at Hyannis._
　Mid June-mid Sept.: 4 trips daily
　_Late May-early June & late
　Sept.-late Oct._: 1 trip daily
　Trip time: 1 hours
Hyannis-Nantucket
_Connects w/Plymouth & Brockton buses
from Boston at Hyannis._
　Mid June-early Sept. 6 trips daily
　_Early May-early June & mid- Sept.-late
　Oct._: 1-3 trips daily
　Trip time: 2 hours
**Martha's Vineyard (Oak Bluffs)-
Nantucket**
　Mid June-mid Sept. only: 3 trips daily
　Trip time: 2 hours

Island Queen
**Falmouth-Martha's Vineyard
(Oak Bluffs)**
　Mid June-early Sept.: 7-8 trips daily
　_Late May-early June & mid
　Sept.-Columbus Day:_ 2-5 trips daily
　Trip time: 30 min.

Massachusetts Bay Lines
Boston terminal: Rowes Wharf
Boston-Hingham
See _"MBTA Commuter Boat" in Chapter 18._
Hingham-Georges Island
　Summer: 3 trips daily
　Spring & fall: weekends only
　Trip time: 30 min.

Steamship Authority
Hyannis-Nantucket
_Connects w/Plymouth & Brockton buses
from Boston at Hyannis._
　Late May-early Sept. 6 trips daily
　Rest of year: 3 trips daily
　Trip time: 2 hours

**Woods Hole-Martha's Vineyard
(Oak Bluffs)**
_Connects w/Bonanza Bus from Boston
at Woods Hole._

Late May-late Sept. only: 4 trips daily
Trip time: 45 min.
**Woods Hole-Martha's Vineyard
(Vineyard Haven)**
*Connects w/Bonanza Bus from Boston
at Woods Hole.*

Mid March-late Oct.: 9-14 trips daily
Rest of year: 6-7 trips daily
Trip time: 45 min.

Buses

Buses operated by Regional Transit Authorities are listed in Chapter 20. See Brockton Area Transit *(BAT)*; Berkshire Regional Transit Authority *(BRTA)*; Cape Ann Transportation Authority *(CATA)*; Cape Cod Regional Transit Authority *(CCRTA)*; Franklin Regional Transit Authority *(FRTA)*; Greater Attleboro-Taunton Regional Transit Authority *(GATRA)*;

Also, Greenfield-Montague Transportation Area *(GMTA)*; Lowell Regional Transit Authority *(LRTA)*; Martha's Vineyard Transit Authority *(VTA)*; Montachusett Area Transit Authority *(MART)*; Merrimack Valley Regional Transit Authority *(MVRTA)*; Pioneer Valley Transit Authority *(PVTA)*; Rhode Island Public Transit Authority *(RIPTA)*; Southeastern Regional Transit Authority *(SRTA)*; and Worcester Regional Transit Authority *(WRTA)*.

Airways Transportation
Logan Airport-Boston hotels
Serves all downtown and Back Bay hotels.
   Daily: every half hour until 10:00 pm
6:00 pm Sat.)

American Eagle Motor Coach
Boston terminal: Peter Pan
Boston-New Bedford-Fairhaven
Some trips stop at Taunton (Silver City Galleria Mall)
   M-F: every 2 hours until 11:30 pm
   Rush hours: every 15 min.
   Sat: every 2 hours until 9:00 pm
   Sun: every 3 hours until 8:00 pm
   Trip time: 1 1/2 hours

Barrett's Tours
Barrett's Tours operates summer-only local buses on Nantucket.
   June 15-Sept. 1.

Brockton Area Transit (BAT)
12 Ashmont–Brockton
Dorchester: Dorchester Ave., Lower Mills; *Milton:* Randolph Ave.; *Randolph:* Main St., Crawford Sq.; *Avon:* Avon Sq., W. Main St. (some trips via E. Main St.); *Brockton:* N. Main St. (No local stops between Ashmont and Randolph/Avon line.) *Connects w/Red Line at Ashmont.*
   M-Sat: every 40 min.
   Rush hours: every 20 min.

Nights: every hour until 11:40 pm M-F (until 10:50 pm Sat)
Trip time: 40 min.
12X Ashmont-Brockton *(express)*
Via Rt. 24; *Brockton:* Pleasant St.
Connects w/Red Line at Ashmont.
   M-F rush hours only: every 20 min.
   Trip time: 32 min.
See Chapter 20 for BAT local buses in Brockton and Stoughton.

Beverly Shoppers Shuttle
Shoppers Shuttle Commuter Bus
*Beverly:*loop via Beverly Depot, Cabot St., Balch St., N. Beverly (Sat. only), Herrick Rd., Beverly Hosp., Brimball Rd., Essex St., Montserrat, Colon St., Elliott St., Bridge St. *Connects w/T-Commuter Rail at Beverly Depot (Rockport/Ipswich Lines) and Montserrat (Rockport Line).*
   M-Sat: every hour

Big W Trans, Inc.
Boston-Northborough
Post Road Line
From Sudbury St., Essex St., Park Plaza, and Copley Sq.; via Mass. Pike, Rt. 20, Weston, Wayland, Sudbury, Marlborough.
   M-F rush hours only: 1 trip
   Trip time:1-1 1/4 hours

Bloom Bus Lines
Boston terminal: Peter Pan
Boston-Taunton

Via Raynham; some off-peak trips stop at Westgate Mall, Brockton. Stops at Silver City Galleria Mall in Taunton.
> Daily: every 2-2 1/2 hours
> Rush hours: every 30 min.
> Trip time: 1 hour

Bonanza Bus Lines
Boston terminal: Back Bay Station
Boston-Newport, RI
Via Fall River. *Also serves Logan Airport.*
> Daily: every 2 hours until 10:00 pm (until 11:45 pm Fri & Sun)
> Rush hours: to Fall River every 30 min.
> Trip time: 1 hours

Boston-New York, NY
Via Providence, RI (change buses), Hartford, Danbury, CT.
> Daily: 5 trips
> Trip time: 5-6 1/2 hours

Boston-Providence, RI *(express)*
Via Pawtucket, RI.
> Daily: every hour until 12:15 am
> Trip time: 1 hours

Logan Airport-Providence, RI
Via Foxborough, MA, and Pawtucket, RI. *Does not stop in downtown Boston.*
> Daily: every 1-2 hours until 11:45 pm
> Trip time: 1 hour

Boston-Wareham
Express; rush hour trips also serve Buzzards Bay.
> M-F: 5-6 trips
> Sat-Sun: 3–4 trips
> Trip time: 1 1/4 hours

Boston-Woods Hole
Via Bourne, Otis AFB, Falmouth. *Also serves Logan Airport.*
> Daily: every 2 hours until 10:00 pm
> Rush hours: every hour
> Summer: daily, every hour
> Trip time: 1 3/4 hours

New York, NY-Hyannis
Via Providence, RI, Fall River, New Bedford, Bourne; connecting buses to Falmouth and Woods Hole. *Does not stop in Boston.*
> Daily: every 2 hours
> Trip time: 6 1/2 hours

Brush Hill Transportation
Boston terminals: Park Plaza; South Station
Boston-Milford
Via Rt. 109, Westwood, Medfield, Millis, W. Medway.
> M-F rush hours only: 2 trips
> Trip time: 1 1/4 hours

Burlington People Mover
Local buses serving the town of Burlington. All buses depart from the Common at Cambridge & Bedford Sts., where they connect w/T- Buses 350 and 352. Buses 1, 5, and 6 also connect w/T-Bus 350 at Burlington Mall. Service operates Mon-Fri 8:00 am-6:30 pm. Odd-numbered buses depart on the hour; even-numbered buses depart on the half hour.

1 South	2 North
3 Northwest	4 Southeast
5 South	6 Southwest

C & J Trailways
Boston terminal: Peter Pan
Boston-Durham, NH
Via Logan Airport, Newburyport, Seabrook, Portsmouth, and Dover, NH.
> Daily: every 1-1 1/2 hours (13 trips) until 9:50 pm (11:20 pm Fri & Sun)
> Trip time: 2 hours

Boston-Portland, ME
Via Logan Airport, Portmouth, NH.
> Daily: 5 trips
> Trip time: 2 3/4 hours

Carey's Bus Lines
Boston-Whitman
From South Sta. and Govt. Ctr.: via E. Braintree, Weymouth Landing, S. Weymouth; 1 trip serves Rockland; 2 trips serve N. Abington, Abington Ctr.; 3 trips serve Whitman Ctr., E. Whitman.
> M-F rush hours only: 5 trips
> Trip time: 1-1 1/2 hours

City Transportation
Logan Airport-Downtown Boston
Serves all Boston hotels.
> Summer: daily, every 30 min. 'til 9:00 pm
> Winter: every hour

Concord Trailways
Boston terminal: Peter Pan
Boston-Concord, NH
Via Londonderry, Manchester, NH; through buses to Laconia, Conway, Littleton, NH, and other northern New Hampshire points. *Also serves Logan Airport.*
> Daily: every 1-1 1/2 hours (13 trips)
> Rush hours: every 30 min.
> Trip time: 1 hours

Boston-Portland, ME
Express. *Also serves Logan Airport.*
Daily: 7 trips.
> Trip time: 2 hours

Boston-Bangor, ME
Via Portland, ME. *Also serves Logan Airport.*
> Daily: 4 trips.
> Trip time: 4 1/4 hours.

Boston-Amherst, Novia Scotia
Via Portsmouth, NH; Portland, Bangor, ME; St. John, Moncton, NB.
> Daily: 1 trip
> Trip time: 15 1/2 hours.

Contran
Contran provides local bus service in Concord, connecting to shopping areas in neighboring towns. Buses operate Mon., Wed., and Fri. mornings, except holidays.

Crystal Transport
Framingham-Milford
Via Rts. 126 & 16, Ashland, Holliston. *Connects w/Peter Pan & Logan Express at Shoppers World, Framingham; connects w/T-Commuter Rail (Framingham Line) at Framingham.*
> M-Sat: every 2 hours
> Trip time: 40 min.

Dedham Local Bus
Operated by Hudson Bus Lines.
Spring St.-Readville Manor
Dedham: Riverdale, Bridge St., Ames St., Dedham Sq., High St., Dedham Mall, E. Dedham Sq., Oakdale Sq., Cedar St., Endicott Cir., Sprague St., Trenton Rd. *Connects w/T-Bus 36 at Spring St. (W. Roxbury) and w/T-Bus 34E at Dedham Sq.*
> M-F: 9 trips
> Trip time: 30 min.

H. T. Drummond, Inc.
Commuter van service to downtown Boston from Abington, Cohasset, Duxbury, Hanover, Hingham, Kingston, Marshfield, Pembroke, Plymouth, Rockland, Scituate, Weymouth, and Whitman. *Monthly tickets only.*

Green Harbor Transportation
Logan Airport-Plymouth
Via Braintree, Rockland, Pembroke, Kingston, Plymouth Ctr.
> Daily: every hour (15 trips)

Greyhound Lines
Boston terminal: Greyhound
Suburban terminal:
Riverside *(Green Line-D)*
Boston-Albany, NY

Via Riverside, Worcester; some trips also serve Springfield, Lee, Lenox, Pittsfield.
> Daily: 4 trips
> Trip time: 3 3/4–4 3/4 hours

Boston-New York, NY*(express)*
Via Riverside, Hartford, CT.
> Daily: every hour (11 trips)
> Trip time: 4 3/4 hours

Boston-New York, NY *(local)*
Via Riverside, Worcester, Hartford, New Haven and other Connecticut points; White Plains, NY.
> Daily: 2 trips
> Trip time: 6 1/2 hours

Boston-Portland, ME
Via Newburyport, Portsmouth, NH; 2 trips stop at Biddeford/Saco ME; through buses to Bangor, ME; summer service to Bar Harbor, ME, Moncton, NB.
> Daily: 5 trips
> Trip time: 2 1/2 hours

Gulbankian's Bus Lines
Boston-Hudson
From Park Plaza and Copley Sq.; via Mass. Pike, Southborough, Marlborough.
> M-F: 3 trips
> Trip time: 1 1/4 hours

Framingham-Hudson
From Shoppers World, via Southborough, Marlborough.
> Sat only: 1 trip
> Trip time: 35 min.

Hudson Airporter
Logan Airport-Bedford
Via Woburn, Burlington.
> M-F: every hour (14 trips)
> Sat morning: 4 trips
> Sun: 12 trips
> Trip time: 50 min.

Logan Airport-Chelmsford
Via Andover, Tewksbury, Lowell.
> M-F: 19 trips
> Sat: 10 trips
> Sun: 14 trips
> Trip time: 1 hour

Logan Airport-Manchester, NH
Via Nashua, Merrimack, Bedford, NH.
> M-F: 19 trips
> Sat: 10 trips
> Sun: 14 trips
> Trip time: 2 hours

Logan Airport-Needham
Via Newton Corner, Auburndale, Riverside.
> M-F: every 45 min. (22 trips)
> Sat: 9 trips
> Sun: 15 trips

Hudson Bus Lines
See also "Dedham Local Bus."
Boston-Lexington
From Park Plaza and Haymarket, via I-93; Medford: Medford Sq., High St., W. Medford; Arlington:Medford St., Arlington Ctr., Mass. Ave., Arlington Hts.; Lexington: Mass. Ave., Lexington Ctr., Hartwell Ave.

> M-F: extended rush hour service, 5 trips, plus 2 "reverse commute" trips
> Trip time: 1 hour

Boston-Peabody
From St. James Ave. and Haymarket; via Lynnfield.

> M-F rush hours only: 1 trip
> Trip time: 1 hour

Boston-Salem, NH
From South Sta. and Haymarket; also serves Windham, NH.

> M-F rush hours only: 1 trip
> Trip time: 1 hours

Boston-Stoneham
From Park Plaza and Haymarket, via I-93; Medford: Medford Sq., Governors Ave., Elm St.; Stoneham:Woodland Rd., New Engl. Memorial Hosp., Pond St., Stone Zoo, Franklin St., Stoneham Sq., Pleasant St., Washington St., High St., Broadway, Redstone Plaza. Midday route (10:00 am-2:00 pm): from Haymarket only, to New Engl. Memorial Hosp. only; omits Stone Zoo, Stoneham Sq., Redstone Plaza.

> M-F: every hour
> Rush hours: every 30 min.
> Trip time: 50 min.

Fulton St.-Meadow Glen Mall
*Medford:*Highland Ave., Fulton St., Medford Sq., Riverside Ave.

> Mon-Sat: every 30 min. 10:00 am-2:00 pm: every hour
> Trip time: 15 min.

Mattapan-Canton
Milton: Blue Hill Ave.; Canton:Washington St., Canton Ctr., Cobbs Corner. *Connects w/Red Line at Mattapan.; connects w/BAT 14 at Cobbs Corner.*

> M-Sat: hourly (except no service M-F 10:00 am-2:00 pm)
> Trip time: 30 min.

Interstate Coach
Boston-Middleborough
From Park Plaza and Lincoln St.: via Bridgewater, W. Bridgewater; 1 midday trip also serves Easton and Stoughton.

> M-F: rush hours, every 30 min.; 1

midday trip; 1 "reverse commute" trip
> Sat-Sun: 3 trips
> Trip time: 1 1/4 hours

Island Transport
Island Transport operates seasonal local buses on Martha's Vineyard.
Vineyard Haven-Edgartown via Oak Bluffs
Connects w/ferries at Vineyard Haven and Oak Bluffs.

> Late June-Labor Day:
> Daily: every 15 min.
> Nights: every 30 min. until 11:30 pm
> *Memorial Day-Late June & Labor Day-Columbus Day:*
> Daily: every 30 min. until 6:00 pm
> Trip time: 30 min.

Vineyard Haven-Edgartown via Martha's Vineyard Airport
Connects w/ferries at Vineyard Haven.

> Late June-Labor Day
> Daily: every hour
> Trip time: 30 min.

Vineyard Haven-Gay Head
Via Oak Bluffs, W. Tisbury, Chilmark; 1 trip via Edgartown. *Connects w/ferries at Vineyard Haven and Oak Bluffs.*

> Late June-Labor Day
> Daily: every 2 hours (4 trips)
> Trip time: 1 1/4 hour

Lexpress
Lexpress operates local buses in Lexington; one route also serves Burlington Mall. All buses depart from Depot Sq. in Lexington Center, where they connect w/T-Buses 62 and 76. Service operates Mon.-Fri. 7:00 am-6:00 pm and Sat. 10:00 am-5:30 pm; there is no Sat. service in July or Aug. Even-numbered routes depart on the hour and odd-numbered routes on the half hour.

1 Southeast	2 South
3 Southwest	4 West
5 North	6 North
7 Burlington Mall	8 East

LIFT
Local Intra-Framingham Transit
LIFT operates local buses in Framingham, Ashland, Hopkinton, and part of Natick. Service operates Mon-Fri 6:00 am-6:30 pm and Sat 9:00 am-4:45 pm. All routes operate hourly. All LIFT routes depart from Concord & Howard Sts. in downtown Framingham, where they connect w/T-Commuter Rail.

Routes 1-4 also connect w/Peter Pan buses to Boston, w/Logan Express, and w/the Natick Neighborhood Bus at Shoppers World.

1 Pinefield express
Via Concord St., Shoppers World.
> M-F: 6:30 am-5:00 pm

2 Malls via Nobscot
3 Nobscot via Malls
Via Union St., Framingham Ctr., Edgell Rd., Nobscot, Water St., Pinefield, Saxonville, Shoppers World, Natick Mall, Sherwood Plaza, Concord St.
Route 2 operates in a clockwise loop; Route 3 operates counter-clockwise.
> M-F: 8:30 am-6:20 pm
> Sat: (Route 2 only) 9:30 am-4:30 pm

2X Industrial Park Express
Via Union Ave., Framingham Ctr., Rt. 9.
> M-F rush hours only: 2 trips

4 Mall Shuttle
Via Concord St., Shoppers World, Natick Mall, Sherwood Plaza.
> Sat only: 9:00 am-4:45 pm

5 Framingham-Hopkinton
Via Rt. 135. *Framingham:*Waverly St.; *Ashland*: Union St.; *Hopkinton*: Main St.
> M-F: 6:00 am-6:30 pm

Logan Express
Logan Airport-Braintree
Express to Forbes Rd. (Rt. 128/I-93 at Rt. 37). Operated by Plymouth & Brockton.
> M-F: every 30 min.
> Nights: every hour until 11:00 pm
> Sat: every hour
> Sun: every 30-60 min.

Logan Airport-Framingham
Via Mass. Pike, express to Shoppers World. Operated by Peter Pan.
> M-F: every 30 min. until 11:45 pm
> Sat: every hour until 11:00 pm
> Sun: every 30-60 min. until 11:45 pm

Logan Link
Boston Terminal: South Station Massport initiated this rush-hour shuttle bus from South Station to Logan Airport on a six-month trial basis in May 1992. Seven shuttle buses a day are coordinated with peak-hour commuter rail service.

Lower Cape Bus
Lower Cape Bus operates summer-only local buses in Provincetown and Truro.
Town Loop
Via MacMillan Pier, Bradford St.

Daily: every hour until 12:00 mid
Beach Loop
Via MacMillan Pier, Bradford St., Herring Cove Beach
Daily: every hour until 6:30 pm

Lynn East/West Loop Bus
Lynn: Central Sq., Broad St., Lewis St., Eastern Ave., Timson St., Union St., Rockaway St., High Rock St., Washington St., Lynn Hosp., Boston St., Broadway, Wyoma Sq., return to Central Sq.
> M-F: 6 trips
> Trip time: 35 min.

West Lynn Loop
Lynn: Central Sq., Franklin St., Lynn Hosp., Boston St., Cottage St., Barry Park, Summer St., Neptune Towers, return to Central Sq.
> M-F: 5 trips
> Trip time: 25 min.

M & L Transportation
Logan Airport-Merrimack, NH
Via Boston (Quincy Market), Woburn, Burlington, Bedford, Lowell, Chelmsford, Nashua NH.
> M-F: every 30 min. until 11:00 pm
> Sat-Sun: every 30-60 min.
> Trip time: 1 1/2-2 hours

Mass Limousine Co.
Logan Airport-S. Attleboro
Via Middleborough, Taunton, Foxborough, Mansfield.
> M-F only: 5 trips
> Trip time: 1 1/4 hours

Metrobus
Cambridge-Longwood Medical Area
Cambridge: Harvard Sq., Mass. Ave., Central Sq., MIT; to *Fenway:* Ave. Louis Pasteur, Longwood Ave.; some night trips via *Brookline:* Coolidge Corner.*Tickets must be purchased in advance at Harvard, MIT, or Longwood Galleria. Limited to students, faculty, and staff of Harvard, MIT, and other Medical Area institutions.*
> M-F rush hours: every 10 min.
> Midday: every 30 min.
> Nights and Sat: every hour
> Trip time: 25 min.

Michaud Bus Lines
Peabody-Northshore Shopping Ctr.
Peabody: Lake Shore Pk., Lynn St., Washington St., Main St., Peabody Sq.,

Central St., Andover St.
 M-Sat: every 1-3 hours (7 trips)
 Trip time: 20 min.
Salem Belt Line
Salem: Riley Plaza, Broad St., Jackson
St., Jefferson Ave., Shaughnessy Hosp.,
Little Peach, Canal St., return to Riley
Plaza.
 M-Sat: every 1-3 hours (7 trips)
 Trip time: 20 min.
Salem-Northshore Shopping Ctr.
Salem: Riley Plaza, Washington St.
Bridge St., Boston St.; *Peabody:* Main
St., Peabody Sq., Central St., Andover St.
 M-Sat: every 1-3 hours (6 trips)
 Trip time: 25 min.

Mission Hill Link Bus

Serves the Mission Hill neighborhood of
Boston. All buses depart from Osco
Drug on Tremont St. near Brigham
Circle, where they connect w/Green
Line-E trains and T-Buses 39 and 66.
Service operates Mon-Fri 5:45 am-9:30
pm and Sat 5:45 am-7:00 pm.
Baptist Hospital Shuttle
Brigham Cir.-N. E. Baptist Hospital
 M-Sat 5:45 am-6:59 am: on demand
Green Route
Via Tremont St., St. Alphonsus St.,
Calumet St., Parker St., Fisher Ave.,
Wait St.
 M-Sat 2:00-6:40 pm: every 20 min.
Blue Route
A variation of the Green Route which also
serves Roxbury Crossing*(Orange Line)*,
Parker St., Hillside St.
 M-Sat 7:00-9:30 am: every 30 min.
 M-F 7:30-9:00 pm: every 30 min.
Red Route
A variation of the Green Route which
also serves Ward St., Annunciation Rd.,
Parker St., Hillside St.
 M-Sat 10:30 am-1:30 pm: every 30 min.

Natick Neighborhood Bus
Natick Common-Shoppers World
Most Natick neighborhoods are served
by either fixed-route or on-request
service. *Connects w/Peter Pan buses to
Boston, Logan Express, and LIFT
(Framingham local buses) at Shoppers
World (Framingham); connects w/T-
Commuter Rail (Framingham Line) at
Natick station.*
 M-F: every hour, 7:15 am-5:45 pm
 Sat: every hour, 10:00 am-4:00 pm

Paul Revere

Paul Revere operates local buses in

Winthrop. Service operates 5:00 am-
1:00 am Mon-Sat and 7:25 am-11:00
pm Sun.
**Orient Heights-Winthrop Beach *via
Centre***
East Boston:Saratoga St.; Winthrop:
Main St., Hermon St., Pauline St.,
Pleasant St., Washington St. *Connects
w/Blue Line at Orient Hts.*
 M-Sat: every 30-35 min.
 Rush hours: every 7-15 min.
 Nights: every 40 min.
 Sun: every 80 min.
 Trip time: 15 min.
**Orient Heights-Winthrop Beach *via
Highlands***
East Boston: Saratoga St.; *Winthrop:*
Main St., Revere St., Crest Ave.,
Veterans Rd. *Connects w/Blue Line at
Orient Hts.*
 M-Sat: every 30-35 min.
 Rush hours: every 12-18 min.
 Nights: every 40 min.
 Sun: every 80 min.
 Trip time: 15 min.
Winthrop Beach-Pt. Shirley
Winthrop: Shirley St., Tafts Ave.
Through service from Orient Hts.
 M-Sat: every 30 min.
 Nights & Sun: every 40 min.
 Trip time: 20 min.

People Care-iers
**Hingham Depot-Point Pemberton,
Hull**
Hingham: Summer St., Rockland St.
Hull: Nantasket Ave., Spring St., Main
St., to Pemberton. *Connects w/T-Bus
220 at Hingham Depot; connects w/Bay
State ferry from Boston at Point
Pemberton.*
 M-Sat: every 10-2 hours until 7:30 pm
 (5:30 pm Sat)
 Trip Time: 20-25 min.

Peter Pan Bus Lines
Boston terminal: Peter Pan
Suburban terminal:
Riverside *(Green Line-D)*
Boston-Albany, NY
Via Springfield, Lee, Lenox, Pittsfield; 2
trips via Riverside.
 Daily: 5 trips
 Trip time: 4-4 1/2 hours
Boston-Amherst *(express)*
Via Northampton.
 M-F: 1 trip; add'l trips Fri & Sun during
 the school year
 Trip time: 2 1/2 hours

Boston-Amherst
Via Springfield, Holyoke, Northampton; some trips stop at Riverside, S. Hadley.
Daily: every hour (16 trips)
Trip time: 3–3 1/4 hours

Boston-Greenfield-Bennington, VT
Via Springfield, Amherst, Deerfield.
Daily: To Greenfield (5 trips); to Bennington, VT, (1 trip). Additional service Fri & Sun.
Trip time: to Greenfield—3 1/2 hours; to Bennington—4 1/4 hours.

Boston-Framingham *(express)*
From Peter Pan terminal, Park Plaza, Copley Sq.; some rush hour trips from State House; via Mass. Pike to Shoppers World.
M-F only: every 2 hours until 10:15 pm
Rush hours: every 15 min.
Limited "reverse commute" service
Trip time: 35 min.

Boston-Hampton Beach, NH
Connection available from Riverside.
Summer only: 2 trips daily
Trip time: 1 1/4 hours

Boston-New York, NY
Via Springfield; Hartford and other Connecticut points; some trips stop at Riverside.
Daily: every hour (16 trips)
Trip time: 5 hours

Boston-Springfield
Via Mass. Pike, Chicopee (Quality Inn); some trips stop at Riverside, Worcester, Palmer. *Connecting service from Logan Airport.*
Daily: every hour (17 trips)
Trip time: 2 hours

Boston-Sturbridge
Via Worcester, Old Sturbridge Village.
Daily: 2 trips
Trip time: 1 hours

Boston-Westborough
From Peter Pan terminal, Park Plaza, Copley Sq., and State House ; via Framingham.
M-F rush hours only: every 30 min.
Trip time: 1 1/4 hours

Boston-Westfield
Via Springfield.
School year only: Fri & Sun, 1 trip
Trip time: 3 hours

Boston-Worcester*(express)*
Via Mass. Pike, Millbury. *Connecting service from Logan Airport.*
Daily: every hour (20 trips)
Rush hours: every 30 min.; also stops at Park Plaza, Copley Sq., and Auburn.
Trip time: 1 hour

Boston-Worcester *(Rt. 9 Local)*
From Peter Pan terminal, Park Plaza, Copley Sq.; via Brigham Circle, Brookline Village, Newton Highlands, Wellesley, Natick, Shoppers World, Framingham Ctr., Southborough, Westborough, Northborough, Shrewsbury.
M-F: every 1-2 hours (8 trips)
Trip time from Boston:
Shoppers World, 1 hour;
Worcester, 1 3/4 hours

Logan Airport-Downtown Boston
Connects w/buses to Worcester, Springfield, and other points.
M-F: every hour, 10 trips
Sat-Sun: every 2 hours
Trip time: 20 min.

Logan Airport-Framingham
See "Logan Express" listing.

Logan Airport-Worcester
Via Westborough. *Does not stop in downtown Boston.*
Daily: 4-7 trips
Trip time: 1 hours

Springfield-Bradley Airport
Connects w/buses from Boston at Springfield.
Daily: every 2 hours
Trip time: 30 min.

Springfield-Hyannis
Via Worcester, Bourne; connecting bus to Amherst & Northampton; connecting bus to Falmouth and Woods Hole. *Does not stop in Boston.*
School year: Fri & Sun only, 1 trip
Summer: Daily, 2 trips
Trip time: 3 1/2 hours;

Plymouth & Brockton Street Railway Co.
Boston terminals:
Park Plaza; South Station; Peter Pan
P&B buses make two stops in Boston. One stop is at the Park Plaza terminal. The second stop is either at South Station or the Peter Pan terminal, as noted below.

Boston-Brockton
From Park Plaza & South Sta..; express, via Westgate Mall.
M-F: 4 rush hour trips; 2 midday trips.
Trip time: 1 hour

Boston-Hyannis
From Park Plaza & Peter Pan; via N. Plymouth, Sagamore, Barnstable. *Also serves Logan Airport.*
Daily: approx. every hour (15 trips)
Rush hours: every 10-15 min.

Sat-Sun: every 1-2 hours (every hour in summer)
    Trip time: 1 3/4 hours

Boston-Pembroke Center
From Park Plaza and South Station; via Hanover, Pembroke, Bryantville.
    M-F rush hours only: 1 trip
    Trip time: 1 1/2 hours

Boston-Plymouth Center
From Park Plaza, Peter Pan & South Sta.; via Rockland (Rt. 228), Rt. 53, Norwell, Hanover, N. Pembroke, Duxbury, Kingston.
    M-F: every 2 hours
    Morning: to Boston only
    Afternoon: to Plymouth only
    Rush hours: every 15 min.
    Nights (M-F): every hour
    Trip time: 1 hours

Boston-Scituate
From Park Plaza, Peter Pan & South Sta.; via Rockland (Rt. 228), Hingham, Cohasset, N. Scituate, Egypt, Greenbush; 1 trip via Norwell.
    M-F rush hours: every 15-20 min., plus 1 mid-afternoon trip
    Trip time: 1 1/4 hours

Boston-S. Duxbury
From Park Plaza & South Sta.; via Marshfield, Brant Rock, Green Harbor, Duxbury (Rt. 139). Also serves Logan Airport.
    M-F rush hours only: 2 trips
    Trip time: 1 1/4 hours

Braintree-Marshfield
Via Hanover Mall. Connects w/Red Line at Braintree.
    M-F rush hours only: every 30 min.
    Trip time: 30 min.

Hyannis-Chatham
Via Rt. 28, S. Yarmouth, Dennisport, Harwichport. Connects w/buses from Boston at Hyannis.
    Late May-mid Oct.: 2 trips daily
    Rest of year: 1 trip daily
    Trip time: 45 min.

Hyannis-Provincetown
Via Yarmouth, Dennis, Brewster, Orleans, Eastham, Wellfleet, Truro, N. Truro; 1 trip via Chatham. Connects w/ buses from Boston at Hyannis; connects w/Bay State ferry from Boston at Provincetown.
    Late May-mid Oct.: 6 trips daily
    Rest of year: 2-3 trips daily
    Trip time: 1 1/2 hours

Logan Airport-Braintree
See "Logan Express" listing.

The Coach Company
Operated by Timberlane Transportation. Departs from St. James Ave. and Haymarket.

Boston-Amesbury
Via Newburyport (park and ride); some trips serve Byfield (Newbury) and Seabrook, NH.
    M-F rush hours only: 5 trips
    Trip time: 1 1/2 hours

Boston-Haverhill
Via Danvers Plaza, Boxford, Georgetown, S. Groveland, Bradford; also serves Plaistow, NH.
    M-F rush hours only: 3 trips
    Trip time: 1 1/2 hours

Boston-Newburyport
Via Rt. 1, Topsfield, Ipswich, Rowley, Newbury, downtown Newburyport.
    M-F rush hours only: 3 trips
    Trip time: 1 1/4 hours

Trombly Commuter Lines
Boston-N. Andover
From Park Plaza and Essex St.; via I-93, Andover, Lawrence.
M-F: every 2-4 hours until 9:30 pm
Rush hours: every 30 min.; *some trips from Copley Sq., Cambridge St., North Sta.*
    Sat: every 2 hours until 7:30 pm
    Sun: every 3 hours until 7:30 pm
    Trip time: 1–1 1/4 hours

Vermont Transit Lines
Boston terminal: Greyhound
Suburban terminals (Rutland route): Riverside*(Green Line-D);*
West Concord (Howard Johnson's)

Boston-Rutland, VT
Via Riverside, W. Concord, Ft. Devens, Fitchburg Jct., Gardner, Winchendon; Fitzwilliam and Keene, NH; Bellows Falls, VT; connecting buses to Brattleboro and Middlebury, VT. *Also serves Logan Airport.*
    Daily: 2-3 trips
    Trip time: 4 1/2 hours

Boston-White River Jct., VT
Via Lowell; Nashua, Manchester, Concord, New London, NH; 1 trip via Henniker, Mt. Sunapee, Claremont, NH; through or connecting buses to all Vermont points and to Montreal. *Also serves Logan Airport.*
    Daily: 7 trips
    Rush hours: to Nashua, NH, every 30/45 min.
    Trip time: 2 1/2–3 1/2 hours

Waltham-Lexington Express

Alewife-Lexington & Waltham
Connects w/Red Line at Alewife.
Limited to employees of participating
companies.
   M-F rush hours only: every 45/60 min.
   Trip time: 20-25 min.

Yankee Line

Boston-Littleton
From Essex St., Copley
Sq.; via Acton, Rt. 119.
   M-F rush hours only: 1 trip
   Trip time: 1 hour

Chapter 20

Regional Transit Authorities

Regional Transit Authorities are responsible for transit in Massachusetts communities outside the Boston area. There are 14 RTAs serving 90 cities and towns across the Commonwealth. This chapter also includes services of the Rhode Island Public Transportation Authority (RIPTA).

All RTAs have reduced fares for elderly and handicapped riders, and many RTAs offer discounted monthly passes or multiple-ride tickets.

Besides the regular buses described here, every RTA offers special services for the elderly and handicapped. For details, call your local RTA, city or town hall, or Council on Aging. RTA services are wheelchair accessible.

BAT
☎ 508-580-1170

Brockton Area Transit local buses operate Mon.-Fri. 6:00 am-8:40 pm, Sat. 7:20 am-6:00 pm; there is no Sunday service. Most routes operate every 40 minutes, or every 20 minutes in rush hours and late afternoons. The local fare is 60¢. Transfers are free.

Brockton—12 local routes depart from the Transfer Centre at Crescent and Main Sts. in downtown Brockton.

Stoughton—BAT Bus 14 departs from Westgate Mall, where it connects with BAT Buses 4 and 4A from Brockton.

Brockton-Ashmont, via Milton, Randolph, and Avon—BAT Buses 12 and 12X operate Mon.-Fri. 5:00 am-10:45 pm, Sat. 5:20 am-10:05 pm. Fare, $1.20.

Connecting services: BAT Buses 12 and 12X (Ashmont) connect with the MBTA Red Line at Ashmont. BAT Bus 10 (Lisa & Howard) connects with T-Bus 230 (Quincy Ctr.-Holbrook) at S. Franklin and Howard Sts. BAT Bus 14 (Stoughton) connects with Hudson Bus (Mattapan-Canton) at Cobbs Corner. Plymouth & Brockton buses from Boston stop at the BAT Transfer Centre.

BRTA
☎ 800-292-BRTA; 413-499-BRTA

Berkshire Regional Transit Authority, or "The B," serves Pittsfield, North Adams, and other Berkshire County towns. BRTA buses operate Mon.-Fri.

6:00 am-6:00 pm, Sat. 8:00 am-6:00 pm; there is no Sunday service. Most routes operate hourly. The fare is 40¢, plus 40¢ for each town line that is crossed. Transfers are free.

Pittsfield—11 local routes in Pittsfield, Dalton, Hinsdale, and Lanesboro. Buses depart from Park Square in Pittsfield. *Connecting services:* Greyhound and Peter Pan stop at 57 S. Church St. (413-442-4451), 4 blocks southwest of Park Square. Amtrak stops at Depot St., off North and Center Sts., 2 blocks north of Park Square.

North Adams—2 local routes in North Adams and Williamstown. Buses depart from Main St. in North Adams. *Connecting services:* Peter Pan stops at Angelina's Subs (413-664-0315); one Bonanza trip serves North Adams.

Pittsfield-Great Barrington, via Lenox, Lee, Housatonic, and Stockbridge—hourly, Mon.-Sat. *Also:* Bonanza has 3 daily trips via Lenox, Lee, and Stockbridge. *Connecting services:* Greyhound and Peter Pan stop opposite the police station in Lenox and at 43 Main St. in Lee.

Pittsfield-North Adams, via Lanesboro (Berkshire Village), Cheshire, and Adams—hourly, Mon.-Sat. *Connecting services:* See "Pittsfield" and "North Adams." *Additional connecting services:* Peter Pan stops at the Williams Inn (413-458-2665) in Williamstown. Bonanza has 2 daily trips from Pittsfield to Williamstown via New Ashford (one trip serves North Adams).

CATA   ☎ 508-283-7916

Cape Ann Transportation Authority buses operate Mon.-Fri. 6:15 am-6:30 pm, Sat. 9:00 am-5:30 pm; there is no Sunday service. Most routes operate every 2 hours with additional rush hour service. The fare is 60¢, or 75¢ for two-zone trips. Trips in the "downtown zones," between the railroad station and downtown in both Gloucester and Rockport, cost only 25¢.

Gloucester—3 local routes depart from Dunkin Donuts at the corner of Rogers St. and Manuel Lewis Dr. in downtown Gloucester. *Connecting services:* The T-Commuter Rail station is on Railroad Ave., off Washington St., 1/2 mile north of downtown. (See map on page 67.) All but one of CATA's routes stop at the train station. CATA's Green Line (Business Express) offers shuttle service from the train station to downtown, every 30 min. Mon.-Fri. The Sat. Business Express schedule is irregular but there is service to downtown from arriving trains. Rush hour trains are met by specially-scheduled trips on 3 CATA routes. The AC Cruise boat from Boston lands at Rocky Neck, across the harbor from downtown Gloucester. CATA's "East Gloucester" bus stops at 1 Wonson St., 3 blocks from the Rocky Neck dock.

Gloucester-Rockport—hourly service via 3 different routes. In Rockport, buses depart from the Richdale store on Broadway. *Connecting service:* The T-Commuter Rail station is behind Whistlestop Mall, off Railroad Ave., 1/2 mile from Dock Sq. and Bearskin Neck. CATA's Blue Line bus (Rockport-Gloucester via Lanesville) stops on Railroad Ave. and makes good connections with most trains. (See map on page 68.)

CCRTA   ☎ 800-352-7155; 508-385-8326

Cape Cod Regional Transit Authority, the "b bus," operates one scheduled route:

Hyannis-Woods Hole, via Centerville, Osterville, Marstons Mills, Cotuit, Mashpee, Waquoit, E. Falmouth, Teaticket, and Falmouth—5 trips Mon.-Fri., 3 trips Sat., no Sun. service. Fares on the 25-mile trip range from 75¢ to $4.00. *Connecting services:* CCRTA stops at bus stations in Hyannis, Falmouth, and Woods Hole, and at Steamship Authority ferry terminals in Hyannis and Woods Hole. (See Hyannis and Falmouth maps on pages 66 and 67.)

Hyannis-Chatham and *Hyannis-Provincetown*—see "Plymouth & Brockton" listing in Chapter 19.

CCRTA also operates door-to-door service by advance reservation, Mon.-Sat., throughout Cape Cod. This service is open to the general public.

FRTA   ☎ 413-774-2262

Franklin Regional Transit Authority operates 3 routes in Greenfield, Bernardston, Charlemont, Deerfield, Northfield, and Shelburne Falls. Service on all routes is limited, 3 or fewer trips per day, with most service operating during the school year only. Buses leave from Court Sq. in Greenfield. The fare is 75¢ plus 35¢ per zone. *Connecting services:* See the GMTA listing.

GATRA   ☎ 508-222-6106

Most **Greater Attleboro-Taunton Regional Transit Authority** routes operate hourly, Mon.-Fri. 6:00 am-6:15 pm, Sat. 9:00 am-5:15 pm; there is no Sunday service. The local fare is 60¢.

Attleboro—3 local routes in Attleboro, N. Attleboro, Plainville, and part of Seekonk. Buses depart from the bus shelter on Union St. *Connecting services:* The T-Commuter Rail station is 1/2 block from the bus shelter. GATRA Bus 2 (S. Attleboro) connects with RIPTA Bus 77 for service to Providence, RI. GATRA Bus 3 (Seekonk) connects with RIPTA Buses 76 and 77.

Taunton—5 local routes depart from the Bloom bus complex bus at 10 Oak St. *Connecting service:* Bloom buses depart from the Oak St. complex.

Attleboro-Taunton, via Norton—Hourly Mon.-Fri., except there is no midmorning service. Fare, $1.20.

Taunton-Providence, RI, via Rehoboth and Seekonk—Every 90 minutes Mon.-Sat. (every 45 min. in rush hour). Fare, $2.25.

GMTA   ☎ 413-773-9478

Most **Greenfield-Montague Transportation Area** buses depart from Court Sq. in downtown Greenfield. The fare is 75¢, plus 35¢ per zone, to a maximum of $1.80.

Greenfield—4 local routes in Greenfield and Turners Falls. Most routes operate hourly, Mon.-Fri 6:00 am-6:00 pm, and every 2 hours Sat. 9:45 am-5:00 pm; there is no Sunday service. *Connecting services:* Peter Pan stops at Barret & Baker, 310 Main St. (413-774-2345). GMTA's "GCC" bus stops at Colrain Rd. and Rt. 2, near Rich's Mall, Mon.-Fri.

Greenfield-Montague, via Millers Falls—5 trips Mon.-Fri.; 2 trips Sat.

Greenfield-Amherst, via Turners Falls, Montague, Leverett—2 trips Mon.-Fri.

LRTA   ☎ 508-452-6161

Lowell Regional Transit Authority operates 18 routes in Lowell, Billerica, Chelmsford, Dracut, Tewksbury, and Tyngsboro. Buses operate Mon.-Fri. 6:00 am-6:00 pm, Sat. 7:30 am-5:30 pm; there is no Sunday service. All LRTA buses depart from the Transit Center between Merrimack and Paige Sts. in downtown Lowell. Most routes operate hourly. The fare is 60¢ in Lowell, increasing to a maximum of $1.00 outside the city limits; transfers are 20¢. *Connecting services:* T-Commuter Rail and intercity buses stop at Gallagher Terminal (508-459-7101), 145 Thorndike St., 1 mile south of downtown. LRTA's 30¢ downtown shuttle bus stops at the Terminal every 12 min. Mon.-

Fri. 6:00am-6:00 pm (every 24 min. in summer); every 24 min. Sat. 10:00 am-4:00 pm. (See map on page 68.)

Lowell-Lawrence—This MVRTA bus stops at the LRTA Transit Center.

MART   ☎ 800-922-5636; 508-345-7711

Montachusett Area Regional Transit serves Fitchburg, Leominster, and Gardner in north central Massachusetts. Buses operate Mon.-Fri. 5:00 am-6:00 pm, Saturday hours vary by route. There is no Sunday service. Most routes operate hourly. The local fare is 50¢.

Fitchburg—3 local routes depart from the Intermodal Center, 100 Main St. *Connecting services:* T-Commuter Rail stops at the MART Intermodal Center (508-343-3064); this is also the stop for buses to Concord, NH and New York, NY. Vermont Transit stops at Bickford's restaurant (508-537-6669) at Rts. 2 and 12, halfway between Fitchburg and Leominster. From here MART Bus 2 (Main Line) operates to both cities, every 30-45 min. Mon.-Sat.

Leominster—3 local routes depart from Monument Sq. *Connecting services:* The North Leominster T-Commuter Rail stop is off Main St., over 1 mile north of Monument Sq. MART Buses 1 and 3 (Circle Line) operate hourly from Main St. to downtown Leominster and to Fitchburg. MART buses to Leominster leave every half hour from the *Fitchburg* Commuter Rail station.

Gardner—2 local routes operate in a loop, Mon.-Fri. 7:25 am-4:25 pm and Sat. 9:25 am-3:25 pm. *Connecting services:* T-Commuter Rail and Vermont Transit stop at the Family Pharmacy (508-632-1158), 19 Union Sq., on both local MART routes.

Fitchburg-Leominster—frequent service by 3 different routes.

Fitchburg-Gardner—3 trips Mon.-Fri. with additional service during the school year; 2 trips on Sat.; $1.00.

Leominster-Fort Devens—2 trips Mon.-Fri.; $1.00.

MVRTA   ☎ 800-231-RIDE

Merrimack Valley Regional Transit Authority serves Haverhill, Lawrence, and Newburyport, north of Boston. Buses operate Mon.-Fri. 5:00 am-6:00 pm, Sat. 9:00 am-5:20 pm; there is no Sunday service. Most routes operate hourly on weekdays, and every 80 min. on Saturday. The local fare is 75¢; transfers are free.

Haverhill—7 local routes in Haverhill and Plaistow, NH. Buses depart from the Transit Station in Washington Square. The T-Commuter Rail station is at Railroad Sq., 3 blocks west of the MVRTA Transit Station. Buses to New York, NY, and Portland, ME, stop at the MVRTA Transit Station (508-372-3900).

Lawrence—11 local routes in Lawrence, Andover, N. Andover, and Methuen. Buses depart from the Intown Mall on Essex St. (westbound) and Common St. (eastbound). A 25¢ downtown shuttle bus operates every 15-30 min., Mon.-Fri. The T-Commuter Rail station is across the river from downtown Lawrence, a 1/2-mile walk across the Parker St. bridge. Trombly buses from Boston stop at 36 Jackson St. (508-686-9577) in the Intown Mall, as do buses to New York, NY, Concord, NH, and Portland, ME.

Newburyport—Buses from Boston stop at the Park and Ride off I-95, 2 1/2 miles west of downtown. (Some The Coach Co. rush hour trips stop in downtown Newburyport.) MVRTA provides rush-hour connections from the Park and Ride to downtown Newburyport and to Amesbury.

Andover—Two free local buses operate every half hour, Mon.-Fri.; plus MVRTA Bus 32 from Lawrence, Mon.-Sat. MVRTA local buses serve T-Commuter Rail stations at Andover and Ballardvale. Trombly buses stop on

Main St., served by all MVRTA routes.

Methuen—A local route connects with MVRTA buses from Lawrence at Methuen Sq. and at Methuen Mall.

Newburyport-Haverhill, via Amesbury—every 60-70 min., Mon-Sat.; $1.00

Haverhill-Lawrence, via Methuen Mall—Every 40 min., Mon.-Sat.; $1.00

Lawrence-Lowell, via Merrimack Plaza (Methuen)—Every 40 min., Mon.-Fri.; every 80 min., Sat.; $1.00

Lawrence-Salisbury Beach, via Methuen Mall, Haverhill, Merrimac, and Amesbury—2 trips Mon.-Sat. in July and Aug.; $2.00.

PVTA ☎ 413-781-PVTA

Pioneer Valley Transit Authority serves 20 cities and towns in the Connecticut River valley, including Springfield, Holyoke, Northampton, and Amherst.

Springfield—20 local routes in Springfield, Agawam, Chicopee, E. Longmeadow, part of Holyoke, Longmeadow, Ludlow, Westfield, W. Springfield, Wilbraham, and Enfield, CT. Most buses operate Mon.-Sat. 5:00 am-9:00 pm, with no Sunday service. Most routes operate every 30-40 min. Buses depart from Baystate West at Main St. and Boland Way in downtown Springfield. The fare is 65¢, plus 15¢ per zone to a maximum of 95¢; transfers are free within one zone. *Connecting services:* Peter Pan and Greyhound stop at 1776 Main St. (413-781-3320), 4 blocks north of Baystate West. PVTA Buses 101, 102, 103, 105, 107, 109, 217, 221, 401, 402, 403, 404, and 406 stop on Main St. near the bus station (see map on page 69.)

Holyoke —9 local routes in Holyoke, Chicopee, Granby, S. Hadley, and Westfield. Buses operate Mon.-Fri. 5:30 am-6:00 pm, Sat. 7:00 am-6:00 pm; there is no Sunday service. Most routes operate hourly. Buses depart from Maple St. The fare is 65¢, or 80¢ for 2-zone trips; transfers are free. *Connecting services:* Peter Pan stops at Rt. 5 ABC Pizza, 1735 Northampton St. (413-533-3674). PVTA Bus 204 stops at Northampton and Dwight Sts., 1 block from the bus station, every 80 min. PVTA Buses 217 and 221 offer frequent service to downtown Holyoke from the Springfield bus station.

Northampton —3 local routes in Northampton, Easthampton, Williamsburg, and part of Holyoke. Most routes operate every 1-2 hours, Mon.-Fri. 6:00 am-6:30 pm, Sat. 7:00 am-6:30 pm; there is no Sunday service. During fall and winter semesters, service is free; at other times, the fare is 65¢. *Connecting services:* Peter Pan stops at 1 Roundhouse Plaza (413-586-1030), off Old South St., 1 block from the PVTA bus stop and 3 blocks from Smith College.

Amherst—13 local routes in Amherst, Belchertown, Hadley, S. Deerfield, S. Hadley, and Sunderland. During the college year, buses operate Mon.-Sat. 7:15 am-12:45 am, Sun. 10:30 am-12:00 mid; during school vacations, there is no Sat. or Sun. service. Service in Amherst operates every 10-20 min. on school days and every hour on weekends and during vacations. Service outside the town operates much less frequently. Buses depart from N. Pleasant St. adjacent to the University of Massachusetts. The Amherst buses are free.

Five Colleges —Frequent shuttle buses during the school year, connecting Amherst College, Hampshire College, Mount Holyoke College, Smith College, and UMass/Amherst. Service operates Mon.-Thurs. 6:30 am-12:00 mid; Fri. 6:30 am-2:00 am; Sat. 10:00 am-2:00 am; Sun. 9:00 am-10:30 pm. This service is free and open to the public. *Connecting services:* Peter Pan stops in Amherst Ctr. at 79 S. Pleasant St. (413-256-0431), at the UMass Hotel (413-256-0431), and at the Hampshire College Bookstore (413-549-4600). It runs 18 trips daily from Springfield, via Holyoke, Northampton, and Hadley. The Amherst-Greenfield GMTA bus stops at UMass.

Springfield-Holyoke—3 routes: via Chicopee, via W. Springfield, or express in rush hour; every half hour, Mon.-Fri. 5:00 am-7:30 pm; every 45 min. on Sat. 7:30 am-5:45 pm. Fare, 90¢.

Northampton-Amherst, via Hadley—Same schedule as Five Colleges buses during the school year; reduced service in summer.

RIPTA   ☎ 401-781-9400
The **Rhode Island Public Transit Authority** operates all public transit service in Rhode Island, both local and intercity. The system serves 36 of the state's 39 cities and towns. The fare is 85¢ for one zone (25¢ for a "short zone" in Providence), increasing to a maximum of $2.50 for 4 zones; transfers are 15¢.

Providence—28 local routes in Providence, Centredale, Cranston, E. Providence, Johnston, and N. Providence. Service operates Mon.-Fri. 5:15 am-12:10 am, Sat. 6:00 am-12:10 am, Sun. 7:00 am-11:00 pm. Most routes operate every 15-30 min. Mon.-Sat.; every hour nights and Sun. All buses depart from Kennedy Plaza in downtown Providence. *Connecting services:* Amtrak and T-Commuter Rail trains stop at 100 Gaspee St., 1/4 mile north of Kennedy Plaza; RIPTA Buses 56 and 57 stop on Gaspee St. in front of the train station. The Bonanza bus terminal is at 1 Bonanza Way (401-751-8800), 2 miles north of downtown Providence. Bonanza buses to Boston stop at both the Bonanza terminal and Kennedy Plaza. Buses to other destinations, including Logan Airport, stop only at the Bonanza terminal, but passengers may use the hourly Boston bus for connections from Kennedy Plaza. RIPTA Buses 98 and 99 (Providence-Pawtucket) stop at Cemetery and N. Main Sts., 1/2 mile from the Bonanza terminal. (see map on page 70.)

Pawtucket—9 local routes in Pawtucket, Central Falls, Cumberland, and Lincoln. Service operates Mon.-Fri. 6:00 am-7:15 pm, Sat. 6:45 am-7:15 pm, and Sun. 10:00 am-5:20 pm. Most routes operate every 30-45 min. Mon.-Sat. and hourly on Sun. Buses depart from Main & Roosevelt Sts., where they connect with RIPTA Buses 98 and 99 from Providence.

Newport—3 local routes operate every 45 min., Mon.-Fri. 6:25 am-7:15 pm; Sat. 6:45 am-7:15 pm; and Sun. 10:00 am-5:20 pm. Buses depart from Gateway Center at 23 America's Cup Ave. *Connecting service:* Bonanza buses from Boston stop at Gateway Center.

Woonsocket, Wakefield, and *Galilee*—local buses operate Mon.-Sat.

Providence-Pawtucket—every 10-30 min. until 12:10 am Mon.-Sat.; until 11:00 pm Sun.

Providence-Newport, via Bristol, Warren, Middletown, and Portsmouth—every hour, Mon.-Sat.; every 90 minutes Sun.; until 11:00 pm daily.

Providence-Woonsocket—every 1-2 hours, daily until 9:00 pm.

Providence-Kingston, via S. Kingstown—4-6 trips daily.

Other Providence services—Mon.-Sat. to E. Greenwich, Galilee, Jamestown, Narragansett, N. Kingstown, Wakefield, Warwick; Mon.-Fri. to most other points in the state.

Newport-Kingston, via Jamestown, Narragansett, Wakefield—every hour Mon.-Fri.; every 90 minutes Sat. This bus serves the Amtrak station, which is 2 miles west of downtown Kingston.

SRTA   ☎ 508-999-5211

Southeastern Regional Transit Authority serves New Bedford and Fall River in southeastern Massachusetts. The fare on all SRTA buses is 75¢ per zone.

New Bedford—14 local routes in New Bedford, Acushnet, Dartmouth, Fairhaven, and Mattapoisett. Buses operate Mon.-Sat. 5:00 am-6:00 pm, with limited service Sun. 8:00 am-8:00 pm. Most routes operate every 20-30 min. Mon.-Sat. and every 40-60 min. on Sunday. Buses depart from the Transportation Center at Elm and Pleasant Sts. *Connecting service:* American Eagle stops at the SRTA terminal (508-990-0000).

Fall River—13 local routes in Fall River, Somerset, and Swansea. Buses operate Mon.-Sat. 6:00 am-5:40 pm; there is no Sunday service. Most routes operate every 30 minutes Mon.-Sat. Buses leave from the SRTA terminal at 221 Second St.*Connecting service:* Bonanza stops at the SRTA terminal (508-679-2335).

New Bedford-Fall River, via Dartmouth and Westport—Daily, every hour until 6:00 pm.

VTA   ☎ 508-627-9663

Martha's Vineyard Transit Authority operates two summer-only routes in Edgartown:

Downtown loop—Every 10 minutes, 7:30 am-11:30 pm, daily, late May-mid Sept.; 25¢.

Katama Beach shuttle—Every half hour, 9:00 am-5:30 pm, daily, mid June-early Sept.; $1.50. *Connecting services:* See "Island Transport" in Chapter 19. All buses stop on Church St. in Edgartown, next to the police station.

WRTA   ☎ 508-791-WTRA

Worcester Regional Transit Authority operates routes in Worcester, Auburn, Boylston, Brookfield, Clinton, E. Brookfield, Holden, Leicester, Millbury, Shrewsbury, Spencer, and W. Boylston. Buses operate Mon.-Fri. 5:00 am-8:00 pm; Sat. 6:00 am-8:30 pm; Sun. 10:30 am-5:30 pm; with service on a few routes until 11:00 pm Mon.-Fri. Most routes operate every half hour on weekdays, hourly at night and on Sat., and every two hours on Sun. Buses depart from Worcester City Hall. The fare is 75¢, plus 25¢ per zone outside Worcester to a maximum of $1.50; transfers are 25¢. *Connecting services:* Peter Pan and Greyhound stop at 75 Madison St. (508-754-4600), 4 blocks south of City Hall. WRTA buses 6S, 19S, 26S, 30S, and 33 stop at Main and Madison Sts., 2 blocks west of the bus station. The Amtrak station is at 45 Shrewsbury St., 1/2 mile east of City Hall. (See map on page 70.)

Index

Transit Telephone Numbers

All telephone numbers in this book are in area code 617 unless noted otherwise. A "1" means the number is a toll call from Boston, but still in the 617 area. Toll-free "800" numbers are valid from eastern Massachusetts unless noted. "TDD" numbers are for the hearing impaired.

MBTA

Travel Information Line	722-3200; 800-392-6100
TDD	722-5146
Commuter Rail	800-392-6099
from RI	800-882-0090
Commuter Rail Group Travel	722-3663
MBTA General Offices	722-5000
Monthly Pass Program	722-5218
Customer Relations, Commendations and Complaints	722-5215
Senior Citizen ID cards/Transportation Access Pass	722-5438
TDD	722-5854
Transportation Access/The Ride	722-5123
TDD	722-5415
Lift-Bus Info & Reservations	800-LIFT-BUS
Elevator Service Update	451-0027
MBTA Police Emergency	722-5151
MBTA Police Business Office	722-5747
Bikes on the T Program	722-5799

Lost & Found:

Blue Line	722-5533	Buses	
Green Line	722-5220	Cambridge, Arlington, Belmont, ...	
Orange Line	722-5403	Watertown	722-5560
Red Line	722-5317	Charlestown, Everett, Malden, ...	
Red Line—Mattapan	722-5213	Medford, Revere	722-5607
Park Street Station	722-5672	Dorchester, Kenmore, Harvard- ..	
Trackless Trolleys		Dudley, Mass. Pike	722-5203
Cambridge, Belmont, Watertown.		Lynn & North Shore	722-5263
	722-5562	Quincy & South Shore	722-5367
Commuter Rail		West Roxbury, Jamaica Plain, ...	
North Station	722-3600	Newton	722-5819
South Station	345-7456		

COMMUTER INFORMATION

Caravan for Commuters, Inc.	CAR-POOL; 800-248-5009

LOGAN AIRPORT INFORMATION

Ground Transportation Information	800-23-LOGAN
Public Information Office	561-1800
Airport Handicap Van	561-1769
Airlines	See Chapter 6

VISITOR ASSISTANCE

Boston Visitor Information	See page 42
Travelers Aid Society	542-7286
U.S.O.	720-4949

RAILROADS

Amtrak	482-3660; 800-USA-RAIL
TDD	800-523-6590

FERRIES

A. C. Cruises 426-8419; 800-422-8419
Airport Water Shuttle 330-8680
Bay State Cruise Co. 723-7800
Boston Harbor Commuter 740-1253
Boston Harbor Cruises 227-4321
Cape Island Express 508-997-1688
Cuttyhunk Boat 508-992-1432
Harbor I. Water Taxi 740-1605

Hy-Line 508-778-2600
Island Queen 508-548-4800
Massachusetts Bay Lines 542-8000
Steamship Authority
    Hyannis 508-771-4000
    Woods Hole 508-548-3788
    TDD 508-540-1394

BUSES

Airways Transp. 267-2981
American Eagle . 426-7838; 508-993-5040
Barrett's Tours 508-228-0174
BAT (Brockton) 508-580-1170
Beverly Shoppers Shuttle ... 508-921-0040
Big W 508-881-4627
Bloom Bus 426-7838; 508-822-1991
Bonanza 720-4110; 800-556-3815
BRTA 800-292-BRTA
    Pittsfield 413-499-BRTA
Brush Hill 986-6100
Burlington People Mover 270-1965
C & J Trailways 426-7838
    from NH 603-742-5111
Carey's 471-4098; 1-447-5555
CATA (Gloucester) 508-283-7916
CCRTA 800-352-7155
    Hyannis 508-385-8326
City Transp. 236-1888
Concord Trailways 426-7838
    from NH 800-852-3317
Contran 508-369-1538
Crystal Transport 787-1544
Dedham Local Bus 326-5770
H. T. Drummond Inc. 1-293-6264
FRTA (Greenfield) 413-774-2262
GATRA
    Attleboro 508-222-6106
    Taunton 508-823-8828
GMTA (Greenfield) 413-773-9478
Green Harbor Transp. 1-837-1234
Greyhound
    Boston 292-4700
    Riverside 969-8660
    national schedules 423-5810
Gulbankian's 508-485-8988
Hudson Airporter 395-8080
    from NH 603-883-4807
Hudson Bus 395-8080
Interstate 1-344-2231
Island Transport 508-693-0058
Lexpress 861-1210
LIFT (Framingham) 508-620-4852
Logan Express 800-23-LOGAN

Logan Link 800-23-LOGAN
Lower Cape Bus 508-487-3353
LRTA (Lowell) 508-452-6161
Lynn East/West 598-4000 x305
M & L Transp. 665-7791
    from NH 800-225-4846
MART 800-922-5636
    Fitchburg 508-345-7711
    Gardner 508-632-7373
Mass Limousine ....
    .... 508-823-9328; 800-342-5894
Metrobus 732-2384
Michaud ... 508-745-1000; 800-MICHAUD
Mission Hill Link 445-1657
MVRTA 800-231-RIDE
    Haverhill 508-372-3900
Mybus 356-5170
Natick Neighborhood Bus .. 508-651-7262
Paul Revere 536-1993
Peter Pan 426-7838; 413-781-3320
    Riverside 965-7040
People Care-iers 361-1515
Plymouth & Brockton Street Railway ....
    .... 773-9400; 800-328-9997
PVTA
    Springfield 413-781-PVTA
    Northampton 413-586-5806
RIPTA
    Providence 401-781-9400
    Newport 401-847-0209
    from RI 800-662-5088
SRTA 800-352-7192
    Fall River 508-672-6071
    New Bedford 508-999-5211
The Coach Co. 800-874-3377
    from NH 800-582-0885; 603-382-4699
Trombly 508-686-9577
Vermont Transit 292-4700; 800-451-3292
    Riverside 969-8660
VTA (Edgartown) 508-627-7448
Waltham-Lexington Express .. 890-0093
WRTA (Worcester) 508-791-WRTA
Yankee Line 268-8890

Jump Aboard!

...our train, bus or boat (pick your own car-free metaphor) by joining the Association for Public Transportation, the publisher of *Car-Free in Boston*.

APT, a private, non-profit corporation, works for better transit in the Boston area. Our goal is simple: a transit system good enough to reduce traffic and pollution problems, not just keep them from getting worse.

We invite you to join us. Your tax-deductible donations to APT are an investment in better transit for greater Boston.

In return, we'll keep you informed with our newsletter *mass. transit*. Plus, you'll receive a free copy of the next edition of *Car-Free in Boston* when it is published. APT members are also encouraged to attend our monthly meetings and participate in our work.

To join APT, fill out the form on this page and mail it to:

Association for Public Transportation
PO Box 1029
Boston, MA 02205

You can help us improve *Car-Free* (and be eligible for a valuable prize) by entering the contest described on page 170. You do not have to join APT to enter this contest.

Help! Improve *Car-Free* and Win a Valuable Prize.

By answering the questions below you'll help us improve *Car-Free* and public transit in New England. The information will be used to help us design future editions of this book to better meet your needs and assist our ongoing efforts on behalf of public transit.

To show our appreciation, 28 respondents will win a free Boston Passport, which provides a week of unlimited travel on MBTA subways and buses. If you prefer, you may receive a cash prize of equal value — $18 as of September 1992. We will also send all respondents a free copy of our newsletter, *mass. transit*, which includes a summary of all the latest changes in MBTA and other transit services. Simply fill out the form and mail it to:

Association for Public Transportation
PO Box 1029
Boston, MA 02205

Thank you very much for your help. We publish this book for you, the transit users of Greater Boston and New England — your input is valuable to us.

— — — — — — — — — — — — — —

NAME

ADDRESS

CITY   STATE/PROVINCE

ZIP/POSTAL CODE   COUNTRY
AGE: ☐ UNDER 25 ☐ 25-34 ☐ 45-59 ☐ 60+
OCCUPATION: _____ ☐ STUDENT ☐ RETIRED
HOW OFTEN DO YOU USE PUBLIC TRANSIT?
☐ AT LEAST 3 TIMES WEEKLY ☐ AT LEAST 1 DAY A WEEK
☐ AT LEAST 1 DAY A MONTH ☐ NEVER
WHERE DID YOU PURCHASE *CAR-FREE*?
(CITY)_____ (STORE) _____

HAVE YOU PURCHASED *CAR-FREE* BEFORE? ☐ YES ☐ NO
HOW DID YOU HEAR ABOUT *CAR-FREE*? ☐ NEWSPAPER
☐ FRIEND ☐ SAW IN BOOKSTORE ☐ OTHER:_____
PLEASE RATE THE USEFULNESS OF EACH OF THE FOLLOWING *CAR-FREE* SECTIONS (FROM 1-5, WITH 5 BEING BEST):
I._____ II._____ III._____ IV._____ V._____

DRAWING DETAILS
1. DRAWINGS WILL BE HELD 4 TIMES — ON JANUARY 15, 1993, JUNE 15, 1993, JANUARY 15, 1994, AND JUNE 15, 1994. AT EACH DRAWING, 7 NAMES WILL BE SELECTED AT RANDOM FROM ENTRIES RECEIVED. EACH WINNER WILL RECEIVE A "BOSTON PASSPORT" OR CASH EQUIVALENT.
2. THE EARLIER YOU ENTER, THE MORE CHANCES YOU'LL HAVE TO WIN. UNSELECTED ENTRIES WILL BE ELIGIBLE FOR ALL REMAINING DRAWINGS UNTIL JUNE 15, 1994.
3. ALL ENTRIES MUST BE RECEIVED BY JUNE 15, 1994.
4. ONE ENTRY PER HOUSEHOLD, PLEASE.
5. WINNERS WILL BE NOTIFIED BY MAIL.
6. NO PURCHASE NECESSARY. FOR AN ENTRY BLANK, PLEASE WRITE TO US AT OUR ADDRESS.

170